THE GODFATHERS TRIANGLE

3 Books in 1 - The Rise and Fall of Three Mafia Empires

MAFIA LIBRARY

TABLE OF CONTENTS

The Patriarca Mafia Crime Family

The Magaddino-Todaro Mafia Crime Family

The Bufalino Mafia Crime Family

THE PATRIARCA MAFIA CRIME FAMILY

MAFIA LIBRARY

INTRODUCTION

One evening, in late September of 1916, a husband and wife were walking back to their home in the Boston suburb of Brookline, Massachusetts. A respected member of the community, the man would have been easily recognizable around town. He had been successfully operating a produce importing company in the city and had important political connections both in Boston and in his native hometown in Sicily, where his ships loaded tons of fruit destined for the Boston Harbor. His name carried a lot of weight, particularly in the Italian neighborhoods of urban Massachusetts. Specializing in citrus fruits, he was fondly nicknamed "The Lemon King." His real name was Gaspare DiCola, and the woman he was walking home with that evening was Antonina, his wife (although it seems that the pair were never officially married). The couple certainly wasn't looking for trouble that night—Gaspare was 50 years old in 1916 and Antonina was just a few months behind him. They were unassuming, and looking forward to a peaceful night at home. But, before they could reach their house on Fairbanks Street, two unseen figures approached the DiColas from behind and shot five rounds from their pistols into Gaspare before fleeing the scene.

Gaspare and Antonina were returning from the local Massachusetts Dante Alighieri Society, an organization founded back in 1889 to promote the culture and language of Italy abroad, especially in

Italian diaspora communities. Gaspare, who had emigrated from his hometown in Palermo, Sicily to the United States sometime between the late 1880s and early 1890s, clearly had pride for his Italian roots even after he became a naturalized U.S. citizen around 1896 at a ceremony in Boston. Still, America was his home, and he had already made a name for himself in the 20-odd years since he first stepped onto American shores. His importing headquarters on Boston's North End waterfront was well-known, and since 1911 he had served on Boston's Board of Children's Institutions and Services, a position he had been personally appointed to by the city's Mayor, John F. Fitzgerald (who happened to be the grandfather of future U.S. President John F. Kennedy). He was even President of the Boston chapter of the Italian Red Cross committee, an international humanitarian group. There is no obvious reason that someone would have wanted this high-profile member of the community gunned down in the street, but it has long been suspected that Gaspare DiCola was, in fact, the boss of a New England Mafia Family.

In 1916, the Mafia was a concept about which the public knew very little. Many who lived in the communities in which the Mafia operated had a general notion that there was *something* connecting the seemingly organized criminal activity in the major cities across the United States, but it would be nearly half a century before an actual member of *La Cosa Nostra* (literally meaning "our thing," or "this thing of ours") would publicly admit that the Mafia existed and had a national structure. After all, one of the central tenets of the Italian-American Mafia was *omerta*, an oath of silence that forbade its members from speaking about the "business" to anyone who was not a member, especially law enforcement, a rule that went almost completely unbroken for decades.

Still, there are a few major reasons to suspect that DiCola was one of those prominent and upstanding citizens who liked to make a living on the side, in Boston's criminal underworld. First and most obviously, Gaspare's shooting was certainly not random. His assailants took no chances and got close enough to their target to identify him before shooting. The shooting was clearly planned—someone wanted Gaspare DiCola dead. Second, as the 50-year-old lay in his hospital bed in Boston, in critical condition, he refused to cooperate with Boston police in any way. If he spoke to them at all, it was to reassure them that somehow neither Gaspare nor his wife could recall a single identifying detail about their attackers. This is a major red flag, as in these early days the sense of duty that bound mafiosi to *omerta* was strong, and it was taboo to work with the police even if it was against your enemies or killers. In the Mafia world, disputes were settled amongst themselves, not outsiders. Lastly, and perhaps most striking, the eventual death of Gaspare from his injuries the next morning was followed shortly after by the rise of another bona fide Mafia boss in Boston: Gaspare Messina. If DiCola's death created a void in the criminal underworld leadership, it had now been filled.

DiCola's story—at its base—is not unique, though it is one of the earliest in New England's history. More or less the same tale would play out again and again over the next hundred years in major cities across the country. A mafioso begins building an empire for himself by creating connections and a base of power until eventually his enemies (or sometimes, his friends) decide that he has gotten too greedy. He's taken out, replaced by another "made" guy, and the cycle repeats until he's either killed or put in prison. In New York, Boston, Chicago, Philadelphia, Los Angeles, and elsewhere, the history of the Italian-American Mafia is written in blood and betrayal. Although Mafia bosses have generally been considered untouchable for most of the Mafia's history, greed and selfishness slowly eroded what made the organization successful. But, although the Mafia in the 21st century is a shell of its former self, it has proven incredibly resilient in the face of decades of infighting and aggressive legal prosecution. Many Mafia families are still active today in whatever illicit markets they can penetrate, and the vast majority of them can—in one way or another—trace their lineage back to New York City; the national hub of Mafia activity in America. Even the Rizzuto Family of Montreal, Canada began as an extension of the Bonanno Family, one of New York City's infamous "Five Families." The Mafia in New England was no exception.

American port cities at the beginning of the 20th century were lands of immigrants. As the underclass of Europe sought better lives for themselves and their families, they poured in on immigrant ships through coastal cities like Boston, New Orleans, and especially New York. Though America is a melting pot of cultures, these men and women invariably brought their own culture and values with them to their new homes. Sicily and the southern Italian mainland (where the Mafia first began) was a major source of immigrants to America in the 20th century, and so many people were coming in that, inevitably, some had been connected to the Sicilian Mafia. Most newly arrived immigrants tended to make their homes in communities where their fellow immigrants lived, resulting in close-knit enclaves—Italians with Italians, Irish with Irish, Chinese with Chinese, etc.—allowing their shared culture to grow and flourish. Complicating matters was the fact that these immigrants were often discriminated against and had no hope of securing anything other than the lowest-paid, most dangerous jobs. As a result, the Mafia was eventually reborn in America, most powerfully in New York City. Here, five large families came to dominate the city's criminal ecosystem, and the oldest of these, the Genovese Family, traces its heritage all the way back to Giuseppe Morello, one of the earliest-known mobsters who began his first gang in the 1890s. From this nucleus, the Mafia grew and took root in other cities. Importantly for our story, Boston, Massachusetts, and Providence, Rhode Island were two of these cities.

Regardless of what region they controlled, Mafia Families tended to follow a similar structure. At the bottom of the hierarchy were the "associates," the non-members who were still valuable to the Mafia and were known to work with them. Sometimes associates were those who simply hadn't been "made" yet, sometimes they were unable to ever be "made" because they were non-Sicilian (or non-Italian). Regardless, associates were typically organized into crews run by soldiers, who occupied the lowest rank of the "made" men. Associates helped organize heists and run the Mafia's several criminal operations. Whatever they made, they kicked up a portion to soldiers, who in turn kicked up to the Family's *caporegimes*, otherwise known as captains. *Capos* acted as a kind of middle management for the Mafia, overseeing larger operations and running their own crews which consisted of lower-ranking members. They earned more money and had plenty of people paying them, but they also had to kick up to the boss (the man in charge of the entire Family and its operations) and their second-in-command, the Family's underboss. In the early years of the Mafia in New England, after the death of Gaspare DiCola and before the factions were organized into a single Family unit, there were two bosses trying to build crime empires: Messina in Boston, and later, Frank Morelli in Providence.

Messina and Morelli built their own crews independently, but their respective cities eventually became two centers of a united organization that spanned across several northeastern states at the height of its power. In this region, huge portions of all criminal activity—from union racketeering to paid assassinations—were monopolized by the New England Mafia for decades. During the 1920s, the power of both the Boston and Providence crews grew even more as a result of the federal prohibition on alcohol that began in 1920 and lasted for 13 years. Those in the criminal underworld were presented with a lucrative opportunity to keep the booze flowing through the streets of America's cities, and this period began the criminal careers of many infamous gangsters, including Al Capone and Charles "Lucky" Luciano, to name a few. The new source of wealth that came with bootleg alcohol production and rum running sustained the more successful Families for years, and they could now purchase more political connections than ever before. After much infighting and bloodshed through the early 1930s, the national Mafia was consolidated and became even stronger as a result of the Castellammarese War and the creation of "The Commission."

The Commission was the brainchild of Lucky Luciano and was his attempt at making the national organization more centralized, cohesive, and even democratic. It brought together the most powerful and respected Mafia bosses from across America's cities with a simple mandate; to govern national Mafia activities and to serve as an arbiter for disputes which, in prior decades, had torn Families apart from within. Along with the forming of the Commission came a major restructuring of the American Mafia as a whole, which had huge implications for New England's disconnected and fragmented criminal underworld in the 1930s. The organization that would eventually become known as the Patriarca Crime Family first coalesced in this period, and these early years will be the focus of our first chapter.

CHAPTER 1

THE GODFATHERS OF NEW ENGLAND

Long before the legendary Raymond Loreda Salvatore Patriarca stepped into the commanding role of a united New England organization, the Mafia's presence and power in Massachusetts, Rhode Island, Connecticut, and elsewhere were relatively weak. Further, they were plagued by frequent wars with other ethnic gangs in the city, most notably with Boston's Irish Mob. It would take a few decades before the Sicilian-American Mafia in New England would come to rival the power of their counterpart Families in New York City, but the activities of the two regions were highly connected during this time, and events in NYC would forever change the landscape of crime along America's northeast seaboard. Messina had strong Mafia ties to New York, which proved invaluable during Prohibition and helped to grow the influence of the faction in Boston; the city that became the headquarters of the Family until Patriarca took over operations in the 1950s. Messina also personally had an important role to play during the Castellammarese War in NYC. His counterpart in Providence, Frank Morelli, had a much more modest role and power base, but as we'll see, the Rhode Island faction also underwent some drastic changes in these early decades.

Prohibition and the Castellammarese War

Prior to approximately the late 1940s and early 1950s, relatively little is known about the inner workings and finer details of the New England Mafia, at least in comparison to the Five Families of New York. There is, however, much speculation and conflicting stories about these years, as is the case with the circumstances of Gaspare DiCola's death. Despite so many signs pointing toward DiCola being one of Boston's first crime bosses, there exists little to no actual evidence from the time linking him to the city's rackets and other known criminals. Yet, his role as one of New England's earliest "Godfathers" has nevertheless made its way into the region's Mafia lore. Whatever events preceded DiCola's murder, we do know that Gaspare Messina was the new big man in Boston after 1916. Again though, Messina is a character about whom we know frustratingly little for certain.

What we do know about him is that, like DiCola and many other early mafiosi, Messina was born in southern Italy in the town of Salemi, an inland commune of western Sicily. About 13 years DiCola's junior, Messina left his southern Italian home and immigrated to the United States sometime around 1905. His was one of many immigrant ships destined for the harbors of New York City (specifically, Messina with his wife and brother landed on the famous Ellis Island), and it was here that Messina made his first American home. He began to build a life for himself and soon settled down in Brooklyn, where he would remain for about a decade. He made an honest living to support his family, opening up a neighborhood bakery in Brooklyn that he ran with his family. Before long though, Gaspare was supplementing his salary with more illicit income. It's unclear when, but at some point during his early years in New York City, Gaspare Messina had joined the Mafia. He was the newest member of the Bonanno Crime Family.

Messina would retain life-long business and personal connections to New York, but he was not destined to remain in the city forever. By 1915, he and his family had relocated to the major New England city of Boston, Massachusetts (some sources claim the move wasn't made until later in the decade). Boston was another popular immigrant city at the time and had a healthy population of Italians, but in Boston, the Irish healthily outnumbered the Italians. The result was higher competition between ethnic gangs over resources and criminal rackets, which often boiled over into gang wars. When Messina first moved to the area though, the Mafia there often had more to fear from their own people rather than outsiders. Coincidence or not, within just one year of Messina's arrival in Boston, Gaspare DiCola would be brutally and publicly murdered on his own neighborhood streets. Not long after DiCola's death, Messina began seizing much of the criminal operations throughout Boston's North End, particularly gambling, counterfeiting, and a few years later, bootlegging. Unfortunately for Messina, it's unwise to live lavishly with no way to explain to the government how you earned all of your money, and so he reopened his old family bakery in his new home to serve as one of his several "front" businesses (essentially, fronts were establishments designed to give the appearance of legitimate and legal income—profits from criminal activities could be reported to the Internal Revenue Service as income generated from legal business, thus cleaning or "laundering" the money).

The exact circumstances and rationale surrounding Messina's arrival in Boston are, for the most part, unknown. It's possible that he decided to relocate purely of his own volition, seeking out a smaller city where he could more easily carve out a place for himself to operate. It's possible, though unlikely, that Messina was fleeing New York due to either safety concerns or pending legal investigation. What's more likely though is that Messina was asked to make the move by the leadership of the New York Families. It was not uncommon for the most powerful organizations to send their own men to other cities in order for the Family to both gain a foothold in and oversee the area's racket operations. Messina was probably sent to New England as a *rappresentante*, or "representative" of the national Boss of Bosses, known in Italian as the *capo di tutti capi*. Prior to the creation of the Mafia Commission, the Boss of Bosses was a title typically given to the most powerful and respected boss of the New York Families. At the time Messina left New York for Boston, that man would have been Salvatore D'Aquila, boss of the organization that would become known as the Gambino Crime Family. Having a made guy like Messina in another city to represent both the interests of the Bonannos as well as D'Aquila would not have been unusual. Of course, it would have also been a very lucrative opportunity for Messina himself.

Whatever the reason for his entrance into Boston's North End, Messina quickly set to work intimidating and extorting his way to a commanding position within Boston's underworld. The remainder of the decade was spent pursuing this goal, but the 1920s soon brought a new, incredibly profitable source of income for those willing (and able) to break the rules. In 1919, the Protestant

Christian groups in the United States that had long been calling for an end to the sale and production of alcohol, including the Women's Christian Temperance Union, finally succeeded on a congressional level. These groups blamed everything from family violence to political corruption on the scourge of alcohol, and Congress finally gave in to pressure with the ratification of the 18th Amendment. No longer could American citizens legally purchase liquor, outside of religious purposes. The problem was that Americans still very much enjoyed alcohol and were not willing to give it up. And so, the underground black market for beer and liquor became big business, especially for the Mafia.

In major cities across the country, various Mafia Families came to dominate the bootlegging markets, and Boston was no different. The city was a big market and Messina ensured a steady flow of bootleg liquor through its North End districts. It was apparently so profitable that he and his associates needed new streams of legitimate revenue. To that end, Messina established sometime in the early 1920s the Messina & Company Grocery on Prince Street. His partners in this venture were two of his associates, Paolo Pagnotta and Frank Cucchiara. Pagnotta had to leave the partnership before long due to his publicized 1925 arrest, along with two of his associates who ended up receiving charges for carrying concealed handguns. These early years also were not *entirely* kind to Messina either. In 1923 he became the suspect in a large investigation into approximately $500,000 USD in counterfeit bills flooding Boston's economy. Not much appears to have come of it, but it seems very likely that the investigators were looking into the right person. Messina was known to have a hand in the counterfeiting business, and aside from that, he mysteriously vanished from the state once the investigation picked up steam. He had gone back to his native Sicily before returning stateside in late 1924.

When Messina arrived back in Boston, he was facing exactly zero criminal charges relating to his counterfeiting operation. Still, by the middle of the decade, life as the top criminal in Boston had taken its toll on the boss, and the stress was beginning to affect his health. He decided to step down as boss of the Boston faction based out of the North End. In future decades, the Mafia Commission would have stepped in to handle a situation like this, convening and ultimately voting to select and confirm a new boss to fill the void. In the 1920s though, no such apparatus existed and when it came to disputes, it was the Wild West. Messina's absence led to a power struggle in the region for control over the businesses and rackets that were formerly his domain. The North End's illegal gambling clubs and card games, loan sharking, and the highly lucrative bootlegging were all up for grabs. Fighting ensued, but ultimately it was the gangster from east Boston Filippo (Phil) Buccola who rose above the rest and inherited the commanding share of Messina's fledgling empire. He then set to work consolidating and reorganizing the fractured criminal world Messina left behind. Unfortunately for some, this included going to war with the city's other gangs.

One of the biggest rivals to Buccola's faction of the Mafia was operating out of South Boston, a neighborhood familiarly known as "Southie." In this part of the city, it was the Irish gangs that ruled. Of these, it was the Gustin Gang, run by the Irish Wallace brothers, that posed the most serious competition for Boston's underworld.

The Wallace brothers earned their early reputation mostly with robberies and hijackings (the eldest, Frank, was involved in a high-profile case in Detroit where he had been accused of robbery of over $10,000, but he and his brothers had a lot of important friends and none of the charges ended up sticking to Frank). When Prohibition hit, the Wallaces found a new way to profit from their illegal hobby—they began tracking and hijacking the trucks belonging to rival bootlegging gangs and stealing their shipments of liquor. This was clever, as criminals have little recourse when they themselves are victimized, and the Bureau of Prohibition was not in the business of helping bootleggers recover their stolen, illegal whiskey. Further, the Wallaces were known to dress up as law enforcement when they raided their rivals, complete with police-style weapons and fake badges, so oftentimes they would simply assume that the law had confiscated their product, meanwhile the Gustin Gang was reselling the contraband to other establishments. Among the many smuggling trucks that the Wallaces hit throughout the 1920s, several of them belonged to the Italians—it's no surprise that this manner of hit-and-run thievery did not sit well with Buccola's Family on the north side of the city.

Instrumental in Buccola's war against the Irish rum-jackers was his underboss, Joseph Lombardo (sometimes Lombardo is referred to as his *consigliere*, a kind of close personal advisor to a boss—it's possible that he held both roles at different times, or simultaneously). Born sometime in the late 1890s, Lombardo was another native of Salemi, Sicily, and as such he carried similar "Old World" values. During his time in Mafia leadership, Lombardo became a very highly respected elder statesman kind of figure both regionally in Massachusetts and at a national underworld level. He was known to be diplomatic and was often consulted as an arbiter in gangland disputes, but ironically, he is easily best known for his role in orchestrating a double homicide (although it was his goal to murder three that day). As a result of the Gustin Gang's repeated hits on Buccola's trucks (including the most recent hijacking in which the North End mob lost approximately $50,000 in merchandise to the Irish), Lombardo called a meeting with Frank and his top guys just a few days before Christmas, 1931, to discuss a resolution. The Wallaces were no fools and they expected a backstab, so when Frank showed up at Lombardo's office building, he, Tim Coffey, and "Dodo" Walsh were all armed to the teeth. Still, it was Lombardo who got the drop on them. As the Irish gangsters waited for Buccola's underboss to usher them into his office, a hail of bullets blasted through closed doors and cut down both Frank and Dodo. Coffey was luckier and managed to hide before he caught a bullet.

With Frank out of the picture, his younger brother Steve Wallace came to head the now-emaciated Gustin Gang. It soon became obvious to their rivals that Frank was the true power in the gang, and Steve was never able to recover the influence that his brother had garnered for their family. It's unclear what the role of James, the youngest brother, was exactly, but his presence was evidently not too beneficial. The market formerly controlled by the Irish out of Southie was now up for the taking by Buccola and Lombardo. Unfortunately for them and other bootleggers, the 18th Amendment was not long for this world in 1931. The entrance of organized crime into the bootleg liquor business caused years of gang violence and public bloodbaths in the streets of cities across the country. To make matters worse, Prohibition simply wasn't working. Bootleggers, and especially the Mafia, had become so adept at eluding law enforcement that just about anyone who wanted booze would be able to get it. By 1933, the once powerful and vocal support for Prohibition had diminished to a whisper.

The 21st Amendment officially repealed Prohibition, and gangsters everywhere lost the most valuable source of income they had yet known. Still, the profits generated from the 13 years of bootlegging built the legacies of mobsters that would last for decades. Gaspare Messina had profited handsomely while he sat atop Boston's gangster totem pole, and even though he had assumed a background role by the late 1920s, he had created quite a life for himself. Around the late 1920s and early 1930s, he became president of Neptune Oil, his own petrol company based out of the Boston harbor. Buccola too had built himself an empire that would sustain him over 20 years later. But the bosses weren't the only ones making big moves during Prohibition. In the nearby Rhode Island city of Providence, where the Mafia faction was even weaker, a young small-time thug named Raymond Patriarca was cutting his teeth hijacking liquor trucks and running them out of state. A protege of the powerful Don Iacone who operated out of Worcester, MA, and Providence, Patriarca would soon become a pivotal figure in the history of the New England Mafia.

It seems that by 1932, Gaspare Messina, one of the Godfathers of New England, was fully out of Mafia life. After he had stepped down as the boss in Boston, he was called on once more around 1931-32 to serve the Mafia at a national level. His reputation and the respect he commanded were valuable during this time, as the New York-based Families were embroiled in a massive conflict that came to be known as the Castellammarese War. With the rise in power and status of the American Mafia, the old Families back home in Sicily decided to make a play for control of U.S. territory from their immigrant cousins across the Atlantic. The Sicilian faction from the coastal Castellammare Del Golfo region of the island had sent representatives to New York to try to wrest control away from the Families who at the time were headed by *capo di tutti capi* Giuseppe Masseria, also known as Joe the Boss. The Castellammarese faction was headed by the Sicilian lieutenant Salvatore Maranzano, who was representing the interests of his boss in Italy. For a brief period during the turmoil caused by the war, it was Gaspare Messina who was selected to serve as "boss of bosses," likely in the immediate aftermath of Joe Masseria's murder. Messina was likely living in New York City at the time, and so his role here didn't directly affect the New England Families, but as we'll see, the events following Maranzano's victory in the Castellammarese War had massive implications for both Buccola in Boston and Frank Morelli in Providence.

One Family

In the immediate aftermath of the war in New York City, the Mafia's presence in New England was still fractured, and Buccola and Morelli each ran their own separate operations. Buccola, who had only been in America since about 1920, had first begun earning income by managing professional boxers and prizefighters. He partnered in this with an associate based in New York, the city where Buccola had initially entered the U.S. Born in 1886, Buccola was already in his thirties when he immigrated out of Sicily but he wasted no time entering the criminal underworld once he was there, which suggests that he very likely was already a made member of a Family in Sicily when he left. When he eventually made his way to Boston, he initially set up his base of operation in the East Side of the city where he grew his power during Prohibition until he came to replace Messina as Boston's kingpin.

In 1932 when Messina permanently retired, Buccola was recognized by the New York Families as his legitimate successor. However, according to Mafia turncoat Vincent Teresa, Buccola was being used as a front man by the true Boston don, Joe Lombardo, sometimes known as Big Joe L. There's not much besides Teresa's word that substantiates the claim that Lombardo was the man behind the curtain, and all signs point to Buccola instead. During the 20s and early 30s, Buccola was still, for the most part, sharing the wealth, especially with "King" Solomon, a Jewish gangster from the West End who was heavily active in the city's rum-running operations. After Buccola became boss though, this arrangement didn't last.

Solomon was a true founding father of organized crime in New England and had made a fortune peddling narcotics even before Prohibition began. He was influential too, holding sway in New York among the Mafia intelligentsia and elder statesmen, and his nature of arbitrating disputes supposedly influenced the creation of the so-called National Crime Syndicate coalition. At the beginning of 1933, his time was up. After a long night at Boston's Coconut Grove nightclub, which was a notorious hotspot for organized criminals between 1927 and 1942, Solomon and his entourage of women made for the Cotton Club in the South End. After a while at their new location, Solomon at some point stood up and went to the bathroom before being followed by two men sitting at a nearby table. There was muffled gunfire followed by screaming before the two men ran out of the bathroom and fled the club. A few moments later, a severely injured Solomon staggered out, covered in blood, and collapsed. He had been hit several times in the neck and torso at close range, and he died soon after. Neither of the gunmen, John Burke or Jimmy Coyne, were Sicilians, but it has long been understood that Philip Buccola was the man who orchestrated and authorized the killing. Buccola doesn't appear to have made a play for the Jewish kingpin's former territory, but his faction was significantly weakened.

This was Buccola's Boston in the early 1930s. In Rhode Island, criminal operations were organizing themselves and becoming more centralized, but Providence's Frank Morelli was an entirely different breed from his Boston counterpart. For starters, he wasn't an immigrant like the majority of his colleagues at the time. It was for a long time assumed that Morelli had come from the Foggia region of southern Italy in the late 1890s, but evidence suggests that his parents made the move to America long before he was born—Morelli (originally spelled Molarelli, and Frank's given name was Adolfo) was born, and died, in Providence. He and his brothers (he was the youngest of five) seem to have begun their criminal careers in the 1910s, when Frank, who was born in 1896, was still young. The eldest brother, Joe, had started a loosely organized gang of neighborhood youths after the passing of their father Gennaro, which included several, if not all, of his brothers. The gang was petty at first, committing nighttime burglaries and theft, but they eventually graduated to far more brazen robberies. Their favorite targets ended up being large freights, which were profitable when successful, but they also brought more serious charges. Given that the cargo was often bound for out-of-state cities, robbing them would have been considered an interstate crime, and thus would carry federal punishments. The brothers' recklessness soon caught up with them.

In 1919, an investigation into the hijacking of a large shipment of shoes from a transport train led to the arrest of a number of Morelli gang members, including the leader Joe. Another wave of arrests hit the gang soon after, this time for the robbery of a truck carrying the payroll of a local shoe factory. Rhode Island police had suspected that the two crimes were linked, and so the Morellis were under investigation once again. Frank got picked up by police and was convicted in 1920, but this was getting off very easy in comparison to two of his fellow gang members. Complicating the payroll heist case was the fact that, in the course of the crime, someone from the Morelli gang (or all of them) decided that witnesses couldn't be tolerated, and so the drivers of the truck were shot dead. Law enforcement decided that this warranted making an example of the Providence gangs, and so they made their case and pursued it aggressively. Their selected villains were gang associates Nicola Sacco and Bartolomeo Vanzetti. Court proceedings were hotly contested and six years passed before a final verdict was rendered. The court eventually determined that Sacco and Vanzetti were the chief victimizers in the robbery, and their sentence was the electric chair. In the summer of 1927, the two men were executed by the state for double homicide.

Frank himself was out of his Atlanta prison cell by the end of February 1924, and the world he was re-entering was already steeped in Prohibition-era bootlegging. Relocating back home to Providence, Morelli quickly proved that the American justice system of the early 20th century was less than effective. He was rearrested just months later for armed assault, and his violent incidents would continue for years. Some of his brothers appear to have still been committed to their robberies and hijackings, but Frank had bigger things in mind when he went back to Rhode Island. He began a bloody turf war in Providence in an attempt to seize control of the majority of the city's rackets. His main games appear to have been Prohibition, but especially gambling. Just like his young self, his crimes were brazen. Once again there is little evidence, but Frank is generally considered the man who organized the 1931 bombing of the home of a notorious Providence gangster who oversaw much of the illegal gambling in the city. His luck wasn't over quite yet though, and he escaped that investigation with nothing but suspicion. In less than five years after his former co-conspirators were put to death, Frank had taken over much of Providence's racketeering and he had become a pioneer of the Mafia in Rhode Island.

So, in the early 1930s, things in Boston and Providence were developing nicely for their respective bosses. But, just as operations were becoming more steady and consolidated across the two states, they were about to be shaken up again. After the Castellammarese War, the Mafia landscape was altered everywhere. Charles "Lucky" Luciano, the New York boss who was pivotal in ending the war in 1931, had petitioned the Mafia community to create the Mafia Commission. Luciano had seen firsthand the kind of mutual destruction that came as a result of all-out turf wars, namely loss of profit, and the Commission was his solution—the mandate of those serving on the Commission (which would consist of the most respected bosses across the nation) was to intervene in, mediate, and settle high-profile gangland disputes before they could ever evolve into another Castellammarese War. This was meant to be in the best interest of the entire national Mafia. But if this was to be possible, the Mafia needed to be more centralized and there needed to be more authority vested in a smaller group of powerful men. This applied across the country. In New York City, the Five Families-style organization was officially implemented to contain competition in the massive city. In New England, it was decided that neither Boston nor Providence, the two main hubs for Mafia activity in the region, were large enough to justify having separate Commission-approved Families and bosses. The national leaders insisted that the two factions be merged under a single Family banner.

The question still remained: Which boss would receive the blessing of the newly-created Commission? Which city would become the new nexus of crime in New England? The obvious choice was Buccola's faction in Boston. His city was a much larger market than Providence, and the Mafia's presence there was already more substantial and growing faster. On top of this, Buccola was Sicilian-born like much of the old leadership in NYC and elsewhere, plus Morelli's history with violence and run-ins with the law were considered potential liabilities for a regional boss. The only negative was that despite the best efforts of Buccola and his predecessors, the Irish still outnumbered Italians in Boston, and Irish gangs still posed a considerable threat to Mafia operations. Nevertheless,

Morelli was passed over for the position of boss. Given Morelli's reputation, it's possible that this could have evolved into a war over the position of New England boss but as the story goes, it was Joe Lombardo who apparently visited Morelli and convinced him to accept the determination of the Commission and to take himself out of the running. It's also possible that Morelli was simply bowing to more experienced leadership. In any case, New England was now set to face the rest of the 1930s under a united Mafia Family led by Philip Buccola and Joe Lombardo out of Boston. Frank Morelli still remained the top man in Providence, but he now had his own boss to answer to. Until 1954 when he finally retired, that man was Buccola.

The Gustin Gang was destroyed, Charles "King" Solomon was dead, Frank Morelli was reduced to a regional lieutenant, and Buccola was the most powerful mafioso in New England. Lombardo, who had escaped prosecution for the murders of Frank Wallace and his henchman, was trying his hand in the restaurant business in the North End while Buccola operated out of his home territory in the East End. Lombardo also headed most of the family's loan sharking operations as well as their illegal gambling for years before he stepped back from crime in the mid-1950s. In Providence, Morelli remained in a very powerful local position until he too retired in 1947, making Buccola even more powerful. Not much is known for certain about the New England Family in the 1940s, but that decade did see the rise of many mobsters who would end up becoming important figures in later years. One of these men was Joe Barboza, who would go on to cause major headaches for the family in the future. But of all the mafiosi who were out to make a name for themselves in these years, one Worcester-born member of the

Providence faction rose above the rest. He had the mentoring of the respected don Iacone, won the position that Frank Morelli had vacated in Providence, and eventually was selected to run the entire New England operation. His name was Raymond L. S. Patriarca.

CHAPTER 2
THE RISE OF RAYMOND PATRIARCA

Raymond Patriarca is, without a doubt, the mafioso that we know the most about from the New England Family. Whereas his predecessors always carried an aura of mystery around them, making it difficult for historians to recover evidence about how they operated, Raymond Patriarca ended up becoming something of a celebrity in his lifetime. Notoriety and face recognition aren't the best qualities to possess when trying to run a criminal empire, but Patriarca nonetheless succeeded in taking the New England Mafia to all-new heights. He was so influential that the organization he ran ended up adopting his name—even today, the New England Mafia is known as the Patriarca Crime Family. Patriarca was certainly a successful man, and his reign coincided with a period that is generally regarded as a golden age for both the regional and national Mafia, but he and his contemporaries had to face new challenges that the bosses of the 1920s and 30s never did. Most notably, a coordinated and concerted effort by law enforcement to expose and destroy organized crime, which was an effort supported at the highest levels of government. Putting the names and faces of bosses all over the media was a part of this effort, and served to make Mafia leadership feel uneasy, paranoid, and exposed. So, before Patriarca's reign was over, he had become a public figure. He had always been a respected and recognizable member of his community in Providence, but the Patriarca name became tainted. However, before all this, Raymond was just a small-time gangster making a living in Worcester and Providence, and it didn't seem that he was destined to become boss. What does seem likely is that he was always destined to be a criminal.

"I Guess I Drifted a Little..."

In February of 1938, a robbery took place at a jewelry store in Brookline, Massachusetts, just west of Boston. It wasn't a typical nighttime robbery with discretion and a degree of finesse. It was flagrant, out in the open, and right in the middle of business hours. Well over $10,000 in cash, jewelry, and gold was stolen from the displays and store vault by two armed men. They forced the owner and employees of Wallbank Jewellers to cooperate under threat of death. One of these men holding the guns was 29-year-old Raymond Patriarca. With the considerable haul secured, the pair then decided to force the witnesses in the store to remove their clothes which they then also stole, likely to prevent them from exiting the store and witnessing their escape. To top things off, Patriarca and his co-conspirator tossed their loot into the back of the store owner's car and made off with that too. Just 11 months earlier, Raymond and his crew were involved in a payroll heist at Oxford Print. The men threatened the workers, stole yet another car to make their getaway, and this time they even took a hostage to make sure they gave up the payroll prints. If it wasn't already clear by the late 1930s, it was now: Raymond Patriarca loved stealing.

His relationship with theft went back a long time, dating back to at least his teenage years. But even he would admit later in life that something happened to him that may have helped make him the way he was. Born in Worcester, Massachusetts in 1908, Patriarca lived in a predominantly Italian ghetto that would have a considerable Mafia presence in later years. His surroundings were much the same when the family relocated to Atwells Avenue in Providence, Rhode Island. His father, Eleuterio, originally ran a liquor store and so became an active illegal liquor distributor during the early years of Prohibition, but he was not a big player in the city. He lived outside the law to provide for his family, but it did not necessarily doom young Raymond to a life of crime. Eleuterio's sons were already getting into trouble as teenagers, but their father was always there to help them and bail them out of jail when necessary. Then, in 1925, the senior Patriarca suddenly died, and Raymond was left without a father. According to Patriarca himself, this is when his life began to truly go off the rails: "I lost my father, and I guess I drifted a little..." (quoted in Songini, 2015).

It wasn't long after Eleuterio's death that Raymond devoted himself fully to the criminal lifestyle which he had only dabbled in in childhood. His crimes got bigger and what was once petty theft became armed robbery and grand theft auto. He even followed in his late father's footsteps and got involved in Prohibition-era bootlegging. Given his talents, it's unsurprising that Raymond spent most of his time hijacking transport trucks and stealing liquor shipments from other gangsters running booze through Rhode Island. In fact, Prohibition has the honor of being the first law that Raymond was put away for violating. It was just a year after his father's death, and he was slapped with just a one-month stay in a

Connecticut jailhouse and a couple hundred dollars in fines. Evidently, it was not nearly enough to deter the young man, as he began his lifelong trend of violating his probation almost immediately after leaving jail and making his way back to Providence. He earned a reputation around Providence as a notorious gambler and he also joined with his brother Joseph in several pimping ventures, all of which got him in trouble at some point. These run-ins with the law would plague him for decades to come.

At some point, Raymond linked up with the Providence-based Morelli brothers, Frank and Joe, and their gang. At the time, the Morellis were a relatively small-time group of disorganized thugs and heisters, but these were the years that Frank was working to bring the city's rackets under his control. With Patriarca's help, the gang began to take on the look of an actual *organized* crime Family. In later years, when Morelli began to step back from his active role in overseeing crime in Providence, it was to Raymond Patriarca that he chose to cede most of his lucrative enterprises to. Around the same time that Patriarca was associating with the Morellis, he also began working under the respected Worcester boss Frank Iacone, who mentored him in running a crew and crime empire. Raymond did plenty of bootlegging in those days and spent a lot of time running rum interstate from Rhode Island into Massachusetts on behalf of don Iacone. Aside from this, he also began making money on the side. In fact, he played both sides of the rum-running game: He both hijacked other gangs' liquor trucks and worked security for the liquor shipments of other gangs, including the Irish (although it's been reported that Raymond made himself available to those planning to ambush his shipments and, for a fee, he would allow the trucks to be stolen without a fight). He also did some pimping across state lines with his brother, which carried surprisingly little return considering the severity of interstate human trafficking. All of these things got him in trouble (for the transportation of women across state lines, both he and his brother earned a stay in a penitentiary in Atlanta) as he piled up an impressive rap sheet. Despite his recklessness, Raymond Patriarca was heading into the 1930s well-positioned for a meteoric rise through the criminal underworld.

Il Patrone, A Made Guy

With Iacone's tutelage, the time had come by 1929 to initiate Raymond Patriarca as an official member of the Mafia. When he was "made," it wasn't just a New England affair. By the 1930s, Raymond was already well-known in New York Mafia circles. This was before the days of the Commission, so it wasn't necessary for Patriarca's induction to be approved, but he nonetheless had the blessing of the New York leadership. The weight that Patriarca's name carried in New York only increased in later years, and although he had proven to be a somewhat careless and brash criminal at times, he had also earned a reputation as a calculated, diplomatic, and even-handed leader. This allowed him to be a trusted voice and confidant later in his career, and he even bragged at one point that he held sway over the Five Families and that few big decisions in the Big Apple weren't made without his approval. This may have been an exaggeration on his part, but it is certainly true that his opinion mattered to many high-ranking bosses.

Raymond Patriarca was now a made man, and as such, he was more powerful than ever. Considered untouchable (except by other made guys and, of course, law enforcement), he could operate in his home territory with much more confidence. If anyone crossed him, they would have the Providence faction to deal with, and later, it would be the entire New England Mafia. He had a sense of security, impunity, and power, and his taunting and menacing of law enforcement rose in kind—by the early 1930s, Raymond was already atop Providence's list of public enemies. He and his crew dabbled in just about everything from bootlegging (until 1933) to extorting illegal gambling clubs, but his guilty pleasure was always stealing. Sometimes it didn't even matter what he was stealing (as we've seen, he was not above lifting the literal shirt off a man's back). When Raymond staged the bold and successful daytime heist at the Wallbank Jewellers, it took him less than a week to plan and stage yet another robbery scheme, this time at United Optical, a company that produced luxury eyeglasses. He and his partner at least had the good sense to wait until nightfall to attempt the break-in, but the plan was doomed anyway. Loud noises convinced nearby residents to report suspicious activity and before Raymond could grab the goods and make a getaway (likely in yet another stolen car), a dispatch of officers entered the building. Raymond hid but was eventually discovered and arrested after trying to conceal his identity. As it turned out, Raymond was still a bit reckless: When the officers searched his vehicle, they found merchandise that would eventually be linked back to the jeweler in Brookline.

So, Raymond was off to jail again to await his fair trial. He wasn't there for long before he got someone to post his bail so he could at least be a free man until he faced the jury for his failed eyeglass heist.

Almost immediately though, Raymond was implicated in the jewelry store robbery, which was confirmed personally by the owner of the establishment who immediately recognized Raymond's apparently unmasked face. Rhode Island police were given the order to arrest him once again, and luckily for them, Raymond was a reliably compulsive gambler who did a poor job controlling his habits. They found him quickly and easily, betting on the horses at a Rhode Island racetrack. Raymond was back in jail and when it came time to take the stand and defend himself for the crimes he had been convincingly accused of, he chose to plead guilty. The sentence he received carried a maximum penalty of five years in a prison cell. The punishment likely would've been much harsher had he chosen to fight the charges, which would've been a lengthy process. Besides, the indisputable incriminating evidence suggested that he didn't stand much of a chance in court anyway. Raymond was off to Charlestown State Prison in Boston.

Neither Raymond nor the Family were keen to have him behind bars for the long haul. Joe Patriarca—Raymond's brother and frequent criminal accomplice—together with the New England mob enlisted the help of a Boston lawyer, Dan Coakley. Coakley had less than a stellar reputation in the legal community, especially among Massachusetts' state prosecutors, but there's no doubt that he had a talent for making the problems of criminals disappear, so long as they had the cash and were willing to bend the rules. It was decided that even though Raymond had essentially admitted to the charges, his legal team would pursue a pardon. Amazingly, Coakley actually pulled it off. With some faked letters and a bit of underhanded legal chicanery, Raymond was released from prison just a few days before the end of 1938, well before he served even a fifth of his sentence.

Raymond wasn't completely out of the woods in 1939. There were still serious questions regarding his involvement in past crimes, particularly his affinity for stealing cars (it was something he did both on its own and during the course of other crimes). Authorities in Massachusetts were, unsurprisingly, not happy with the result of Raymond's previous conviction and were out to nab him on anything that would put him back in a jail cell. Outwardly though, Raymond was trying to go straight. The saga of his multiple arrests, guilty plea, and ultimate release had become headline news by this point, and the media in New England was eager to hear his input on the situation. He told them his sole focus was making amends and settling down for a quiet life, the latter of which he actually did when he married Helen Mancini (her last name is sometimes spelled "Mandella"). As for his going straight, he at least wasn't in New England long enough afterward to cause much more trouble. After the wedding ceremony, he and his new wife took off for Miami for an extended honeymoon while Rhode Island and Massachusetts police were still investigating him. Unfortunately for him, his notoriety stretched past New England and police in southern Florida would be keeping a close watch on the newlyweds.

It should have been easy for Raymond to at least avoid arrest while he was in Miami—so long as he did nothing wrong, there would be no reason to apprehend him unless authorities in New England indicted him again and issued an extradition request. Yet for some unknown reason, when he was stopped and questioned about his business in Miami and where he lived, he offered them a fake home address. Already suspicious of Patriarca, it didn't take much digging to find the empty parking lot where the mafioso had claimed his house should be. It was a bizarre thing for him to do while being actively surveilled but in any case, it was enough for the police to pick him up on suspicion.

While in custody, Florida authorities got in touch with their counterparts in New England, and it was determined that Raymond should be sent back to Massachusetts to face trial once again. Police there had a fresh indictment for grand theft auto waiting for him when he arrived back in the state with his Boston police chaperone (his new bride was still back in Miami, stranded and probably very confused). Also waiting for him was a parade of media paparazzi trying to get photos and sound bites of the notorious criminal who, as the papers correctly suggested, may have received a pardon under false pretenses. The issue with his pardon was becoming a serious concern—if forgeries were discovered in the documents, it could endanger the careers of several New England politicians and other officials who had been in the Mafia's pocket.

The media attention that followed Raymond's forced arrival back in New England caused a cascading effect on his legal woes. His name and face constantly being in the papers led to more folks recognizing him, which led to him being implicated in even more past crimes. Raymond would spend the rest of 1939 as well as the early 1940s trying desperately to evade charges and clear his name, but it was no use. He was going to face serious charges, and among them was attempted murder. This charge was likely the result of his constantly threatening those he was robbing with death if they didn't cooperate. He was constantly being released and rearrested and whenever one of the cases against him fell apart, it seemed another charge was always there to take its place. Ultimately, Raymond went to trial for two cases of robbery which he once again pleaded guilty to. Near the end of 1941, Raymond was off to prison once again and this time there would be no phony letters from community priests testifying to his character, nor would there be any ill-gotten pardons to get him out early. He served his time and was finally released into the public in May of 1944.

Raymond was a free man (at least for now) and had a lot of work to do. As it turned out, he got busy building up both his own family and his Mafia Family—just a year after his release, the woman that Raymond unwillingly abandoned in Miami about six years prior gave birth to his son, Raymond Patriarca Jr., who was commonly known simply as "Junior." Junior would also have a significant role to play in the fate of the New England Mafia, and in later years he would be the one to inherit his father's criminal empire. But before that could happen, Raymond Sr. needed to build such an empire. Another testament to the misguided nature of the American justice system of the early decades of the 20th century, exactly no one was convinced that Raymond's stay in prison would reform him or correct the wayward path he had been on since at least the early 1920s. Indeed, upon his release he was more ambitious in his criminal activity than ever before and sought to regain control of his former rackets that had been divided up amongst the Family since his conviction. It was at this point that Raymond began collecting his close-knit group of associates who would later form the bulk of the leadership when the Patriarca name was on top. Among these men were Louis Taglianetti and Henry (originally Enrico) Tameleo, a made guy who was tied to the Bonannos in New

York but was active in Massachusetts, Rhode Island, and likely Connecticut as well. Tameleo had earned himself the nickname "Referee," or "The Ref," for being a conciliatory voice between the New England and New York Families.

Together, these three men—along with their crews—began to bulk out the Providence faction, at this point still controlled by the aging Frank Morelli and his brothers. By the time Raymond was out of prison in '44, it was clear that the Morelli era in Providence was near its close, as its leadership became reckless and was plagued with infighting. Luckily, in his effort to establish connections and support across the regions, Raymond had ingratiated himself with Phil Buccola, the boss of the combined Boston-Providence operations. So, when it became obvious in 1947 that it was time for Morelli to step aside, it was Raymond Patriarca that Buccola favored to fill his spot and become the next Providence underboss. Raymond now had the favor of Worcester wiseguy Frank Iacone and the boss in Boston, but the connections he made in these years went beyond New England: He had also associated himself with Frank Costello, head of the organization that later became the Genovese Family. With huge support both within Rhode Island and out of state, Providence was Patriarca's for the taking.

Aside from Raymond's campaign to reorganize the Providence faction under him, Mafia activity had been steady, quiet, and profitable for years. The beginning of the 1950s, however, marked a new age for the Mafia. It was the beginning of the era of celebrity prosecutors and public figures trying to make a name for themselves through high-profile, often televised, investigations and trials. This phenomenon continued for decades and was perhaps the most destructive development for the American Mafia. In the 1980s, lawyers such as Rudolph Giuliani leveraged their success in prosecuting mob bosses to transition into successful political careers. For instance, Giuliani used his success in taking down New York City's Five Families as a launching pad to become the city's mayor. In Patriarca's era though, it was the Kefauver Committee hearings of 1950 that first sounded the alarm. Estes Kefauver, a relatively unknown senator out of Tennessee, introduced a resolution that proposed the formation of a senate committee with a mandate to investigate Mafia-related interstate crime. His proposal very nearly fell apart before it saw the light of day, but after some maneuvering and a razor-thin senate vote, the Kefauver Committee was created. Its members were mostly lawyers by trade and included senators Alex Wiley, Lester Hunt, Charles Tobey, Herb O'Conor, Rudolph Halley as Chief Counselor, and Kefauver himself.

Beginning in New York, the committee started calling in alleged Mafia bosses to testify before the Senate. The hearings were televised and highly publicized, which put even the most stone-faced mafiosi under a crushing amount of pressure; the likes of which they had never experienced. Plenty had been to court, but none had ever had to defend themselves while, for all they knew, the entire nation was watching and reporters captured their every move. Unfortunately for Raymond, his closest ally in NYC—Frank Costello—was the most tripped up by the affair. The successor of the legend Lucky Luciano made a fool of himself as cameras caught him fidgeting, sweating, repeatedly contradicting himself, and generally coming off as extremely suspicious. In 1950, no one from within the Mafia had yet admitted publicly to its existence—La Cosa

Nostra still had an aura of mystery surrounding it, but this embarrassment gave the entire nation a hint that the Mafia was indeed real, and that the stories they had been hearing for decades were true. Costello's reputation never recovered after his testimony and as a result, the Patriarca influence in New York was weakened. But Raymond had much bigger problems on the horizon. After the hearings were wrapped up in New York City, it was announced that Kefauver, his committee, and the myriad film crews were packing up and heading for New England.

This news was troublesome to everyone in Massachusetts and Rhode Island with an empire to lose. This was particularly true for those who had been mentioned by name, which included the elders Buccola and Iacone, plus Raymond himself. Buccola, being at his advanced age and being the man in charge of the entire regional operation, was particularly stressed. He knew that he wouldn't be able to continue in his position for much longer without health complications interfering. Besides, it would have been in his best interest to vacate the top spot to let the heat die down. Buccola seems to have favored Patriarca, his underboss in Providence, as his heir. Raymond was one of the few gangsters in Rhode Island who held sway and commanded respect. Given his reputation in Massachusetts and New York, it was logical to choose him. Sometime in 1952, prominent veterans of La Cosa Nostra met to discuss the affair, and ultimately they decided to accept Buccola's nomination of the big man in Providence as successor to the New England Mafia. The decision was met with much fanfare as Iacone arranged a large celebration in Raymond's honor which attracted big underworld names from New York, Philadelphia, Chicago, and elsewhere. By 1954 when Buccola fully retired and went back to his native Sicily, Raymond Patriarca was the boss of his own Mafia Family, one which would eventually carry his name.

CHAPTER 3

THE PATRIARCA CRIME FAMILY

After the celebrations were over and bosses from all over the eastern states had paid their respects to New England's newest don, Patriarca began the most significant reorganization of the region's criminal underground since the creation of the Commission and the merging of the Boston and Providence factions. It was a new era for the Family, one which brought plenty of new fortunes but also fresh, potentially fatal challenges. Patriarca was an effective leader and he operated a relatively smooth business, but certain aspects were outside of his control. After surviving the publicity nightmare caused by the 1950 Senate testimonies, things would only get worse for organized crime in America. A new generation of crusaders rose to confront and expose the Mafia that had been shrouded in unanswered questions for years. Police and federal agents began using aggressive tactics and tools to nab their guys, and frankly, they terrified the Family bosses. By the mid-1960s, Mafia life had changed permanently. Before Raymond was even out of the game, the empire he created was already beginning to crack under the pressure that had been building since Frank Costello first stammered his way through his self-defense against Estes Kefauver and his personal Justice League.

The New Providence Regime

When Raymond fully inherited Buccola's empire in 1954, he was already beginning to tire of the demands of Mafia life. Now that he was boss, this pressure was felt even more acutely. He would now personally face more scrutiny from law enforcement than ever before and now, he had much more to lose. Raymond was already quite reserved and generally wary of people he didn't know, but now he was forced to trust even fewer people—one new tactic of the government was the relentless pursuit of potential informants or disgruntled mafiosi willing to flip and become state witnesses. As a result, the new regime in Providence was defined by an utmost commitment to secrecy and discretion. Raymond kept his inner circle incredibly tight, and those outside of Providence were often on the outside looking in. He also moved the New England Family's "headquarters" away from Boston to his home city. Although the criminal marketplace was considerably bigger in Boston, Providence was where Raymond felt the most comfortable and secure, qualities that seemed more valuable than ever in those days. This was a drastic change: The Family's seat of power would remain in the Rhode Island capital city for decades.

Raymond operated a bit differently from other bosses. He proved to be adept at keeping his top guys and their underlings strictly in line, despite the incredibly wide distribution of the Family operations across several New England states. Further, his general trust issues led him to completely disregard the long-standing Mafia tradition of working exclusively with Italians (in some more strict cases, even Italian heritage wasn't enough—one needed to be full-blooded Sicilian on both sides). The Patriarca Crime Family, as it came to be called, was known to work and associate with anyone, regardless of their ethnicity, so long as they were deemed reliable and could be trusted by Raymond. Honor and character were paramount, and employing those with loose lips or questionable integrity was out of the question. Unfortunately, as we'll see, more than a few rats slipped through Raymond's vetting attempts. For now though, business had to go on and Raymond was tasked with guiding his Family through a new decade and a new era.

Fearing the potential downfall of his ally Costello in New York City, Patriarca soon began building new relationships to avoid being isolated from the Families out west. He formed close ties with the Profaci (soon to be renamed Colombo) Family which gave Patriarca a valuable support base in the event anyone challenged his new position. In the interest of closing the ranks, he began filling his subordinate leadership positions with the crew he had first begun to assemble when he was released from prison in the 1940s. Tameleo was made underboss of operations in Providence, and it seems that Anthony Santaniello was given charge of the now-subsidiary Boston faction. The promotion of Tameleo with his close ties to the Bonannos also helped garner support in the Empire State. After Vito Genovese predictably overthrew Costello (he willingly stepped down after Genovese orchestrated a failed hit on him), Patriarca still maintained a working business relationship with the Family.

With the Providence-NYC connection secure, Raymond had his own Family affairs to tend to. For the most part, the Patriarcas continued to be active in all the typical Mafia rackets, which included gambling, loansharking, labor unions (eventually), prostitution, and even the production of pornography. The days of bootlegging alcohol were long dead, but Patriarca men eventually found new addictive substances to peddle. According to the mafioso-turned-witness Vincent Teresa, Patriarca had warned all of his men to stay away from the narcotics trade but just like with liquor prohibition, the potential profit to be made off of drug prohibition was too tempting to resist. If it is true that Patriarca was vehemently against drug dealing, it was a wise move—when the 1980s hit, their involvement in the narcotics industry became one of the main reasons for the Mafia's eventual collapse.

Part of the transformation of the New England Family into the Patriarca Family was the creation of several new, large front businesses. Raymond had to try to rehabilitate his image as an upstanding, honest businessman and at the same time needed to launder all the illicit profit that he was keen to take in. The two largest of these fronts were two sides of the same coin: The National Cigarette Service, which obviously distributed cigarettes, and the Coin-O-Matic Distributing Co., which installed coin-operated machines in businesses. These included pinballs and arcade-style machines, as well as vending machines which, of course, dispensed his cigarettes. These companies alone were profitable and the Family used classic Mafia extortion tactics to ensure that it was Raymond's cigarettes that people were buying and that it was Raymond's machines that sold them. Coin-O-Matic formed the backbone of Raymond's "legitimate" business empire and, tending to live modestly and avoid excess, he conducted the vast majority of the Family business out of his small Coin-O-Matic office room. This room became almost like folklore: Eventually it, and the entire Patriarca Family, would be referred to simply as "The Office." Aside from these businesses, the Family's other fronts included a dump, some nightclubs, and a textile plant.

As part of his effort to create a favorable image of himself, Raymond kept up a decent public persona throughout the 1950s. He was philanthropic and was often involved in high-profile charity work (at least when business fortune allowed). The facade of an upstanding and respectable man that Raymond wore was successful, and over time he came to be seen as a leader in his community. His reputation for being a skilled arbitrator already made him a trusted presence in disagreements between other gangsters and mafiosi, but folks would often turn to Raymond to settle even non-Mafia disputes in Providence. Henry Tameleo, the Patriarca underboss, seems to have functioned as a sort of diplomat or envoy for Raymond personally. According to Barboza, the enforcer and hitman-turned-witness, Tameleo was the one who ensured that the public image of both Raymond and his associates remained admirable and impeccable. He was also tasked with making sure Patriarca underlings remained happy with leadership, toed the line, and did not turn rebellious.

For years after Raymond took over, this strategy and regimen were very successful. As a result, his power grew considerably in these years and Providence was no longer a backwater of the Mafia world. Where the New England Mafia was once small and disorganized, it was now powerful, centralized around Rhode Island, and earned the respect of the Five Families in New York. The clearest sign of this is that, even in the wake of Buccola's retirement, Patriarca was able to keep the other powerful New York and New Jersey Families from encroaching on his territory. Most importantly, he accomplished this through diplomacy rather than violence. What could have evolved into an interstate turf war was settled with an agreement that the bosses respected for decades. Using the Connecticut River as a dividing line, the eastern portion was the domain of the Patriarcas, and everything to the west was free game for the other friendly Families. Some Families were able to operate across the river as well, so long as they had the blessing of Il Patrone. The Genoveses, for example, directly controlled Springfield, MA, as well as regions of Connecticut, including the city of Hartford.

The overlaps ran even deeper: In Worcester (one of the main Patriarca Family cities and a place that Raymond used to frequent) it was Carlo Mastrototaro who was selected to take over for the elderly Frank Iacone. It turns out that Iacone had joined Frank Costello in the club of victims of the Kefauver Committee. When the panel of senators held their planned hearing for the Worcester don, something about his testimony left them unsatisfied and suspicious. Under the direction of Chairman Kefauver, the Internal Revenue Service launched an investigation into Iacone's tax returns and came up with enough to indict him for evasion—they reportedly found a discrepancy of hundreds of thousands of dollars worth of unpaid income tax. In early 1953 he was facing charges to which he pleaded guilty. Iacone, who had been active since the Prohibition days and had long dominated much of Massachusetts' illegal gambling, was gone and his position vacated.

This was definitely a blow to the Family, as Iacone brought to the table huge profits, reliable counsel, and more than a few important connections he had built over the decades. Especially within Worcester, he was nearly untouchable by local law enforcement.

Most notably, Worcester police Lieutenant Bill Massei had formed a close personal and business relationship with Iacone. Incredibly, since 1940 Massei was the appointed head of the crime unit specifically meant to tackle the city's organized gambling rackets, which were run by Iacone. As a result, he was for years able to operate with near impunity, all the while the man who was supposed to be investigating him assured the city's residents that illegal gambling in Worcester was a myth. Indeed, Iacone was a difficult man to replace; and not only because of the people he had in his pocket. Ultimately though, Worcester native Mastrototaro filled the void. Mastrototaro was a seasoned, decorated veteran of the Second World War (he had been a Marine since 1939 when the war began) and was also a long-serving captain in the Genovese Family. With Raymond's approval, Mastrototaro replaced his former mentor and apparently performed admirably, holding the position for decades. In this role, the new Worcester don served the interests of both the Patriarcas in Providence and the Genoveses in New York.

Clearly, Raymond knew how to make peace and, despite his notorious temper, he could be very tactful. But when all else failed, the Patriarcas relied on intimidation and violence just like every other Family. When they needed intimidation and muscle, they turned to their enforcers. The most prominent of these were John Nazarian and Joe Barboza. Nazarian was known to be crazy, which earned him the nickname "Mad Dog." This usually meant that the threat of Nazarian coming after you was more than enough to make sure you paid what was owed to the Family. On the surface, it appeared as if Raymond's "legitimate" businesses were the sources of the Family's wealth, but behind the scenes it was Mad Dog

Nazarian and his ragtag crew of questionably loyal thugs who ensured they saw steady flows of profit. Because Nazarian's name was known across the eastern states as belonging to an erratic criminal who killed for cheap and didn't care about witnesses, Raymond had the difficult task of keeping him at arm's length to avoid being implicated in his wild exploits, yet still close enough to control him and ensure his violent tendencies were directed in the best interests of the Family.

Joe Barboza was no less frightening than Nazarian. A son of Portuguese immigrants, Barboza was never a made man in the Family (nor was Nazarian for that matter), but he did end up having a significant impact on its future. He was quite a bit younger than Nazarian, but his affinity for delivering savage beatings (and the account in which he reportedly bit the ear of a man after being told by Tameleo to keep his hands off him) had also earned him an unfriendly nickname. He was "The Animal," and he was a reliable hitman for hire to all manner of New England criminals in the late 1950s and 1960s. He was an imposing figure too, with a large frame that he used during his stint as a pro boxer. This made him a valuable extortionist and, like Nazarian, his reputation often got the work done for him. In fact, Barboza's criminal history was even more sensational than Nazarian's in some ways. He had been breaking the law since before he was a teenager and his first prison sentence came before he was even legal drinking age. But before his sentence—which was handed down to him at 18 years old—was concluded, he had formed a crew of several other inmates and together they staged a daring escape. They broke out of their cells, assaulted and beat the guards, and slipped out into the streets of Boston before they were all rounded up again. By 1958, he had linked up with the Patriarcas and Stephen Flemmi, a member of the notorious Irish Winter Hill Gang. Winter Hill was founded in the mid-1950s by Buddy McLean and was ruled between 1966 and 1979 by the infamous Irish-Italian gangster Howard Winter.

With these two brutes in his arsenal, and with his most trusted guys running operations in Providence, Boston, and Worcester, things were looking solid for Raymond Patriarca and his Family as they entered the 1960s. The income from their diverse array of rackets enabled them to expand their influence across multiple states. They gained ground in their home states of Rhode Island and Massachusetts, as well as in peripheral territories such as Connecticut. Later, they extended their reach to Maine and New Hampshire, where Orlando Napolitano's Portland Family became affiliated with the far larger and more powerful Patriarcas. Despite the Kefauver hearings causing a stir in the underworld from Los Angeles to Providence, things carried on in a relatively familiar fashion for years (although Raymond was a bit more paranoid) and the New England Mafia prospered under steady, even-handed guidance. But this peace too came to an end, and things quickly threatened to spiral out of control. The coming years would see Raymond, as well as plenty of other top Mafia guys, become terrified of law enforcement and their new tools and techniques, including witness hunting, wiretaps, and electronic surveillance devices. It was yet another new era, one where some bosses went mad from the constant fear that they were being monitored by someone or something. Much of this can be traced back to events in New York City, particularly the infamous and ill-fated Apalachin Meeting of 1957.

The Witness You Can't Kill

On the 25th of October in 1957, Albert Anastasia was shot dead in his chair by two men as he awaited a haircut at a Manhattan barbershop. Anastasia was one of the most veteran figures in the American Mafia and in New York, he was considered royalty of the old school. He was head of the powerful organization that would soon be known as the Gambino Family, and he was the most powerful gangster in New York's waterfront districts. Unfortunately for him, the power he had accumulated over the years stood little chance when confronted with the ambition of the younger generation. Vito Genovese, apparently unsatisfied with the failed hit on Frank Costello months earlier, banded together with Carlo Gambino to carry out the assassination of Anastasia. With the seasoned veteran out of the picture, it was Gambino who took over the remnants of his former empire. But as it turned out, the hit was also part of a grander scheme, orchestrated by Genovese, to become New York City's premiere Mafia boss.

With Anastasia out of the picture, the question of what to do with the rackets he controlled and the people from whom Anastasia was still owed money was a troubling hurdle to overcome. His empire was vast, and the solution wasn't as simple as appointing a new head of the Family, though Gambino probably would have preferred that to be the case. Further, developments in the government's assault on Mafia activities had gone unaddressed for too long. For these reasons, Vito Genovese called a meeting of Family heads from across the nation, as well as their top made men. The purpose was ostensibly to discuss these issues which were pertinent to the functioning of the Mafia across the states (as well as in Montreal,

Canada—the home of the Rizzuto Family), but it's generally agreed that this was part of a major power play by Genovese to solidify himself as the de facto *capo di tutti capi* of the underworld. Genovese was a new boss in New York and had to replace the widely-respected Costello, so organizing and calling this meeting was meant as a signal to bosses across the nation that he was capable of calling the shots and arbitrating on vital matters. So it was that in November of 1957, the nation's foremost made men from New York, New Jersey, California, Ohio, Florida, Illinois, Pennsylvania, Kansas, and elsewhere convened at one of the biggest criminal meet-ups in American history.

The meeting was held at the home of Joseph Barbara, known by his friends as Joe the Barber. He was another mobster of the old school and was originally of the Castellammarese faction decades ago, so his hosting was a natural choice. It wasn't Joe's only home—he was the boss of the Bufalino Family based out of the Scranton Wilkes-Barre area of Pennsylvania, but he always maintained a presence in NYC. His Empire State home was in the Apalachin neighborhood in New York's Tioga County. As a result, the summit would go down in history as the "Apalachin Meeting." Unfortunately, it didn't go down in history as a resounding success, but rather as one of the biggest blunders in organized crime. Before everything was said and done, dozens of mafiosi and bosses from across the country were detained by New York police and some 20 of them were charged, convicted, and fined. What was originally meant to be Genovese's grand gesture of domination had become a farce, and both his and Barbara's reputations took a hit. It also seriously damaged the credibility of the decades-old claim that the Mafia was imaginary and that organized crime was a non-issue—reportedly, there were over 100 of the nation's most wanted criminals at Barbara's estate that day.

There are many theories that have been formed in the years since Apalachin that contend that the entire calamity was a setup, likely by another mafioso. This would make sense given that there were likely more than a few rival mobsters who would've liked to see Vito Genovese's ego cut down to size, but such a move would have jeopardized the operation of the entire Mafia, everywhere. And, since so many bosses were known to be in attendance, the destruction of the leadership of nearly every major Family could've been achieved in one fell swoop. It was also assumed for a long time that local police simply happened upon the meeting after noticing the strange number of fancy, out-of-state luxury vehicles parked at the vast property. As it turns out though, New York state troopers had already been keeping an eye on the Barbara estate for quite some time. After a high-ranking member of the Bonanno Family was recorded visiting and leaving Barbara's home, law enforcement made it a habit to include the estate in their routine patrols. Further, a state trooper by the name of Edgar Croswell had been pursuing leads on Barbara, and prior to the meeting's scheduled date he had discovered a suspicious number of room reservations made at hotels across the city, all under the name of Barbara's son. He relayed this information to his superiors who realized immediately that something big was about to happen.

When patrolmen reported the strange fleet of vehicles at the estate, it was time to move. Officers began preemptively running the plate numbers of the vehicles which, before long, revealed that more than a few of them belonged to either wanted criminals or criminal suspects. This was all the pretext that was needed, and so a roadblock was set up and officers prepared to forcefully enter Barbara's estate. All the while, inside the house Vito Genovese was unwittingly making his long-awaited grandstand in the presence of the nation's premiere criminals. Unfortunately for the New England Family, Raymond Patriarca and his consigliere Frank Cucchiara (the same Cucchiara that Messina had partnered with years earlier) were among those criminals in attendance. Police attempted to arrest everyone in attendance, but that didn't stop dozens of them from attempting to escape. Some shuffled past officers to their vehicles only to drive directly into a roadblock. Some of the more frantic and desperate decided to make a getaway on foot, attempting to sprint through the fields behind Barbara's manor. Dozens of the most feared men in America, clad in expensive shoes and designer clothes, were reduced to dodging cops like petty street thugs. It's not clear exactly what happened to Raymond at the meeting, or how and if he attempted an escape, but he was identified as an attendee and if he was apprehended, he was soon a free man.

Despite years of fighting unfavorable media coverage and (correct) accusations of malfeasance, this was the most exposed Raymond, and the Mafia, had ever been. The entire underworld was shaken and the Patriarcas now feared more severe legal action. With Raymond's criminal history, it would be a difficult task convincing anyone that his presence at a meeting of known gangsters was pure happenstance. Perhaps the biggest knock-on effect of the Apalachin Meeting, though, was the fact that Director of the FBI J. Edgar Hoover was now *forced* to take the threat of the Mafia presence in America seriously. This was largely due to the insistence of Robert

F. Kennedy, future Attorney General and brother of future U.S. President John F. Kennedy. For years, Hoover had repeatedly and publicly denied the possibility that an extensive criminal network like the Mafia could exist in the United States. There are a couple of potential reasons for this. Many assumed that the Mafia's growth during Director Hoover's tenure at the Federal Bureau was a source of shame for him. If this is true, it would have been easier to simply deny their existence rather than admit that they were there and he was powerless to stop them. More likely, though, is that Hoover denied their existence because he himself had gathered more than a few Mafia connections as a result of his alleged degenerate gambling habits and affinity for prostitutes. Whatever the case may be, his hand was forced after Apalachin. Neither he nor mafiosi themselves could credibly claim that La Cosa Nostra was nothing more than a legend from the old country.

The aforementioned era of anti-Mafia crusaders was definitely in full swing. The year after the abortive Apalachin Meeting, the U.S. Senate called Raymond Patriarca to testify before the McClellan Committee on labor crime. It was a select committee that was formed in early 1957, meant to investigate organized crime and American labor unions. The committee took the name of John McClellan, a Democratic senator out of Arkansas who had been investigating the Teamsters; one of the nation's largest labor unions. Its goal had broadened since its formation and in February of 1958, the committee had their eyes on Patriarca. The answers he presented to the panel were less than satisfying—when asked how he acquired enough money, without taking loans, to start his various business enterprises, he credited his mother who apparently left him tens of thousands of dollars in cash as an unofficial inheritance. When asked why he chose a life of petty crime and robbery in his earlier years when he had so much money waiting for him, he once again blamed the tragedy of his father's death. Finally, when questioned about the well-known extortion tactics that Patriarca's underlings used to funnel revenue into his National Cigarette Service corporation, he simply pleaded ignorance. The chairmen, particularly Robert Kennedy, were incensed. Later, Raymond received a subpoena from another Senate committee.

The increased scrutiny on Patriarca in particular in years following his senate testimonies likely wasn't a coincidence. Around this time, probably in 1960, Raymond was allegedly chosen by national bosses to serve on the Mafia Commission. At the time, the government had an idea that the Commission existed but it was still a nebulous concept. Unfortunately, the combined stress of his senate subpoenas and his appointment to the Commission seems to have taken its toll on him in 1960 when he suffered cardiac arrest and was hospitalized. He remained in bad health for a while and to make matters worse, his underboss in Boston, Santaniello, died that same year. Now with two senior members out of the picture, the Family was in crisis. Needing a strong influence to keep order in Boston, it was Gennaro "Jerry" Angiulo who rose to fill Santaniello's spot. Jerry, the most prominent of his troupe of criminal siblings, was a Boston native and big-shot nightclub owner in the city. He was also a restaurateur, and his most popular place was a bar and grill called Jay's Lounge on Tremont Street in Boston. Because it was such a well-known Mafia hangout, it later became the target of extensive FBI wiretaps. Angiulo had steadily risen through the ranks of the Boston faction since the end of WWII and, even though he was not part of Raymond's insulated inner circle of counselors, he did eventually become the Family's underboss.

Unfortunately, Santaniello's death wasn't the only problem for Raymond in Boston. Unbeknownst to him, one of his guys there, Vincent Teresa, had become a police informant. Teresa, whose Mafia lineage went all the way back at least to his grandfather in Sicily, was well-connected and worked his way up to becoming a trusted enforcer in Henry/Enrico Tameleo's crew. He was a long-time criminal whose history of burglaries dates back to his grade school days. Though he did enlist in the Navy during WWII, he only did so at the tail end in 1945, and even then he was dishonorably discharged within 3 years. Needless to say, he was a bad egg. He managed to top out working as a kind of debt collector for Tameleo in Boston and Worcester, but this gig never seemed to be enough for him. He was definitely the right guy for the job, as few knew more about debt than Vincent Teresa: He was a full-blown, lifelong gambling addict since before he was kicked out of school in the 9th grade. He spent his free time racking up endless debt from various hustlers across Boston's North End and elsewhere, and when the money he earned collecting from other debtors wasn't enough to pay them back, he stole; which meant that he stole a lot. Unsurprisingly, this made him plenty of enemies in Massachusetts. But all of it couldn't feed his habit successfully—he was perpetually teetering on bankruptcy and he simply couldn't steal enough to keep him afloat.

All of this meant that Teresa was a perfect target for the FBI's witness hunt. Hoover had been begrudgingly directing his Bureau's agents to aggressively pursue any leads on made men or associates who might be willing to flip and inform on their bosses. Teresa, who plenty of people wanted dead and who was buried to his neck in debt, needed little convincing to begin feeding (often fabricated) information to his federal handlers. Promised a place in federal witness protection after his tenure was over, he also had less to fear from ballooning his list of enemies. By the first few years of the 1960s, Vincent Teresa had become a full-fledged Mafia rat. The campaign to flip inside guys accelerated after the election of John F. Kennedy to the White House in 1961. He quickly made his brother, Bobby Kennedy, the Attorney General and with this new executive and judicial power, Bobby set to work recruiting as many made guys as possible from across the Mafia hubs and building cases off of the information he received. When it came time to prosecute, the state would have a robust arsenal of first-hand witnesses willing to expose their peers to save themselves. Again, greed proved to be one of the Mafia's most self-destructive characteristics. The effects of this witness hunting process were felt most acutely in New York state, but Boston and Providence were clearly not spared.

In 1963, Teresa ratted out both Henry Tameleo and Jerry Angiulo to the FBI in exchange for a cash payment. Apparently, the two high-ranking Patriarca members were involved in a cartoonish scheme to heist valuable ivory and Chinese Ming dynasty-era jade. The reported value of the stolen goods ranged from about $50,000 to well over a million, but it was a significant amount regardless. Teresa was questioned in the investigation, during which he told police exactly where they could find the loot and was willing to implicate his own boss and the top guy in Boston. Vincent appears to have told the truth about this, at least: Both Tameleo and Angiulo's fingerprints were successfully lifted off the car in which they found the jade and ivory stashed, presumably as the pair waited for a suitable buyer. The police seized the goods, which of course caused problems in the Family as no one understood how the Feds could have known where it was.

Raymond ended up summoning both Tameleo and Angiulo to his Providence office to explain themselves and the debacle. The pair offered up excuses and theories, and it was suggested that perhaps someone ratted, but ultimately the two turned on each other under Raymond's disapproving gaze. Angiulo accused Tameleo of being reckless, and vice versa. It led to suspicions between Family members that would last for years and began a period of distrust between even the closest of associates. The Patriarca don, however, came to his own conclusion: The Feds must have discovered the location of the stolen goods by eavesdropping on his underlings via electronic surveillance devices. Raymond was already a paranoid man, but it seems that it went into overdrive after the jade bust. The New England boss told all his guys to be vigilant and utterly discrete in their dealings, and he closed off his inner circle even further. Frankly, he was terrified of wiretaps and hidden video recording devices, which he likened to witnesses that couldn't be killed, intimidated, or bribed. They were, in his eyes, a mafioso's kryptonite.

Angiulo was also succumbing to paranoia around this time, and was apparently frantic about the possibility of an IRS indictment. When he crunched his own numbers, he realized he could easily be found liable for over two years worth of tax fraud. With all of the media attention and high-profile, nationally televised senate hearings, all it would take is one tax agent to take an interest in the Angiulo name and his entire Boston operation could be in jeopardy. Then, also in 1963, an article published in the *Saturday Evening Post* dropped the jaws of just about every gangster from Providence to Boston. In uncomfortable detail, it described the illicit operations of Raymond Patriarca's empire and the myriad rackets they controlled for all their subscribers to read. Raymond's public image took yet another beating along with those of his top underlings. Even their "legitimate" rackets, especially National Cigarette, began to bleed profit because Raymond's name being attached to them scared business away (plus, with the strong-arm tactics of Nazarian directly exposed by the McClellan Committee, intimidation as a method of securing customers became less effective). Aside from the fronts, Raymond and Angiulo also personally lost a lot on some joint ventures, including some golf courses and a large investment in Vegas.

Financial woes continued for most of the top brass in New England, but the worst of 1963 was still to come. In October of that year, the efforts of Hoover and RFK paid dividends as the McClellan Committee gave way to the McClellan Hearings. These crusaders had long been searching for someone, a made man with enough credit (and dirt on them) who was willing to spill everything they knew about La Cosa Nostra. They eventually found their man in Joe Valachi, a soldier in the Genovese Family. Valachi was willing to tell all (even some fabricated bits) and his testimony was so consequential that the entire hearing process came to be known as the Valachi Hearings. During the hearings, Valachi became the first man in organized crime history to admit to the world, from the inside, that the Mafia existed. He went into great, frustrating detail about how the Mafia operated and how it was structured. He even detailed the most sacred of Mafia rituals which they performed at initiation ceremonies for new members. He spoke mostly about the Five Families, but in his testimony he also pointed to Raymond Patriarca by name as the top gangster of all the northeastern states.

Afterwards, Walter Stone—an official of the Rhode Island police—publicly poured salt in the wound by describing Patriarca as dangerous, underhanded, and absolutely not to be trusted. Angiulo got it bad in Boston too, where commissioner Ed McNamara publicly dropped Jerry's name when describing the illegal operations he was investigating. Jerry also had to fear for his safety after a botched attempt on his life at his home. The incident caused even more infighting in the Family, as Jerry began pointing fingers at other Patriarca members, specifically a made guy named Iacone. Some accounts claim that the veteran Frank Iacone was the one Jerry accused of the hit, but this is impossible since estate records detail Iacone's death in 1956. The name could have been a coincidence, but it's more likely he was a relative of Frank since, during an earlier encounter, Raymond clearly showed favor to him. During a meeting between this Iacone and Angiulo, Angiulo had supposedly severely insulted the other. When Iacone told Raymond about the run-in, he gave him explicit permission to murder Angiulo (Raymond's top man in Boston) on the spot if he ever spoke to him in that manner again. Raymond of course had to mediate the dispute, but his hasty and violent suggestion to Iacone was a sign of times to come—Raymond was losing his ability to arbitrate peacefully between his men.

Angiulo, still deeply troubled by the law and his various enemies, even considered fleeing the country to get away from it all, believing that "this thing of ours" would be easier back in Sicily with the old Families or up in Canada with the Cotronis and Rizzutos. The enforcer and Family associate Joe Barboza, too, was growing increasingly paranoid; both of being identified by police and of being murdered in the street. He allegedly went so far as to disguise himself in public for fear of someone recognizing him, often comically dressing up as an old lady. These fears wore him down over the years and eventually, like Vincent Teresa, he flipped. By 1967, Barboza was informing the FBI on the Patriarcas. As the story goes, Barboza was picked up on a weapons charge sometime after being released from jail in 1964. The Patriarcas didn't seem to mind, as they had seemingly grown tired of Barboza's shenanigans anyway. Despite his pleas, no one from the Family visited him or posted his bail. Worse, members of his own crew were suspiciously murdered while they were gathering money to secure his release. Feeling betrayed and with no one else to turn to, Barboza agreed to cooperate with the FBI.

Joe "The Animal" was now on the payroll and the 1960s had plenty of other curveballs for Raymond. He had been dealing with his wife's cancer diagnosis throughout the decade and in 1965, one of his oldest right-hand-men, Louis "The Fox" was indicted for tax evasion, convicted in 1967, and finally shot dead in front of his home in 1970. But before the new decade dawned, Raymond's worst fears had already come true. Teresa did a lot of damage, and Barboza did too when he flipped and ultimately testified, but the "witness" that Raymond couldn't kill proved most destructive at all. His fears of surveillance and wiretaps were justified and, as it turns out, Raymond's decision to cease all meetings at The Office in Providence was a decision made much too late.

CHAPTER 4

THE 1970S, FROM BEHIND BARS

In 1967 it was discovered that for months, the once-revered office of Raymond Patriarca, a room that had literally become synonymous with the New England Mafia itself, was riddled with FBI recording devices. During this period, nearly every conversation Raymond had with associates, whether mundane or criminal, was being eavesdropped upon. This included explicit conversations with other top guys, including Henry Tameleo and Angiulo, about activities related to ongoing investigations. The fact that this had continued on for so long under Raymond's nose was, unsurprisingly, a source of intense embarrassment for the don. His reputation in the public eye had long since been tarnished, but after this, his status as New England's underworld kingpin was also called into question. With the help of these tapes (they were later found to be inadmissible in court, but the damage was already done), as well as the cooperation of Barboza, the law was rapidly preparing to make its move against Il Patrone and his multiple-state-wide empire. The start of the 1970s would be the start of yet another completely new chapter in Raymond's life as his empire threatened to come undone.

Facing Kennedy's Music

Back in 1966, a mob-connected bookie out of Providence by the name of Willie Marfeo was shot dead as he ate lunch at a restaurant that was walking distance from Raymond's office. Marfeo had run afoul with the Patriarca clan several times and had made plenty of enemies from years of dodging his debts. It's not clear exactly who killed Marfeo, nor who gave the order, but it could have been any number of people in Rhode Island. Tameleo was suspected by some of Willie's brothers, and some suspected Barboza. This was a problem for Barboza as he was already worried about being gunned down every time he left his house, plus the Marfeos were, by all accounts, predictably violent. Luckily for him though, he had the FBI on his side and when it came time to prosecute for the murder, he was more than willing to point the finger in any and all directions. In 1969, Raymond Patriarca, Henry Tameleo, and Jerry Angiulo were all forced to defend themselves against the charges levied against them by mob informant Joe Barboza as he accused them all of orchestrating Marfeo's death.

The investigations didn't stop at Marfeo. The FBI was attempting their grand slam and successive charges would help pin down the Providence and Boston crews before they could weasel out of the consequences once again. After Marfeo, it was the murder of the Irish gangster and Bonanno Family associate Teddy Deegan that Barboza and his handlers in the FBI tried to throw at the Patriarcas. Deegan, who operated largely in the small and compact Massachusetts town of Chelsea, had started to become a growing figure in the Boston scene, and so his murder provided a good opportunity to strike at several of the top guys outside of Rhode

Island. Tameleo was once again charged with murder, along with Peter Limone, Louis Greco, Ronnie Cassesso, Joe Salvati, and Willie French. Barboza's testimony against them was damning but in reality, he was only actually aware of the involvement of Cassesso and French (ironically, Barboza himself was also involved in the Deegan hit). By the time Barboza and the federal agents guiding him were finished embellishing and outright lying their way through the court proceedings Tameleo, Limone, Greco, and Cassesso had received sentences of death. The other two were spared execution, but were sentenced to prison cells for the rest of their lives. As for Raymond, the Marfeo case resulted in a sentence of up to 10 years in prison, which is how he began the new decade. The upper echelon of Patriarca leadership had been decimated.

To illustrate the desperation that must have been felt by the Patriarca brass during the trial, one need only look to their defense's strategy in court. Raymond's last-ditch plan was, literally, to make Barboza so angry that he would physically assault them in court. Using potentially fabricated evidence gathered by a private investigator that Raymond hired, the defendants planned to accuse Barboza, among other things, of being a pimp, a drug mule, and of being the son of a prostitute. Everyone knew that Joe "The Animal" was notoriously hot-headed and ideally, an emotional or violent outburst from him would call into question his character and reliability before the jury. If nothing else, it would at least make a brand new trial necessary, thus extending their days as free men a little bit longer.

If Barboza's prior fear of being murdered was unwarranted, it wasn't any longer. The outrage throughout the New England mob against Joe was severe both during the trials and after they concluded. Generally speaking, lawyers were off limits when planning hits, regardless of who they represented. For Barboza, though, they were willing to make an exception. Sometime before the sentences from the Marfeo and Deegan cases were handed down, a car bomb was planted in the car of J. E. Fitzgerald, the man representing Barboza. It detonated as planned and cost the lawyer his leg, but he managed to at least survive the blast. Barboza was clearly a target though, and it had already been clear that he would need to be placed in witness protection at the conclusion of his service as state witness. With Jerry Angiulo being one of the few higher-ups in the Family to make it through Barboza's assault relatively unscathed, it was up to him to lead the unsuccessful hunt to kill the rat Barboza. Unsuccessful, that is, until 1976 when Joe "The Animal" became the first known man to be murdered while under federal witness protection after Jerry's connections learned where he was hiding out in California. In mid-February of that year, Barboza was shot dead and finally put out of his misery.

The entire Barboza situation caused intense stress throughout the high ranks of the Family. It caused members to turn on each other, especially Henry Tameleo, who had apparently been one of Joe's biggest defenders early on and had vouched for him on multiple occasions. Now though, in Tameleo's eyes he was a "weak, dirty piece of garbage," (quoted in Songini, 2015). Still, many—including Raymond—put at least partial blame for the entire situation on Tameleo, claiming that if not for Tameleo's recklessness and poor judgment of character, Barboza never would have been able to be linked to the Family anyway. Angiulo too blamed Tameleo for being the one who talked him down when he originally planned on killing Barboza some time earlier. Regardless of whether all this is completely true, the Family was distressed and needed someone to point the finger at. During and after the Barboza fiasco, the upper tier of the Family began efforts to try to weed out and eliminate any other possible informants hiding among them to avoid a repeat of the situation. The efforts were ultimately in vain, but much time was spent devising ways to identify the rats. This included starting a controlled disinformation campaign, whereby Raymond and the other high-ranking made guys would supply individual members and associates with random, contradictory pieces of information regarding criminal activity. Then, when being questioned or in conversation with the police or federal agents, it would be a simple matter of listening to what the officers accused them of, and then cross-referencing that with whom in the Family they gave that false information—then they would then have their man. It was a solid plan in theory, if a bit risky. Still, the Mafia's informant problem was not going away anytime soon, despite their best efforts.

While Raymond was in prison, he remained the official boss and continued to administer Providence, relaying his orders to his underlings from behind bars while Jerry Angiulo manned the Boston crews. Raymond at least managed to control his violent temper long enough for it to be considered "good behavior," and he ended up serving only about five years of his decade-long sentence. Still, it was a challenging period for him, and nearly everything about running a Family was made more difficult while in custody. Challenging, but not impossible. Several other bosses have done it, including Lucky Luciano and Vito Genovese, and Patriarca would do it too. While he was away though, a new and brutal figure was on the rise in Boston—the legendary Irish-American gangster

Whitey Bulger. He caused problems for a lot of people as he led a bloody war through the streets of Boston, and Angiulo was one of them. Around the same time, a Patriarca associate named Stephen Flemmi began working with Bulger. Flemmi had a sour history with the Patriarcas, as Raymond once had to call a meeting with him to demand that he stop carrying out hits without permission from The Office. Unbeknownst to Raymond, he had also been an informant for the FBI since at least the mid-1960s.

More than one disreputable FBI agent had a hand in all that had transpired in the Family during these years. In Barboza's case, it was his handlers Paul Rico and Dennis Condon who guided Joe through his various false testimonies, and Rico watched silently as The Animal perjured himself, under his own direction, in federal court. Rico was also aware of the Fitzgerald car bombing from the late '60s, and it was he who ensured Vincent Flemmi (Stephen's brother) fled while the investigation took place and saw to it that Frankie Salemme was fingered for it instead. In the case of Bulger and Stephen Flemmi, it was agent John Connolly pulling the strings (or, according to Bulger, perhaps it was the other way around). After Connolly met with the two gangsters and formed their initial understanding, Bulger and the Winter Hill Gang wreaked havoc with a renewed sense of impunity. Connolly was constantly running interference for Bulger's crew, even against other FBI agents, and served as his protector. With Connolly, whom Bulger referred to as "Zip," in their pocket, Angiulo's work was cut out for him. A staggering number of rival gangsters were massacred in Boston's streets during these years, including Joe Notarageli and Spike O'Toole, both of whom were murdered in 1973, as well as Tommy King two years later. Connolly was aware of the majority of these murders either before or after they happened, and he held Bulger and Flemmi responsible for exactly none of them. Rico and Connolly turned out to be borderline criminals themselves and, as we'll see, the law eventually came to recognize that.

Angiulo didn't have a ton of time to deal with the Winter Hill Gang and their violence in his city anyway. He had to prevent the Boston faction from falling out of line and rebelling in the absence of Il Patrone, whose influence from prison was distant enough in Providence, let alone Massachusetts. To this end, Jerry appointed Ilario "Larry" Zannino, a Patriarca *caporegime*, to be his trusted number two in Beantown. Needing a trustworthy and reliable counsel, he also made his older brother and Patriarca veteran Nicolo Angiulo his *consigliere* in 1974. Acquiring a cool and level-headed advisor was wise, as just two years prior in 1972, Jerry inexplicably risked it all over what could have been a non-issue. Off the coast near the Boston Harbor in July of that year, the Coast Guard patrol identified and attempted to stop Angiulo while he was sailing around on his yacht. He could have cooperated and faced no consequences (there was apparently nothing illegal onboard that day), but he instead chose to sail his yacht away for miles, pretending like he didn't notice the Coast Guard ship attempting to hail him down. When he finally yielded and parked his boat near Dorchester, he proceeded to assault the officers attempting to board. When it was all said and done, Jerry had his day in court but only spent a month in jail, continuing his incredible streak of good luck.

In 1974, things were beginning to look relatively back to normal—the heat from the Barboza case and the car bombing was dying down, operations in Boston were continuing despite Bulger's rampage, and the Family was preparing to welcome back its long-time don, Raymond Patriarca, from his latest prison stint.

Patriarca Returns

In 1974, Raymond once again left his cell in Atlanta. He was a free man and was aiming to keep it that way, but he still had scores to settle. Upon his release, Patriarca was incensed at developments in the Mafia world. The rats, both Joe Barboza and Vincent Teresa, had authored expository books about their lives in the New England Patriarca Family which promised to be exclusive "tell-all" accounts. Several of these were published while Raymond was imprisoned, and some hit stores soon after his release, as though to pour salt in his fresh wounds. The real Mafia secrets that the two had exposed definitely would've angered Raymond, but likely far more annoying were the myriad fabrications and outright lies that they had put to their pages. Raymond had always disliked both of them (he reportedly hated Barboza) but now he wanted them dead. Teresa got off lucky and lasted until 1990 before dying of organ failure, but it took under three years to locate and murder Barboza. Joe Russo (not to be confused with the Colombo Family *capo* Joe Russo), a mobster with ties to both the Patriarca and Lucchese Family in NYC, tracked him down to San Francisco with Salemme. Suspecting the former enforcer would likely still be armed while under witness protection and a fake name (they were correct), Russo snuck up behind him to perform the execution.

So, Raymond was out of prison and the centerpiece of the prosecution that helped put him there had been repaid with several shotgun shells in the back. But not all was well in Providence, nor Boston. Raymond was now going to be under intense legal scrutiny for the remainder of his life, a fact that he understood painfully well even before his release. A perpetually stressed man, it wasn't long before his health began to decline. Accusations of misdoings continued to nag him, and in 1978 Teresa decided to speak up once again (he had already testified in 1971 and was responsible for several other made guys and associates being put away). This time, he divulged Raymond Patriarca's involvement in a bizarre, clandestine scheme orchestrated by the CIA to enlist American mafiosi in an attempt to assassinate Fidel Castro, the leader of Cuba. Oddly enough, this wasn't the strangest route the CIA took to try to unseat the communist Caribbean President, but it was probably the most offensive to the American legal system. In any case, the ill-conceived plot was abandoned before it took off, but it would have made sense for both parties. When Castro took over in 1959, he led a mostly successful drive to eliminate the considerable influence of the American Mafia on the island and as a result, Families (including the Patriarcas) lost out on the lucrative Cuban gambling market. It's been alleged that part of the deal included a promise of safe haven for the Mob to operate in post-Castro Cuba. None of it came to fruition (including *any* of the attempts on Castro's life) but Patriarca's name was dragged through the national mud once again.

In 1981, things also started to really go downhill for Angiulo in Boston. That year, Whitey Bulger and Stephen Flemmi offered to draw up an accurate floor plan of Jerry's office on Prince Street and another on Margin Street for the FBI. Along with this, they would outline the best places for their handlers to install listening devices and wiretaps based on where they knew the Angiulo brothers typically discussed business. This allowed the two Winter Hill gangsters' handlers to infiltrate and thoroughly bug the Boston underboss' hideout. Listening intently, the federal agents got a solid three months' worth of recordings which they could sit on for a while to determine how best to use it against the Patriarcas. A number of high-ranking guys including Angiulo and Zannino had their voices identified on the tapes, once again discussing criminal activity and matters relating to ongoing investigations. It's somewhat surprising that Angiulo had allowed this to happen, considering he was well aware that the feds were eyeing his spots—Connolly's colleague Dennis Condon had frequently taunted Jerry by openly surveilling him at his office for years. Regardless, it happened; and among other things, authorities learned from Ilario Zannino's mouth that it was Russo who carried out the hit on Barboza back in 1976. Russo eventually went down for the hit (he was on the lam for some time under Raymond's orders to avoid being picked up for the shooting), but Angiulo was marked too.

In 1983 the FBI made their move on the Boston crime lord, arresting him on a multitude of charges including extortion, gambling, general racketeering, and ordering killings. His Mafia career and the entire Boston faction of the empire were now in jeopardy and Raymond feared losing yet another of his top guys. Despite attempting countless times to convince the judge and jury that he had been set up by Connolly and his Winter Hill stooges, Angiulo received a sentence so severe that, at his current age, he would have been about 112 years old upon his eventual release. The 45-year term was handed down to him in 1986 but before he served half of it, he was released due to poor health and died a couple years later. The Patriarca veteran appears to have been fully removed from operations in Boston post-1986. In the same trial, Jerry's right-hand man Zannino was also handed a conviction, along with several of his brothers. The North End crew was left emaciated and disorganized, a shell of its former self. With their main roadblock removed, Bulger and the Winter Hill Gang, with the help and oversight of Connolly, swept through the Boston scene to seize its rackets. The Italian gangs apparently never stood a chance without Angiulo and his crew in command.

While the legal battle with the Boston faction was underway, Raymond was dealing with his own charges in Providence. Back in 1965, Raymond had personally hired a hitman to gun down a petty street thug named Ray Curcio. Curcio, apparently desperate for cash, had broken into and robbed the house where Patriarca's son, Junior, lived. Some sources, including the *New York Times*, reported at the time that it was actually Raymond's brother's house, which could have been the case considering Junior was just about 20 years old at the time. In any case, Raymond managed to avoid the consequences of this hit when he went to prison in 1969/70, but it had now come back to bite him. Witnesses in tow, the feds charged Raymond with the Curcio murder in 1983, and the next year, he was charged with yet another murder. This time it was the 1968 hit on Robert Candos, a known heister and associate that Patriarca reportedly believed was going to flip and turn witness. The feds were put onto Raymond's trail after the October 1980 arrest of Nicky Palmigiano, an associate of the Patriarcas, for firearm possession. Apparently Palmigiano claimed that he personally murdered both Curcio and Candos, and he was the one who initially fingered Raymond for ordering both of the hits. Raymond had been free for almost a decade, but the entire time likely felt very much like he was still in prison. Now, he risked going back for real. The process of preparing to defend himself once again, combined with the stress of having to try to manage affairs both at home in Providence and in out-of-state Boston was the final straw for Raymond. The two charges against him might as well have been a thousand charges—he would never end up facing the court for any of them.

CHAPTER 5

JUNIOR TAKES THE REINS

When Raymond Patriarca went away in 1970 for the Marfeo murder, his son Raymond Patriarca Jr. was only about 25 years old. Junior was involved in the Family's activities (although allegedly this was in spite of Raymond Sr.'s initial intentions) but was obviously too young to be given charge of Providence's rackets while the don was in prison. During this time it's not exactly clear what his role would have been, but he managed to climb the ladder enough during the 1970s that he became the heir apparent to his father's empire. The only problem was that, by all accounts, his rise was largely a result of Mafia nepotism. Junior appeared to have been ill-suited for mob life and was considered incompetent by more than a few of Providence's gangsters. Based on what he did in his later years after a stint in prison, it doesn't seem like he much considered himself a Mafia "lifer" anyway. According to a Connecticut attorney named Stanley A. Twardy Jr., "there was no reason to believe Raymond Patriarca [Jr.] was not in control of the Family, although there were certain indications he was not devoting all of his energies to running the Family," (quoted in Foderaro, 1989). Indeed, he may have been more of an "armchair boss." But, while many of his Family's top men, including his father, were facing potential legal action in the 1980s, Junior managed to avoid the vast majority of the heat. This put him in a good position to lead a potentially decimated Mafia clan in a worst-case scenario. With his father in poor health and facing a potential life sentence, this opportunity was rapidly approaching.

Gone for Good

In July of 1984, while both he and Jerry were being bombarded with accusations and charges, 76-year-old Raymond Patriarca Sr. suffered a heart attack. He was taken to a Rhode Island hospital where Judge McOsker decided to arraign him as he lay infirm in his hospital bed. The legal system was chugging along as though nothing had happened, but Raymond soon died while being treated. Just two years later, Angiulo was put in prison for good along with many others. According to Songini, "the New England Mafia became a walking corpse whose decay became more obvious every year," (2015). Still, the Mafia couldn't just dissolve, and the organization would need a new leader. The breakdown of the connection between Boston and Providence had unfortunately resulted in a considerable power struggle in the wake of Raymond's death, with one side backing Junior as the natural heir and the other supporting the highly-compromised Jerry Angiulo. It was lucky for Junior that although the Patriarca Family had lost its namesake, his last name still carried weight. Junior enjoyed widespread support in the underworld and the majority of the Providence faction was behind him. In New York, he received support from the Five Families, particularly the Colombos. Even Angiulo's own legally-embattled underboss threw his weight behind Junior for the boss position. Jerry with his crumbling power base in Massachusetts was unable to seize control of the entire operation, and eventually the New York Families stepped in to end the dispute. On a vote, the Mafia Commission elected to cement Junior Patriarca in his father's former role.

Between the two, it was a beneficial decision for the Family. There was a sense of continuity even though Junior simply couldn't command the respect his father did, and as we know, Jerry Angiulo didn't have a lot of time left as a free man anyway. After his conviction, it's been reported that he was actually demoted or removed officially from the Family, likely as a result of his power grab. Being generally opposed to Junior's rise to boss, his veteran counsel probably couldn't be relied on anyway. Apparently, even after his imprisonment, Angiulo was making half-hearted attempts for a while to wrest and maintain control over Boston, none of which were successful. Even Larry Zannino, one of Jerry's top guys, ended up supporting Junior's bid after he himself briefly tried to consolidate power under him. Zannino was also headed to prison soon anyway on a 30-year sentence and, like Jerry, this was basically his death sentence. While his legal fate was still being decided, Larry was serving as the Commission-appointed *consigliere* to Junior in an effort to cool tensions between the now-distant Providence and Boston factions. Another pointless endeavor, as seeking advice and guidance on criminal matters from a man in federal custody proved virtually impossible. With Angiulo and Zannino put away in 1986, control over what remained seems to have been taken by Frank Salemme, who happened to be close associates with members of the Winter Hill Gang, notably Whitey Bulger and Flemmi. The fact that these two friends of his had been informing on his organization for roughly a decade was unknown to Salemme at the time.

Things in Providence weren't developing very smoothly either. It was quickly becoming clear to many that Junior was a Patriarca in name only and that his ability to maintain his father's Family was questionable. There were also a lot of issues with his public image. That, at least, he had in common with his father. But unlike Raymond Patriarca Sr., who only acquired his notoriety later in his life, Junior was already well-known, and he didn't exactly try to be discreet. He was known to call in to Rhode Island radio shows and happily announce who he was, always proud to play up the fact that he was the son of Il Patrone. He even partially owned a local restaurant that was clearly Mafia-themed. Needless to say, Junior's illicit ties to the underworld were a little "on the nose." He also didn't have the social clout that his father had earned from his years of philanthropy and charitable works in Providence and his area in particular. Raymond was known to favor those less fortunate than himself, often funding the school tuition for neighborhood youths, paying medical bills on behalf of struggling families, and donating to various causes and funds in the city. Though Raymond eventually had to cease his philanthropy when Family business started to take a severe downturn in the late 1960s and 1970s, the goodwill he had built up was apparently squandered with Junior in charge.

It was becoming clearer all the time that Junior's time atop New England's gangster totem pole was going to be a short-lived one. Most of the veteran mobsters who had been around for decades and had somehow managed to avoid prison believed Junior was a misguided choice in the first place. After all, Junior simply didn't have the upbringing nor the life experiences that Raymond Sr. did. Il Patrone, like most Mafia veterans, grew up poor and had to claw their way up from virtually nothing. It was survival of the fittest where only the most capable were able to survive and thrive. This, it was believed, developed the kind of character that was necessary to become a successful boss in La Cosa Nostra. Junior, on the other hand, grew up as the son of one of the most successful and powerful criminal kingpins on the eastern seaboard. He grew up in affluence in a safe, wealthy community, as opposed to a poor Italian ghetto, and was at least partially educated—a rare quality in the Mafia underworld. Most importantly, Junior was a part of that generation of mafiosi that came into their own in the post-Valachi period. The Mafia was already exposed, the code of honor and *omerta* that held the Mafia together for decades had dissolved, and it had become commonplace to save oneself by ratting on your friends. It seems that, despite their support for Junior's leadership bid, even the New York Families did not have much faith that the younger Patriarca would last very long.

Junior's Downfall

In the wake of Junior's ascension, it was William Grasso, known as "the Wild Man" or "Wild Guy Grasso," who was chosen to serve as the Patriarca underboss. The circumstances around Grasso's selection aren't known for sure, but it's possible that the decision emanated from New York City. Grasso was a Connecticut-based gangster who operated mostly out of Hartford. This was an area that was under the influence of both the Patriarcas and the Five Families and as such, Grasso ran his rackets for a long time as a member of the Colombo Family, who operated with the blessing of the New England Mafia. It wasn't an obvious choice for Grasso to take over underboss duties from Connecticut, but it's been suggested that one or more New York Families arranged for Grasso to be appointed so that he could oversee operations in Providence. Assuming the leadership in New York doubted Junior's capabilities, this would have made sense. With the Boston crew in shambles and the Irish Winter Hill gang threatening to fully take over the Mafia's rackets there, they needed a more firm grasp on their out-of-state operations.

It was assumed for a long time that "Wild Guy" Grasso was, effectively, the don. It may have been the sort of situation where Junior functioned as more of a figurehead, which was not at all uncommon in the Mafia world, especially in the 1980s and 1990s. This was the era of RICO suits and witness hunting, and so many Families, notably the Genoveses, employed "front bosses," which were individuals meant to be seen as the boss in order for the real boss to operate outside of police scrutiny. Front bosses would be the ones to meet with other made guys and function as the mouthpiece for the real boss, who would rarely expose himself by discussing Family business anywhere besides the most secure locations. Junior would have made for a good front boss, as he drew plenty of police attention, took little issue with people associating him with the Mafia, and literally shared his name with Rhode Island's former public enemy number one. William Grasso, by comparison, was an unknown entity. If this truly was the strategy being used, it was at least partially effective: rival gangsters would get to Grasso well before the law was close to zeroing in on him.

It's impossible to say for sure what degree of control Grasso had over Junior and the Patriarca clan in the years he functioned as underboss from Hartford, but whatever the case was, it's clear that Junior was not regarded as a powerful or intimidating boss. This was true of both his friends and his many enemies, but it was apparently true of law enforcement as well. Even in Connecticut, authorities had long assumed that Grasso was the head honcho of the entire New England operation, which was made clear in the trial of Louis Failla, a low-level soldier of the lesser-known Connecticut faction of the Family. Failla was facing racketeering charges with seven other co-defendants, but Failla was also being charged with conspiracy to commit murder. Apparently he was given orders to murder Tito Morales, the father of Failla's grandson who had apparently run afoul with the Family. It was apparently an open-and-shut case, as Failla's vehicle had been bugged. Embarrassingly, Failla's hoarse, highly distinguishable voice was recorded specifically planning Morales' murder. Not only that, he also was heard bragging about his various illegal operations and rackets, and, inexplicably, even began rattling off the names of various other Patriarca members and associates who he conducted illegal business with. All the while, the prosecutors had been attempting to link Failla's criminal enterprise to William "The Wild Guy" Grasso, and *not* Raymond Patriarca Jr.

In the mid-1980s the FBI had plants everywhere, in various locations and in various ranks of the Mafia. They knew well the kind of reputation that Junior had and the lack of esteem that his fellow mobsters had for him, especially those located outside Rhode Island. In Boston especially, many within the remnants of the former Angiulo crew had grown bitter and resentful toward Junior's appointment as boss—many of the senior members in Boston who had initially supported Junior had since been put in prison. The FBI, still not finished with the Family, sought to exploit the perceived personal weaknesses of Junior Patriarca and explored ways to destroy the New England Mafia from within. In combination with legal prosecution, rattling the cages of the Family leadership would make them more vulnerable, sloppy, and less able to conduct their business. So, the feds began a campaign to sow discontent throughout the ranks of the Family, specifically among those who were less than satisfied with Junior as boss. Using state boundaries to their advantage, they focused their efforts on Massachusetts and Connecticut-based gangsters.

Central to the FBI's plan was the effort by both federal agents and their plants, namely Angelo Mercurio, to convince Patriarca Family members and associates that Junior was preparing to take action against them. Mercurio, nicknamed "Sonny," ended up having nearly as destructive an impact on the New England Mafia as Joe "The Animal" Barboza had years earlier. He was a Boston native who grew up just outside the city and, born in 1936, he was about 9 years older than Junior. Since even before he was confirmed to be associated with the Patriarcas, Mercurio had an impressive rap sheet. At just 18 years old, a Massachusetts judge handed him a sentence of life imprisonment for his role in an armed robbery just outside Boston. That could have been the end of the story, and the Patriarcas would have been better off, but fate once again stepped in. Mercurio received a pardon from the state after about 10 years and was a free man in 1964, the same year Barboza got out. During this time, he definitely became associated with the Patriarcas, if he wasn't already. The problem was that he was also closely associated with the Winter Hill Gang, and often served as a middleman in their dealings during the late 1960s and 1970s.

As it turns out, Mercurio flipping was in itself a payoff of the efforts of the FBI in Boston to recruit from within. When Sonny was sent away on another prison bid around 1978, the Family was already suffering deeply and had been basically forsaking anyone who was unlucky enough to be put away. This meant that even made guys who were in prison often got little support from the Family. In Sonny's case, no one was collecting from his operations on his behalf and his family reportedly didn't see a dime from any Patriarca members while he was incarcerated. The resentment that this bred was fueled by the Winter Hill Gang, whose members Whitey Bulger and Stephen Flemmi made sure his loved ones were taken care of. When Mercurio was out in 1986, he was one of the clearest examples of mafiosi who were dissatisfied with Junior, and this made him an easy target for Connolly and his stooges to manipulate. So, at some point after his release (around 1986 or 1987), Flemmi provided yet another floorplan to Connolly, this time of the basement of Sonny's Italian grocery store in the Prudential Center on Boston's Boylston Street. Once they had enough dirt on Mercurio to get a likely conviction, they charged him with extortion and racketeering. Facing another term in prison, he was presented with the option of instead cooperating and informing on the Patriarcas, which Flemmi coaxed him into accepting. In 1987, Mercurio became the latest Patriarca on the FBI's payroll. Together, Mercurio, Winter Hill, and the feds began causing unrest within the ranks, which included convincing them that Junior was currently planning a purge of the Family and would soon make moves on those he believed were disloyal or otherwise unhappy with his leadership. Chaos soon followed, and this strategy proved to be effective in the coming years.

The 1980s had three more major challenges in store for the Patriarcas before the decade closed, at least two of which Mercurio had a hand in. In June of 1989 Frank Salemme, who had been climbing the Patriarca ranks for years, was advised by Mercurio to attend a sit-down (if you can call it that—it reportedly took place in an IHOP parking lot) between high-ranking members of the now-feuding Providence and Boston factions. Specifically, Salemme was in a struggle with Joe Russo, who was supported by Mercurio, and both of them were reportedly vying for control. Unfortunately for "Cadillac Frank," Sonny's meeting was a setup. As he awaited the other supposed attendants, armed men approached him unseen and fired. Salemme caught two bullets, one in the lower body and another in his chest, though it luckily avoided his heart. Wounded, he frantically shambled into the restaurant and then out through its back entrance as his would-be assassins continued to unload before fleeing the scene. Salemme ultimately survived but he and his crew were shaken, and the bad blood only got worse.

Then, the same month that Frank was very nearly whacked, Junior's underboss "Wild Guy" Will Grasso was murdered. He was shot at close range while en route to Worcester, where he planned to attend to business regarding the remnants of Raymond Patriarca's old Coin-O-Matic vending operation. The shooter was presumably the only passenger known to be in the car with him at the time, Gaetano Milano, a made guy from Springfield, MA. Grasso's body was eventually recovered, floating down the Connecticut River near Hartford, and Milano was later picked up for the murder. When defending himself, Milano claimed that the murder was necessary self-defense, as the Patriarca Family was in a be-or-be-killed situation where everyone was at each other's throats. Believing that

Grasso, the force behind Junior, was soon going to make his move against disloyal elements in the Family, Milano apparently was forced to act first. Clearly, the campaign by Mercurio, Flemmi, Bulger, and the FBI to spread suspicion and violent mistrust was proving to be a resounding success. With these new developments, different factions of the Family began fighting each other more aggressively for dominance and with Grasso gone and Junior weaker than ever, the young boss could not hope to maintain his position. While we don't know if Mercurio had *directly* contributed to the hit on Grasso, his role in the third and final disaster of 1989 was essential.

CHAPTER 6
DISCONTENT IN THE COMMONWEALTH

Needless to say, the 1980s were not friendly to the Patriarca Family. Infighting, treachery, and greed had crippled the connection that once bound the cities of Providence and Boston and as a result, the Family's operation was hobbled. Aside from the murders and murder attempts, the 1980s was also the era of the "crack epidemic" moral panic. Americans in cities across the country were becoming more afraid of the effects of drug abuse and of drugs entering their communities and as a result, the so-called war on drugs was revitalized. Along with that came far more severe punishments for both drug possession and drug distribution. In New England, the Mafia controlled a large portion of both the cocaine and cannabis market, which state and federal law enforcement began to crack down hard on in the 1980s. This, combined with the fact that most dealers in the Mafia were also strung out on their own drugs, made drug peddlers easy targets for witness hunting. The crusade against the drug rackets in New England continued to plague the Patriarcas well into the 1990s, but it still did not have the destructive power of Angelo Mercurio's final backstab. Rather than Family *capos* and underlings, his target this time was Junior Patriarca himself.

Junior's Last Straw

In the 1980s, the Patriarcas' long-standing political and judicial connections began to fall apart. One of the most notable of Raymond's old connections was Joseph Bevilacqua, the former Speaker of the Rhode Island House of Representatives and later Chief Justice of the state's Supreme Court. Bevilacqua, who was born in Providence in 1918, was apparently a close friend of Raymond Sr. for years, and in 1973—one year before Patriarca was released from prison—Bevilacqua testified to his supposedly impeccable moral character and unshakable integrity. There's little doubt that Bevilacqua was a considerable influence in the Parole Board's decision to release Raymond Sr. before his sentence had been fully served (Bevilacqua's connections didn't stop at Raymond Sr.; he was apparently close with the veteran Nick Bianco as well). Politically speaking, his praise of a well-known criminal and accused murderer was certainly a strange move that earned suspicious glances from more than a few of his colleagues. In fact, by the time Bevilacqua was elected to the office of Chief Justice, his connections to Italian-American organized crime were so well-known that he felt obligated to publicly denounce his past and assure his colleagues that he had already moved on from it. However, this was clearly not true, and it became obvious by the early 1980s. He had been identified visiting the homes of known Patriarca Family members several times, was accused of allowing criminals to hide in his home in return for cash payments, and was known to be an avid customer of the Patriarca Family's prostitution establishments. By 1984 he was under intense scrutiny and two years later he was impeached. Bevilacqua resigned from office in

1986, and thus the Patriarcas had lost a vital piece of their legal advantage. The Family could no longer rely on Rhode Island's Chief Justice to run interference for them.

Junior's position was now tenuous, at best. Many rival gangsters wanted to unseat him by force if necessary, and most who didn't directly oppose him still believed that he should probably be removed. The last straw for him came later in 1989 at—of all things—a Mafia induction ceremony; the secretive rites that Joe Valachi had exposed decades earlier. Some time before the ceremony took place, Mercurio tipped off Connolly as to its date and whereabouts. This gave them time to form a plan, and Mercurio ended up agreeing to wear a listening device on his person while he attended the induction in Medford. When the time came, Sonny dutifully concealed the wire and made sure to stand as close as he could to whoever was talking to get the clearest sound quality. The entire hours-long ceremony was recorded, along with the identifiable voices of the roughly dozen mobsters who were attending including Junior, Joe Russo, Nick Bianco, Matt Guglielmetti, Vincent Ferrara, and even Bobby Carrozza, also known as "Baby/Bobby Russo," one of the leading figures behind the Patriarca rebellion. Junior's hobby of calling into popular radio shows and announcing himself came back to haunt him: cross-referencing his radio appearances with the recording made his voice particularly easy to identify. During the ceremony, Junior announced that Russo would be the new official head of the Boston faction, and then Russo carried out the induction rites, which included bloodletting, an oath of both silence and loyalty to the Family, and burning a picture of a Catholic saint while the initiate holds it. And the feds heard every word of it.

This scheme, made possible by the treachery of Mercurio, was the first time that a Mafia induction ceremony had been successfully bugged by the FBI. The most obvious repercussion of this historic bit of espionage was that now the government had undeniable proof that Junior, Russo, and others, were all a part of the same criminal organization, not to mention the brand new recruits Vincent Federico, Ricky Floramo, Rob DeLuca, and Carmen Tortora. This evidence would allow a potential future RICO suit against them to be far more effective. RICO suits, feared by the Mafia since their inception, stood for Racketeer Influenced and Corrupt Organizations. It was a sweeping reform in American criminal justice and allowed for the mass prosecution of an unlimited number of defendants in a criminal case. If one individual was charged with a crime and it was determined that that crime was performed in the service of a broader criminal organization, prosecutors were able to trace a line all the way up to the leader of the organization and charge every single person along the way, all for one criminal action. Further, it allowed federal agents to effectively cripple an organization before a court conviction or even a trial. If a RICO suit was launched and agents suspected that funds possessed by the accused were acquired illegally, the prosecution was allowed to freeze all of those assets, rendering the accused effectively poor. For example, if the government believed that a certain club owned by a Patriarca man was utilized in criminal dealings, assets and income related to the establishment could be seized before they even had a chance to defend themselves. So, with Mercurio's recording, the FBI's job was made very easy, as it was spelled out for them exactly who was in the organization as well as who the leaders were of both the Boston and Providence crews.

When the news broke that the ceremony, which had been approved and overseen by Junior, had been taped by the FBI, whatever respect that was still attached to Raymond Jr.'s last name had vanished along with any hopes he had of reforging his father's crumbling empire. It was a calamity for the entire Patriarca Family and an embarrassment for everyone involved in its planning, but ultimate blame was laid squarely at Junior's feet. The fact that he allowed a sacred Mafia tradition to be sloppily exposed by a rat wearing a hidden wire was beyond disgraceful, and Junior lost all ability to maintain control over his underlings and prevent the splitting of the Family. In addition, with the tape in the hands of the government and with plenty of investigations already ongoing, aggressive legal action was expected before long. Under these conditions, Junior had little choice but to step down as head of the Family. After only five years as don, Junior was out, with neither his tenure nor his legacy having even approached that of his father.

Yet again, the Family was in need of a new boss. Ultimately, the job fell to Nick Bianco, whether he wanted it or not. Interestingly, Bianco was actually the man that most expected would have taken the position of boss in the first place after Patriarca Sr.'s death, as he was respected and had significant ties to the Five Families in NYC. Born in Providence in 1932, Bianco was a venerable gangster whose roots dated back to Frank Morelli and the Morelli Brothers crew. Although he cut his teeth in Rhode Island, he was highly mobile, traveling frequently between his home state and New York where he formed lifelong connections, especially in Brooklyn. Having been associated with the Colombos since the days when they were known as the Profaci Family, he was considered a part of the old school and as such, he outclassed Junior in just about every category that mattered, except he didn't share the Patriarca last name. The popular yet unfulfilled expectation that Bianco would step into the role vacated by Raymond Sr. was not surprising, given that Bianco was asked to return to New England in the early 1970s by his friend Joe Colombo in order to help maintain control while Il Patrone was serving his prison sentence. His time finally did come in 1989 but it was far too late to reverse any of the damage that had already been done—damage which Bianco may have had some outside chance at preventing had he been given control years earlier. Regardless, he didn't have much time left for any kind of course correction.

The Troublesome 90s

Some accounts claim that Nick Bianco was eventually selected to be Junior's successor because he was one of the few high-ranking members not present at the induction ceremony. Others claim that Bianco was in fact present, but he was selected because either he didn't speak, his voice wasn't identified, or because he simply managed to avoid the negative repercussions of the induction recording. In any case, Bianco was in and was cleared of suspicion, at least for the immediate term. Soon, likely as anticipated, the incident in Medford led to legal action against most of its participants, but the results were worse than expected. Junior, as well as nearly two dozen other members and associates, were hit with a plethora of charges in one of the largest single attacks on an organized crime Family in history. Junior was indicted on RICO charges in March of 1990, accused of, among many other things, interstate narcotics dealing, gambling, general racketeering, murder, and conspiracy to commit murder. After everything was said and done, Junior was sent to prison for eight years, which marked the end of his incredibly underwhelming career as a mobster. Even after his eventual release, he showed no signs of wanting to return to the Family he helped drive into the ground. The rest of the defendants, including Ferarra and Matt Guglielmetti, were also put away for years and received hefty financial penalties. Clearly, the Mafia was beginning the new decade with a whimper, not a bang.

The one saving grace of the Medford fiasco was that now, at least, the Family was under the leadership and guidance of a veteran elder statesman mafioso in Nick Bianco. Unfortunately, this wasn't meant to last, and Bianco's brief time as Providence kingpin would be over before he could accomplish anything meaningful. Later in 1990, Bianco was charged with fraud, racketeering, and conspiring to commit homicide. It was another RICO suit and Bianco, as well as numerous other associates, were facing long sentences and harsh fines. In 1991, Bianco was convicted. He was sent off to prison, right behind Junior Patriarca, for just over eleven years. The length of sentence didn't matter too much for Bianco though—within three years he died in prison from complications related to his recent diagnosis of Lou Gehrig's disease. The onslaught didn't stop at the group convictions of Junior and Bianco. In 1993, over 20 other Patriarca associates were hauled before federal court to defend themselves against charges of illegal bookie operations.

With Bianco unseated before he barely had a chance to sit down, the Patriarca power vacuum was opened once again. Frank Salemme, who was still attempting to run operations in Boston, made a bid for the boss position. At least in Massachusetts,

Salemme had few rivals for power. He and his crew had the backing of the Winter Hill Gang, plus Bulger and Flemmi were more than willing to assist an ally in taking over the organization that once posed the greatest threat to them. With their support, Salemme became the next boss of the Patriarca family and for the first time since Raymond Patriarca Sr. took over in 1954, the seat of the Patriarcas' power was shifted back to Boston. Now, the three friends Bulger, Flemmi, and Salemme were in charge of two of the biggest criminal organizations in New England, and at least two of them had a working relationship with the FBI. Unfortunately though, Bulger's long-time FBI contact and handler John Connolly had retired by the mid-1990s. Apparently, with him went Bulger and Flemmi's protection.

In 1995, the criminal trio and three other associates were indicted with a total of 37 racketeering charges against them. Although Connolly couldn't stop the investigation or indictments, he did take a risk by at least letting Bulger know ahead of time that the indictments were coming, just in time for him to make himself scarce and abandon his comrades to the mercy of the law. After Bulger fled the state, Flemmi did not take over leadership of Winter Hill as might have been presumed, likely because it was almost inevitable that he'd be inside of a jail cell before long. Rather, control was given to Kevin Weeks, one of Bulger's closest friends and apprentices. Weeks was highly active in Winter Hill and helped the gang bring the city's drug industry under control in the 1980s. During this period, Winter Hill weren't so much drug *dealers* as they were drug enforcers—instead of selling cocaine and cannabis, Winter Hill simply threatened those who did with death if they refused to kick up to Bulger. Weeks served as the key street man in this operation, being the muscle that kept the city's dealers in line. Weeks was clearly of a rare breed of loyalty, as even after Bulger was running from the law, Weeks continued to wire him tens of thousands of dollars wherever he was, which Bulger then stored in various safes dotted around the country (soon though, Weeks' loyalty would be put to the ultimate test). Salemme, for his part, tried to flee as well but he was far less successful than Bulger, who managed to evade the law for the better part of two decades. Like Bianco, Salemme was hit with eleven years.

Before Salemme was put away though, it was already clear he, like Junior and Bianco, would not be able to prevent the Family's downfall. The infighting was still severe when he took over, and relatively petty offenses (or perceived offenses) were routinely escalating into nearly full-on Mafia civil wars. In 1994, a lowly Patriarca soldier Nino Cucinotta shot dead two of his fellow made guys, Pete Scarpellini and Ronnie Coppola, over a heated exchange during a card game. The same year, one of Frankie Salemme's narcotics guys was murdered over another trivial dispute. While all this was happening, Bulger was still running free across the city, backstabbing and double-crossing until he was forced to go on the lam. Salemme was soon headed on the lam as well though. In 1993 Steve DiSarro, the manager of a nightclub known to be frequented by local mafiosi (DiSarro himself had mob ties too) was murdered. Suspicion of informants lurking among the Mafia was running high by this point, and it's likely that the manager was murdered because he was suspected of cooperating with federal agents (all this was ironic for Salemme, whose closest associates had been rats for decades). Whatever it was that led to the hit on the manager, Salemme was suspected of ordering it. Once he caught wind that the hit was being investigated, he took off for Florida. Before long though, he was apprehended and brought right back. Salemme was off to prison, but his story did not end there like Junior's did. The Patriarca Family was on the precipice of facing a new, even darker chapter of their fall from power.

CHAPTER 7

COLLAPSE: THE MAFIA TODAY

By the mid-1990s and 2000s, the Mafia landscape all over the country had been irreparably altered. The "glory days" were long gone, and all the elder mafiosi could do was complain about the lack of values and respect that the new generation of gangsters seemed to have. In prior decades, prison was not something to be necessarily feared, but rather expected. If you got pinched and had to go to jail, you kept your mouth shut and went to prison. When you were released, things more or less went back to normal. By this new age, the prospect of facing prison time was enough to get the vast majority of mobsters to flip on even their closest friends. Ultimately though, blame for the collapse of the Mafia had more to do with the decision to actually treat organized crime as a threat to America. Their new and aggressive tactics, which had been in development since the mid-1960s, are mostly to blame for this state of affairs. It had put a rapid succession of Patriarca bosses (and other bosses for that matter) in prison, and it was clear that the days of venerable leaders naming Families after themselves and reigning for decades had long since died. Though even now the Mafia has still not been fully excised from American society, the 1990s turned them into the "walking corpses" that they remain today, desperately trying to earn illegal income wherever they can find it. If they could operate without violently turning on each other, that is.

Salemme and the Civil War

Interestingly, Salemme had Angelo Mercurio, the man who recorded the Medford initiation, to (partially) thank for his downfall. While Mercurio had been serving prison time for his participation in the attempted hit on Salemme during Carrozza's rebellion (for his work as an informant, he was serving a significantly reduced sentence), he was brought back into the FBI's service once more in the late 1990s. He was sent from his cell to another Boston court where he divulged everything he knew about Salemme's criminal enterprise. This was actually the first time Mercurio showed his face in court and outed himself as an informant—until now, the Family was unaware that he was the one wearing the wire—and as a result, he had to enter federal witness protection after he was released (his sentence was reduced yet again after his contributions toward convicting Salemme). Mercurio probably didn't feel as secure as he should have, considering Barboza was tracked down all the way on the other side of the country. Mercurio was either luckier than Barboza, or the Family was rendered so weak by the late 1990s that they simply didn't have the resources to search for him. In any case, Mercurio lived out the rest of his natural life, dying in 2006.

After Salemme was apprehended and brought before the courts along with Flemmi, the Family ranks were apparently at their wit's end. With yet another new boss facing RICO indictments and likely over a decade in prison, the rebellion that began years earlier under

Bob Carrozza began to develop into a civil war that lasted until about 1997. The Family split into factions, one consisting of those who continued to support Salemme during and after his trial, and the other consisting of renegade Carrozza loyalists. These factions continued to trade blows for months and left plenty of victims dead in the process, including Richard DeVincent, unflatteringly known as "the pig," who was gunned down in 1996. But before the rebellion could get any bloodier, the FBI made their move. In mid-1997 federal agents swept through New England, specifically the Boston area, picking up over a dozen members of Carrozza's amateurish crew, including "Baby/Bobby Russo" and his top guys. This was good and bad for the Salemme faction. On the one hand, this effectively ended the civil war by decimating the rebellious element and locking up their leader. On the other hand, the FBI's reason for indicting Carrozza's faction was clear: they wanted more state witnesses to use against the Family (i.e., the remnants of Salemme's loyalists). Before everything was done, four of Carrozza's crew agreed to testify against the Family in return for a reduction or absolvement of their potential RICO sentences.

After Salemme's fate was sealed, Louis/Luigi Manochio, also known as "Baby Shacks," was next in line to take over. In a rare case, the Providence-based Manocchio managed to remain in power for quite some time, breaking the trend of recent Patriarca bosses. This was even more impressive considering his advanced age at the time—born in 1927, Manocchio was another veteran mobster who was earning his reputation while the likes of Junior Patriarca were still in elementary school. Still, Manocchio clearly wasn't anyone's first choice, considering he only rose to power after virtually every other capable leader in the Family had been under federal indictment. Still, it was Manocchio that guided the family through the rest of the 1990s, into the new decade and new millennium. Manocchio's record was far from spotless, and in 1996 he and others were charged in connection with various high-profile burglaries in the area. He was facing prison time, but eventually pleaded guilty to all charges in exchange for a three-year term of probation which he miraculously served without being picked up again.

The 2000s brought new challenges for most and new opportunities for some, including Frank Salemme. Having eventually issued a guilty plea for racketeering (the murder charge in the DiSarro case had been dropped in return for the plea and Salemme's assurance that he had nothing to do with it), Salemme was apparently not ready to spend the full eleven years in prison at his age. His way out was familiar—he would have to testify against his former Winter Hill friends and associates. With Manocchio attempting to calm the tensions amidst the Family, Salemme threatened to burn it all down again. Ultimately though, Salemme's bid for freedom worked and Manocchio continued as boss for nearly a decade into the 2000s.

The Patriarcas in the 21st Century

At some point while Frankie Salemme was serving his sentence for racketeering, likely around 1999 or 2000, the former boss finally became aware of the treachery of Whitey Bulger and Stephen Flemmi. Having learned that his close associates had been on the FBI's payroll since the days of Raymond Sr., Salemme was incensed. With the help of agent Connolly, his two Winter Hill associates had orchestrated the Patriarcas' downfall in Boston, all the while they ran their own operations with near-immunity. Initially refusing to turn witness, Salemme was now an eager state participant. He told his counsel that he would be willing to give any information he had, not only on the fugitive Bulger and the imprisoned Flemmi, but on their handler John Connolly as well. Based on his testimony, the government investigated the role that the FBI handlers had played in New England's organized criminal underworld. In addition to Salemme though, former Winter Hill leader Kevin Weeks also flipped while he was in prison for drug-related RICO charges. Apparently, his years of loyalty were destroyed by one conversation with an unnamed, disgruntled, imprisoned former member of the Patriarcas—he essentially told Weeks that he was a sucker for not cooperating because the guys he was protecting would have flipped on him in an instant. This was probably true, and Weeks knew it. From then on, Weeks gave the FBI everything he had on Flemmi, Connolly, and his own mentor Whitey Bulger. Years later, the retired John Connolly was set to face trial and with the assistance of Salemme, it was determined that Connolly was little more than a criminal himself. He was convicted and sent off to prison, put there by the same man he had put in prison years earlier. In exchange for this, Salemme was released from prison in 2003 and placed in witness protection. But at 70 years old, his story was *still* not completed, nor was his criminal record.

Connolly wasn't the only crooked federal agent to face consequences in the new millennium. Harold Paul Rico, the man responsible for handling Joe Barboza (among others), was also under federal scrutiny for his role in the late-1960s convictions of Henry Tameleo, Peter Limone, Louis Greco, Joe Salvati, Willie French, and Ronnie Cassesso. In 2001, four of these men were exonerated for their crimes as the government discovered that the testimony Barboza gave, where he alleged that the accused had ordered the killing of Edward Deegan, was falsified. Unfortunately, Louis Greco had died a few years earlier in 1995 and Tameleo was long gone, having died ten years before him. Limone and Salvati were more fortunate—both lived long enough to be released into society again, and each was awarded tens of millions of dollars in their wrongful conviction settlement. Two years later, former agent Rico was forced to defend himself against the accusation that he was the one who coaxed Barboza into pointing the finger at the Patriarca men (although it's likely that Barboza would have blamed the Patriarcas anyway considering his resentment toward them at the time), and that he obstructed justice by observing Barboza's court perjury and not bothering to report the crime. He was also indicted for instructing Bulger and Flemmi of Winter Hill to organize a hit in Oklahoma back in 1981. While imprisoned awaiting trial in 2004, Rico died at 78.

Back in Providence, where Luigi Manocchio once again rooted the Patriarca Family headquarters, things appear to have gone relatively smoothly for several years, at least for the boss. Little is known about this period of the Patriarca Family history, but we do know that the elderly Manocchio remained boss until 2009. The year before he stepped down, he was under investigation for suspected criminal activity taking place at several of his nightclubs. To avoid being fingered as the head of a multi-state criminal organization, he gave up the reins to Peter Limone, one of the men released from prison in 2001 after his conviction was overturned. At some point, Manocchio followed the footsteps of several New England gangsters before him and fled Rhode Island for Florida. It was here in the

Sunshine State in 2011 that he was apprehended and charged with the extortion of two Providence strip clubs, the Cadillac Lounge on Charles Street and the Satin Doll Gentleman's Club on Aborn Street. The next year Manocchio pleaded guilty and was handed a five-and-a-half-year sentence. In 2013 the Satin Doll was fined and ordered to shut down by the city for allegedly operating a prostitution ring out of their private booths, which led the city administration to consider outlawing all private spaces in strip clubs. Manoccio was eventually released in 2015 before his sentence was completed. Having turned 96 years old in 2023, Manocchio currently lives as a free man.

Boston man Peter Limone had brought the operations back to Massachusetts once again, but his time as a free man lasted less than a year after Manocchio abdicated. Considering he refused to turn witness even after being handed a sentence for a crime he knew for a fact he didn't commit, it was unsurprising that the Family trusted Limone. Still, it was a strange decision for him to return to organized crime at all—he must have been extremely wealthy at this point, having been awarded $26 million himself due to his wrongful imprisonment (Gross, n.d.). Unfortunately he also had serious, new legal problems of his own, so his reign was ill-fated and tenuous from the beginning. Eventually charged with racketeering, he was handed a suspended sentence which meant that any more criminal wrongdoing would result in him dying in prison. It was a light sentence, but one that was warranted considering he already spent three decades in federal custody under false pretenses. The rest of the Family also took hits in these years, including *consigliere* Tony Parrillo, who was arrested for assault in 2011 and eventually sentenced to five years.

After Limone was forced to effectively halt his criminal dealings for the term of his probation, the younger DiNunzio brother, Anthony, became acting boss in his stead. Anthony's older brother, Carmen DiNunzio, had recently been sent away for five and a half years for attempting to bribe law officials. Anthony was headed to prison too before long. The younger DiNunzio had connections in the New York Gambino Family and together they had worked together to seize control of a large swathe of strip clubs in Providence and the surrounding area. The move unsurprisingly drew a lot of heat, all of which came down on him in 2012. He pleaded guilty and received six years in prison, meaning Antonio Spagnolo was next in line. In 2014, Spagnolo and fellow Patriarca member Pryce Quintina, both of whom were in their 70s at the time, were arrested and indicted on extortion charges related to gambling establishments in Boston. Likely due to their advanced age, neither were sent to prison but they were placed under house arrest and forced to wear location-tracking ankle bracelets, effectively eliminating Spagnolo's ability to run the Family.

Anthony DiNunzio's older brother Carmen, nicknamed "Cheese Man," was released from prison just in time to take over acting boss duties from the home-interned Antonio Spagnolo. Carmen, who was an old member of the Patriarcas' North End crew, immediately set out to solidify his position, considering the advanced age of boss Peter Limone at the time which suggested the Family would need a new official boss before long. He inducted a slew of new made guys into his crew, including his own nephew Louis, who earned the affectionate nickname "Baby Cheese," a nod to his uncle. In an effort to make the Boston base of operations more robust, DiNunzio promoted his close ally, the exceedingly overweight Greg

Costa, to captain of the city's North End. Matthew Guglielmetti was installed as Carmen/Limone's underboss, and Joe Achille was made *consigliere*. Both Guglielmetti and Achille were long-time members of the Rhode Island crew, which signaled that the Patriarca Family Boston-Providence connection was not completely fractured, and in fact may have been recovering under Limone and DiNunzio. In 2017, boss Limone died, leaving Carmen to fully inherit the Patriarca clan. Later in 2020, Guglielmetti's health took a turn for the worse and he abdicated his position as underboss, which was then given to Eddie Lato. As far as we know, both Guglielmetti and Lato remain active in their positions today.

In 2018, former boss (and former FBI witness) Frank Salemme, who had been living under witness protection, was yet again coming under federal scrutiny. When he was initially sent to prison for racketeering charges years earlier, he had denied having anything to do with the disappearance of the mobbed-up nightclub manager Steven DiSarro. In 2015 William Ricci, who was associated with the Patriarca Family, was investigated for operating an illegal cannabis growing operation out of the apartment complex that he owned in Providence. During the course of the investigation, authorities received a tip that the building was concealing something more sinister. After a thorough search and digging around the property, authorities discovered DiSarro's decayed remains. The case, which was long assumed to be a homicide but technically considered to be a disappearance, was reopened. They turned their attention toward Salemme and in 2018 they hauled him into court once again.

At the time, Salemme was living under the assumed name "Richard Parker" in Atlanta, Georgia. When the news broke that DiSarro's remains were discovered and that Salemme was suspected, he fled witness protection and holed up in a hotel in Connecticut. Authorities discovered him there, along with tens of thousands of dollars in cash. Testifying against him were the DeLuca brothers, Joe and Bobby. Bobby was a former *caporegime* in the Family (he had also turned witness back in the mass prosecution of 2011), but Joe's standing is not known for certain. Joe told the court that back in 1993, Frank Salemme had contacted him to organize a meet-up and hand off a "package" to Joe. The pair met at a vacant parking lot in Providence and, according to the DeLucas, the "package" was Steven DiSarro's corpse, wrapped haphazardly in a tarp. Joe testified that he was the one who transported and disposed of DiSarro's body on Ricci's property under the direct orders of boss Frank Salemme. With these two star witnesses' testimonies, Salemme was eventually convicted of both DiSarro's murder and of perjuring himself in his trial several years prior when he feigned ignorance of the situation.

The official story was that Salemme's son, Frank Jr., committed the murder by strangling him to death while Patriarca associate Paul Weadick held him down and Salemme Sr. silently observed. Frank Jr. certainly would have faced trial alongside his father, but he had died in 1995. Salemme's defense attorney made unsuccessful efforts to call into question the integrity of those accusing Salemme, although he technically admitted that the mobster was a murderer. Hilariously, part of his defense strategy was to claim that although Salemme of course murdered people in the past, it doesn't mean he murdered *this* person: "Just because he's done these bad things doesn't mean he's done this," (quoted in Telford, 2018). Both 85-

year-old Frank Salemme as well as Patriarca associate Paul Weadick were given life sentences in federal prison and Salemme died in 2022. Weadick, still alive as of the Summer of 2023, is reportedly seeking a new trial for his involvement.

The 2020s also saw more of the Patriarca's former political connections slip away. Deputy Chief of Staff John Conti was put under police surveillance in 2020 under suspicions that he was involved with a known associate of the Patriarcas, Ray Jenkins. Jenkins was known to be involved in a Rhode Island-based cannabis growing racket and Conti was suspected of being either involved or a direct partner in its operation. The surveillance effort was a success, and Conti was recorded associating with Jenkins. It was also revealed later that Conti had also met, on at least one occasion, with Patriarca underboss Matt Guglielmetti, which signals that Conti's ties were not only to low-level made guys and associates. Clearly it has become far more difficult to remain an organized criminal with political safety nets in the 21st century, but the fact that Conti only resigned as late as 2022 goes to show that the Patriarca Family still commands considerable power and influence in their home states, though the days of Raymond Patriarca Sr. supposedly dominating even the Five Families of New York City were very long gone, and that fact remains painfully obvious.

CONCLUSION

More than anything else, the story of the Italian Mafia's history in America is one of violence, betrayal, greed, and honor. Today, it is one of nostalgia—a longing for the "good old days" when mafiosi were seemingly untouchable, police officers and judges were easily plied, and the Mafia was something worth making films about. The general fascination with the glory days of the Mafia is born out of the success of cinematic masterpieces such as *The Godfather* and Martin Scorsese's *Goodfellas* and *Casino.* Francis Ford Coppola's *The Godfather,* which hit theaters in 1972 while the American Mafia was still very much a force to be reckoned with, portrays a highly romanticized version of the Mafia. Set in the 1940s and 1950s, it shows a period where honor, secrecy, and the sacred principle of *omerta* reigned. Unsurprisingly, it is typically this version of the Mafia that even mafiosi today look to as a model for how a Family *should* be run. It's actually an incredible reversal—once, filmmakers looked to the real-life Mafia to guide their vision on screen. Today, mobsters look to these landmark films for inspiration.

The eventual collapse of the Mafia and the nostalgic reaction that it induces has been portrayed excellently on screen by Martin Scorsese in both 1990's *Goodfellas* and 1995's *Casino.* The 1990 film follows the story of real-life former Lucchese Family (one of New York City's Five Families—the film does not explicitly mention the

Luccheses, however) associate Henry Hill, who ended up turning witness and ratting out all of his closest friends, the people he had looked up to and tried to emulate since childhood. *Goodfellas* portrays the perceived romanticism of Mob life, the yearning to become a "respected" made guy, and the eventual downfall of the Mafia due to a combination of drug dealing (and using), RICO suits, and the deterioration of "old school" Mafia principles. The film concludes with a seemingly depressed Henry Hill who, after contributing to the decimation of his own Family's ranks, laments at the fact that he must now live under witness protection, assuming a life of an average citizen, devoid of the thrill of being a "wise guy." For a guy like Henry Hill though, it was probably the best outcome he could have hoped for. The days when it was normal for mobsters to simply retire in their old age and live out their days in the spoils of their criminal career were over. In Hill's era, the life of nearly every mafioso ended in one of just a few predictable ways: you were shot by your enemies, shot by your friends, put in prison, or put in witness protection after betraying the trust of your colleagues.

The 1995 *Casino* also depicts in its closing moments the fading out of the Mafia's national power. Based on the Mafia's involvement in the gambling industry in Las Vegas, Nevada, *Casino* shows the national reach of the Mafia and exorbitant amounts of illicit income that the Families were once capable of "earning." The most powerful of the East Coast families had sent out their top made guys and associates to oversee the operations of casino establishments worth hundreds of millions of dollars, from which stacks of cash were routinely skimmed and sent back to New York City. The Patriarca Family was also involved in the casino business, particularly under Raymond Sr. In this case, his connections were very far-reaching—the vicious and infamous dictator of Haiti, Francois Duvalier, was apparently a partner of Raymond's in the gambling industry. Duvalier welcomed organized crime in his brutalized nation and jumped at the opportunity to ally with someone as powerful as the Patriarca boss. When Raymond was facing the threat of prison time under his several indictments, Duvalier actually offered Raymond a home on his island. It's not clear how active the Patriarcas were in Nevada, though. *Casino* shows an era where the Mafia essentially ran the entire city of Las Vegas, had deep political connections with the city and state's administration, and where running afoul in one of their casinos typically meant a horrific beating rather than a ban. It was, to be sure, a far more violent period, but in the Mafia world it represented (and still represents) an ideal that is simply impossible to obtain in the 21st century. The closing of the film, similar to *Goodfellas*, pines for the loss of the Mafia's influence and expresses regret at the corporatization of Las Vegas (and to a lesser extent, Reno and Atlantic City, New Jersey) which has morphed it from an organized crime paradise to a family-friendly resort town.

Even the era when the American Mafia was crumbling under the weight of the FBI's intense scrutiny and the loss of Mafia principles has attracted critical acclaim and popular attention. The incredibly popular television series *The Sopranos*, which does a masterful job of portraying this period, is a perfect case in point. The lead character, Tony Soprano, is a man dealing with the loss of power and respect that came with the Mafia's severe downturn in the late 1990s and early 2000s. This, combined with various complications with his Family, has led him to seek psychiatric counseling, during which he exposes his deep longing for the days when mobsters like his father had it all, and everything seemed easier. Now as a Mafia boss operating during the turn of the century, he is head of an organization that had been eating itself alive for years. With little integrity, no honor, and an eagerness to avoid consequences by ratting out their friends, Tony Soprano is dissatisfied with his colleagues who comprise his Family. In the very first episode of the series, Tony perfectly sums up the anxiety related to the days when the end of the Mafia entirely seemed to be in sight: "I'd been thinking. It's good to be in something from the ground floor. I came too late for that, I know. But lately, I'm getting the feeling that I came in at the end. That the best is over," (Chase, January 10, 1999).

Indeed, the best was very much over. The once-mighty Patriarca clan has been reduced to a husk, one which used to embody the most powerful aspects of organized crime in America. An old Family dating all the way back to at least Gaspare Messina, the Patriarcas had staged a meteoric rise through the American underworld from the 1930s through to the 1960s and early 1970s and were helmed by one of the most powerful bosses in Mafia history for years. Extending its branches across state borders, the Patriarcas came to dominate Massachusetts and Rhode Island and penetrate the underworlds of other eastern states from Connecticut to Maine in the far northeast. Managing to secure their territory for decades from the other power and money-hungry Families, the strength of the Patriarcas rivaled even that of the legendary Genovese and Gambino Families to their west. As the decades wore on, internal struggles and rival ethnic gangs, particularly the Winter Hill Gang of Boston, became the biggest threat to the Patriarcas.

Though the Family has seemingly recovered somewhat from the brink of dissolving entirely years ago, it remains a highly tenuous organization.

Today, most of the ranks of the Patriarca Family remain a mystery outside of speculation. This is expected, as the inherent secrecy of the Mafia means that the general public typically only learns the truth about events years, even decades, after the fact. That being said, it is generally assumed that Carmen "Cheese Man" Dinunzio, the elder of the DiNunzio brothers, remains boss of the Family to this day. DiNunzio has long been based out of Boston, so if he truly is the current boss this means their base of power remains in Massachusetts. As far as the public is aware, Eddie Lato also remains underboss in Providence. Clearly, then, the Patriarca Family is still a multi-state organization with influence across the seaboard. Guglielmetti, though he has taken a backseat in leadership, is still believed to be active in Rhode Island functioning as a regional captain. He also appears to have formed connections with the Philadelphia-based Bruno-Scarfo Family out of Pennsylvania. Joe Achille, the former *consigliere*, died in 2018 and it's not known who (if anyone) was chosen to replace him as top Family advisor. Costa and Ferrara appear to remain active in the Boston faction, as well as Freddie Simone and Carmen's younger brother and nephew, Anthony (released from prison in 2017) and Louis DiNunzio. Even less is known about the Providence faction ranks, which have likely been weakened as a result of the shift of main operations from Rhode Island to Massachusetts. Connecticut is even more obscure, but it is known that former Hartford underboss Will Grasso's son was involved in the Family's activities at least into the mid-2000s.

Overall, it is difficult to see any faction of the American Mafia, whether in Boston, New York City, Buffalo, or Los Angeles, ever returning to the criminal heyday that has been immortalized in productions like *Goodfellas* and *The Godfather*. Clearly, it is much more difficult to be a mobster these days, as RICO suits are an ever-present threat that could feasibly cripple an entire crew in one fell swoop. Further, there seems to be almost no semblance of the camaraderie and loyalty that once characterized the Mafia. As Songini explained, as far back as the bombshell Barboza testimonies, "the entire organization was eroding with mistrust—its edge was gone," (2015). Mafia Families are unlikely to dominate entire cities ever again, but that is not to say it is not a sometimes lucrative business. Well into the 21st century, the Sicilian-American organization remains active and they continue in most of their old rackets, though some have become infeasible. Corporatization has rendered the practice of extortion a mostly pointless endeavor, but prostitution, loan sharking, and drug smuggling remain typical. There is still plenty of room for organized criminals to build illicit empires, but these days it seems that it always leads to prison.

REFERENCES

Barry, S. (2011, December 11). *Organized crime in Springfield evolved through death and money.* Mass Live. https://www.masslive.com/news/2011/12/organized_crime_in_springfield.html

Carr, H. (2007, October 14). *Mobster of the week: Joseph "J.R." Russo.* Boston Herald. Chase, D. (writer & director). (1999, January 10). Pilot episode (Season 1, episode 1). In Chase, D. (execute producer) *The Sopranos.* HBO.

Critchley, D. (2009). *The origins of organized crime in America: The New York City Mafia, 1891-1931.* New York City: Routledge.

Estate of Iaconi v. Commissioner (1961, April 13). Leagle.com https://www.leagle.com/decision/196152220cztcm5021419

Foderaro, L. (1989, June 18). Mob leader's slaying may signal power struggle. *New York Times.*

Ford, B. & Schorow, S. (2011). *The Boston mob guide: Hitmen, hoodlums & hideouts.* Charleston, North Carolina: The History Press.

Frankfurter, F. (1927, March). *The case of Sacco and Vanzetti.* The Atlantic.

https://www.theatlantic.com/magazine/archive/1927/03/the-case-of-sacco-and-vanzetti/306625/

Jacobs, J. & Gouldin, L. (1999). Cosa nostra: The final chapter? *Crime and Justice* 25, 129-189.

Maher, S. (2009, February 17). *The Worcester mafia and gambling.* InCity Times. https://archive.ph/20131003040242/http://incitytimesworcester.org/2009/02/17/the-worcester-mafia-and-gambling/%23more-859

Meyer, P. (2015). Going beyond the evidence: A skilled trial lawyer uses narrative persuasion to deliver a story to the jury in a complex criminal case. *ABA Journal* 101(2), 26-27.

New York Times (1980, December 6). Patriarca, crime figure, charged as an accessory to 1965 slaying.

New England Patriarca Crime Leaders (n.d.). Mafia History. https://mafiahistory.us/maf-b-ne.html

Peter Limone (n.d.). The National Registry of Exonerations. https://www.law.umich.edu/special/exoneration/Pages/casedetail.aspx?caseid=3383 Senate.gov

Smith, G. (2013, December 11). *City orders Satin Doll closed for 20 days, proposes new limits on strip clubs.* The Providence Journal.

https://www.providencejournal.com/story/news/crime/2013/12/11/20131211-city-orders-satin-doll-closed-asks-for-new-limits-on-operation-of-strip-clubs-ece/35380370007/

Songini, M. (2015). *Boston mob: The rise and fall of the New England mob and its most notorious killer.* New York City: St. Martin's Press.

Telford, T. (2018, September 14). *Boston mobster known as 'cadillac Frank' gets life in prison for an old murder.* The Washington Post.

https://www.washingtonpost.com/crime-law/2018/09/14/long-dark-chapter-ends-boston-mobster-known-cadillac-gets-life-prison-murder/

White, T. (2023, July 13). *Mobster Joe DeLuca, who testified against former mafia kingpin, has died.* WPRI.com

https://www.wpri.com/target-12/inside-the-mafia/mobster-joe-deluca-who-testified-against-former-mafia-kingpin-has-died/

THE MAGADDINO-TODARO MAFIA CRIME FAMILY

MAFIA LIBRARY

INTRODUCTION

In the history books of American organized crime, certain names echo with a particular resonance that makes them hard to forget. We've long been familiar with the Chicago Outfit, the Five Families based in New York, and the Philadelphia Mob. These organizations define the very thing that comes to mind when we think about the criminal underworld. Their stories have been told, retold, and reimagined in countless articles, books, movies, and TV shows, cementing their place in our memories and intertwining them with the very fabric of American organized crime.

However, amid these larger-than-life figures and notorious syndicates, the story of the Buffalo Crime Family has been often overlooked. It's not because their story lacks intrigue or significance. That's far from the truth because the saga of the Buffalo Crime Family is just as compelling as their more famous counterparts. While seemingly hanging on to obscurity, the family actually has always flown just far enough beneath the radar. Maybe they knew how to deflect attention from themselves or maybe all the credit lies with their geographical location. But they had just as much impact as their counterparts on their regions, the United States and Canada, and the Mafia as a whole.

In this book, we are looking at more than a "Golden Age" of a particular outfit. We're going to pull the Buffalo Crime Family out of their shadows and into a new light. It's a journey that takes us through the earliest days when it was trying to take hold in a growing country. It will trace the evolution from the DiCarlo-Palmeri Family and the Magaddino Family to the present-day Todaro Family. That evolution makes this organization one of the most powerful Mafia establishments in the United States. Their story is about power, ambition, betrayal, resilience, and all of it playing against an ever-changing backdrop of US history.

This narrative will start with Angelo Palmeri, who really is the founding father of this branch of the American Mafia. His beginnings, rising up through the ranks across the American landscape to establish an empire that has lasted over a century, echo that of many mafiosos. While his reign didn't speak much of notoriety, his work set the new era of the American Mafia in motion and the stage for the rise of some of the most powerful mobsters.

Palmeri's reign was short, and it was short for a good reason. He was a powerful force, but he lacked direction and a real vision for the future of an empire. So, he passed down the reigns to Giuseppe DiCarlo and took his place as underboss. Under this formidable due, the Buffalo Crime Family would expand its operations, planting roots far beyond the city of Buffalo. Now known as the DiCarlo-Palmeri family, their era was characterized by a ruthless sense of efficiency and a hunger for even more power. This was one of the strongest beginnings of a criminal outfit. They asserted their dominance and left a secure foundation to build on.

However, the DiCarlo-Palmeri reign did not last for very long. DiCarlo was already an aged man, and this meant that a new leader would need to come in and continue to push the family forward into a new regime. Enter Stefano Magaddino. Under Stefano's reign, the Buffalo Crime Family, now infamously known as the Magaddino Crime Family, would find a long period of success and influence. Stefano was a man who had immense charisma and ruthless ambition. Magaddino would further expand the Buffalo region and take the family to heights of power that were unheard of at the time. He, and the family, were a force to be reckoned with in the Mafia landscape.

But all empires reach their end, one way or another. There were already whispers of dissent during his last days, and the death of Stefano Magaddino would not just mark the end of a long era of the Buffalo family, it would also throw the entire organization into disarray. While leaders were still in place, leadership was more about holding the family's operations together. However, rising up through the ranks years before Magaddino's death was a leader who could retake control. Joseph Todaro Sr. would rebrand the Buffalo Crime Family into the Todaro family. "Papa Joe," as he was known, was someone with the vision, determination, and resilience that the family needed. He would take control of the family and help them grow from a traditional Mafia family into a modern enterprise of the criminal underworld.

As such, the Todaro Era took a huge detour from the ways of the old guard and put them onto a path that Joseph "Big Joe" Todaro Jr. is still trying to navigate today. The family now has expanded more into legitimate businesses and taken advantage of the opportunities set out by the modern world. However, no matter the landscape, the Todaro family never strays too far from the roots that are in place. The Buffalo Crime family is one that values loyalty, respect, and honor. While those are pieces of every Mafia family, they are the components that have kept the Buffalo Crime family thriving no matter what challenges are placed before them.

This book will be more than just a chronicle of the constant rise and fall of their criminal empire. Instead, it will be more of a window into a world that rarely comes into the public eye. The Buffalo family is one that exists in the shadows, controlled by its own set of rules and codes. This book is a journey into this specific part of the American underworld, giving you a glimpse at the men who ran it and the events that defined it. From the humble beginnings of the DiCarlo-Palmeri Family to the modern-day enterprise of the Todaro Family, this is the story of the Buffalo Crime Family.

And as you delve into the pages here, you'll find yourself face-to-face with the men who built this empire and a few other figures of the criminal underworld. This is a reminder that every piece of the American Mafia is connected, and one person's story easily blends into another's. Therefore, if you need to, take some time and connect the dots. Watch as you move the pieces around again and again as you try to establish the entire timeline of the Mafia. It truly is fascinating and endlessly intriguing to watch as their world unfolds parallel to ours, almost like a separate, grittier world hiding in plain sight.

So, prepare for a deep dive into a dark spot in the history of Buffalo, New York with the Buffalo Crime Family.

PART I

THE DICARLO-PALMERI ERA

(1910-1922)

CHAPTER 1

THE PALMERI AND DICARLO YEARS

Buffalo, New York boomed with an infectious energy as the US moved into the 20th century. Factories seemed to spring up overnight, industries roared, and opportunity hung heavy in the air. The Erie Canal solidified that opportunity when the watery ribbon sliced through the state in 1825. Buffalo was now a bustling transport hub. This was attractive to many immigrants, as they looked for a better life. They placed their hopes and dreams into the city, looking to have a more peaceful life than what was being offered in New York City.

But that prosperity would come with its own problems and let a darker side in. The city's growth took place at such a rapid rate that social services were spread thin and law enforcement struggled to keep up. This lack of authority opened up the floodgates for criminal activity. Gangs sprouted like weeds, all trying to stake their claim in the growing city. They tried to replicate the movement that was happening in other parts of the country and establish their own empires. Various rackets popped up, with little pushback, but there was a glaring omission from this criminal world: An empire.

This wasn't a unique occurrence, and the back-and-forth dance between ambition and illegal activity was playing out the same way in many growing American cities. However, things were about to change in a very interesting way. The Buffalo Crime Family was a soon-to-be well-oiled machine in the criminal underworld, but it would be a machine built on chance. Being in the right place at the right time would ring particularly true with the unlikely partnership between Benedetto Angelo "Buffalo Bill" Palmeri and Giuseppe DiCarlo.

Palmeri was a Sicilian firebrand with a short fuse and a penchant for violence. He was volatile, which made him feared, but he wasn't boss material. DiCarlo, however, was the embodiment of cool and calculated. He was a strategist who could map a criminal empire as if it were a game of chess. The two men, despite being as different as night and day, were put together by fate. They would form an alliance that set the stage for an operation that still continues today.

But while their legacy would be cemented, their chapter of the story was brief. However, given the era that it was, their personalities and ambition proved to be a force that made the Buffalo Crime Family.

An Unlikely Pairing

The story of the Buffalo Crime Family's rise to power would have never existed without the chance meeting and partnership of two men. Angelo Palmeri and Giuseppe DiCarlo would have vastly different backgrounds and vastly different methods for handling their business. However, when they came together, the stage was set to make the northwestern region of New York one of the most important hubs for Mafia activity.

Angelo Palmeri

Angelo Palmeri, who would establish the Sicilian hold in Buffalo and become the feared figure in the early years of the Buffalo family, wasn't born immersed in the world of petty crime and power struggles. This was vastly different from his contemporaries who rose through the ranks of organized crime, as he found his life to be one of relative comfort.

Angelo was born in January 1878 to Anna and Francesco Palmeri. Francesco was a relatively successful merchant in Castellammare del Golfo, Sicily, and Angelo was able to enjoy the rewards of his father's hard work. There was no story of clawing up from poverty or "humble beginnings" for Angelo.

Despite the comfort of his upbringing, there was a restlessness growing within the young Palmeri. In 1906, with his sights set on something more thrilling, he made a decision that forever changed the landscape of Buffalo. Leaving behind the life of comfort in Sicily, Angelo made his way across the Atlantic toward new horizons. New York City, which was the lively gateway into America for immigrants, was where he first set foot. Here, the son of a Sicilian merchant found himself lost in the reality that was working-class life. Angelo quickly found work on the docks, biding his time while planning his next move.

Six years later, in 1912, Angelo would move farther west. He would plant his roots in the northwest region of New York in Buffalo, a city that was growing, which meant that there were opportunities to take hold of its underbelly. It was here that he took his own steps into the world of business, which would start the dramatic shift in his life and the city's history. He opened a tavern on Dante Place, a seemingly normal establishment where locals could have drinks and share a laugh. However, like most of these ventures, there was so much more behind the "innocent" facade. The tavern on Dante Place was a front for gambling operations.

This venture into the criminal underworld was Angelo putting his feet to the fire. The web of illegal gambling was a risky venture that was constantly catching the attention of local authorities. While this established the future Buffalo family, Angelo's luck would run out in the same year that the tavern was opened. In a meticulously planned raid, Buffalo police targeted the growing gambling scene in the city. Angelo, along with ten other proprietors, were all arrested and convicted. This brush with the law resulted in the young Palmeri paying a fine of $50. It was a setback, but this wouldn't deter the man who was, for all intents and purposes, the founder of the Buffalo Crime Family.

This incident, while minor, exposed a very crucial flaw in Angelo's approach. Palmeri had the fire and ambition to succeed, and while he found minor success, his volatile nature would leave him without any real direction. He needed a guiding force, someone who could manage his impulsiveness while channeling his drive into something more. Angelo's missing piece was there, and once he found it, it would set the pieces in motion to create the silent, yet powerful Buffalo Crime Family.

Giuseppe DiCarlo

Born on October 18, 1873, in the town of Vallelunga, Giuseppe DiCarlo's upbringing stood in contrast to the more privileged existence of Angelo Palmeri. His parents, Francesco and Giuseppa Spera DiCarlo, were working-class people, which meant they were laboring tirelessly to make ends meet and provide for the family. Their humble surroundings and their struggle for survival were all aspects of life shared by those in the criminal underworld. Like many who would become part of the Mafia, Giuseppe's resolve was established by this humble upbringing. It instilled a burning desire to go beyond the life that he knew.

In 1905, Giuseppe took a chance to chase that fortune across the Atlantic Ocean and in the bustling heart of New York City. There, amidst the noise and dizzying pace of life, Giuseppe found his first venture with Salvatore Manzella, a fellow immigrant who was a long-standing produce merchant. Their partnership proved to be more than just a business arrangement; it was one where Giuseppe would learn everything he would need to know. While Giuseppe's time here was brief, his eye wasn't on just being a successful merchant. He wanted more than that; he wanted the American dream.

A year after DiCarlo arrived in the United States, his wife and children, including his son Joseph DiCarlo (who would go on to be a prominent member of the Buffalo Crime Family long after his father's death), joined him in New York. The DiCarlo family didn't find immediate footing in their new home. They moved around a few times, from the busy streets of Brooklyn to the vibrant blend of people in East Harlem. They would eventually settle down in 1908 in Buffalo, the city known for its industrial growth and diverse population. This is when Giuseppe would start to establish himself as a figure in the history of the region.

In 1909, Giuseppe DiCarlo along with Pietro Manzella and Carmelo Cugino established the Buffalo Italian Importing Company. This would be a tremendous step forward, especially for DiCarlo, given his life growing up. This venture would represent all three men's desire to establish their hold on the growing landscape of American Business.

The Buffalo Italian Importing Company's primary focus was going to be on the import and distribution of Italian goods. The business model was aimed at the growing Italian-American community in the region. It would let them chase their own aspirations while being able to have a bit of home there with them. The imports were innocent enough, from olive oil and pasta to wines and cheeses. However, things didn't go very smoothly for the import company.

Not long after the Buffalo Italian Importing Company was founded, there were accusations of fraudulent business practices surfacing. These allegations were heavy for an upstart company, damaging its reputation and slowing operations. There were claims stating that they were involved in unethical activities, which included misrepresenting their finances and engaging in unfair trade practices. A huge shadow was cast upon the business, and the men lost the trust of their clients and trading partners.

The allegations would continue to pile on and the legal scrutiny that followed put tremendous financial strain on the fledgling business. The company, which started with so much potential, suddenly found itself drowning in legal and financial troubles, and it wouldn't be long before the men found themselves before a judge in bankruptcy court.

The legal proceedings marked the end of the Buffalo Italian Importing Company. Whether the three men knew about the shady practices or not, the short-lived venture only marked the beginning for Giuseppe DiCarlo. This was a man who had a mind for business and a knack for strategy, but a great mind alone couldn't get the proper foundation set. For that, he would need someone to put their feet on the pavement while he sat back and pulled the strings. Fortune would favor DiCarlo, as he didn't have to wait long for that person.

The Start of the Buffalo Crime Family

Fate would eventually bring the two halves together, changing the course for the city of Buffalo. Angelo Palmeri married Rosaria Mistretta on October 5, 1913. Rosaria, though, was the cousin of Vicenza DiCarlo, the wife of one Giuseppe DiCarlo. That wedding would be a significant spark for what was to come.

As the year came to an end, Angelo and Rosaria would make a decision that would solidify what started with the wedding. They moved into an apartment located above the DiCarlo family home on Seventh Street. The families would be close, but that move formed a camaraderie between Angelo and Giuseppe. Their friendship started with a personal rapport, but it grew into a mutual respect as the two realized they shared many of the same interests. This personal bond would eventually grow into a business partnership, which was centered in the confines of Palmeri's tavern.

In this partnership, Angelo Palmeri would hand the reins over to DiCarlo. However, he was not without power; he served as an underboss to the DiCarlo organization. He was an advisor and an enforcer—it was a crucial role that fit him perfectly. Angelo provided the necessary support to ensure that the organization ran as smoothly as possible. DiCarlo, now sitting as the leader, got to strategize comfortably, knowing that Palmeri would ensure things were done. It was a new chapter in Buffalo, one with shared responsibilities and mutual growth.

The pairing of Palmeri and DiCarlo was largely characterized by the stark contrasts in how they conducted business. However, that contrast is what made their organization effective. DiCarlo was able to mastermind the expansion of the family, ensuring their growth and influence. He took the helm and made the crucial decisions that shaped an empire that lasted generations.

Meanwhile, Angelo was playing the role of enforcer. It was up to him to keep the rest of the family in line, ensuring that everything that was done adhered to the rules and regulations of the organization and the Mafia as a whole. Palmeri was the strong arm that maintained order and discipline.

While it was an ideal partnership, Angelo was still making waves. His violent nature and love for the American Wild West earned him the nickname "Buffalo Bill." He was not the type of person to shy away from using force when necessary, which gave him quite the reputation. That same violent nature would eventually catch up to him. In 1915, Angelo was arrested yet again; this time for assaulting a police officer.

The Years of Success

A few short months after Angelo was arrested, a small ray of sun peeked through the chaos. He and Rosaria welcomed their daughter into the world. Her baptism in November was an occasion filled with joy, and Joseph (Giuseppe's son) and Sarah DiCarlo served as godparents to the little girl. This ceremony only strengthened the bonds between the Palmeri and DiCarlo families.

The joy would quickly fade away for Palmeri though, as Rosaria fell victim to a brutal one-two punch of influenza and pneumonia. On January 5, 1916, at just 29 years old, Rosaria Palmeri died. Angelo was overcome with grief from losing his wife, and during that grief, he realized that he couldn't raise their daughter alone. It was a difficult choice, but he decided to send his daughter to live with Rosaria's parents in New York City.

Still devastated, Angelo couldn't face returning to Buffalo, so he took a break from the city, finding some solace thirty minutes away in Niagara Falls. Here, he opened a cigar store, but beneath the legitimate business lurked a familiar presence—he was part of the mafia after all. The cigar shop would be a front for the family's gambling operations. It seemed like a perfect combination, and it does leave one very interesting point to note too. A young Willie Moretti, who would become a notorious figure in the Genovese family of New York City, was honing his craft by running craps games for Angelo—a testament to the training grounds that the underbosses provided.

1919 would begin a new chapter for Angelo. He found a new flame and comfort in his new wife, Rosaria's older sister, Loretta. His and

Rosaria's daughter joined them as he moved the family to an apartment in Niagara Falls. By then, it was the age of Prohibition, a golden ticket for the criminal empires in America, and the DiCarlo-Palmeri family wasn't going to pass up this lucrative racket.

Angelo wouldn't be alone either. Besides his new wife and his daughter, Angelo would join forces with his brother Paul to manage the bootlegging empire. They would join hands with a more-than-formidable crew—the Sirianni brothers, Don Simone Borruso, Joseph Sottile, and Rocco Perri, the Canadian mob boss. This was a mafia dream team, and the alliance would become a juggernaut, bringing outlawed alcohol across the border from Canada. Niagara Falls, a place of serenity and scenic wonder, had just become one of the largest hubs in this illicit trade.

Angelo navigated this venture as he had every venture before. It was a great start for the family, and they would see plenty of money flow in, but it wasn't quite where it needed to be. The racket would need a stronger leader to really see the revenue explode. They also needed that leader because bootlegging came with a large cost. Mafia families that were smuggling and distributing alcohol had massive targets painted on their backs. Not only did they have an outraged public and law enforcement breathing down their necks, but rivals and upstart gangs also eyed the territory, wanting a piece for themselves.

The Decline

1921 wouldn't be too kind to Angelo Palmeri either. He found himself facing yet another accusation: This time for the murder of one Emilio Gnazzo. The murder itself was a textbook back-alley job.

Gnazzo was jumped from behind and shot; however, there was a sole witness to the murder—Emilio Gnazzo's wife. The widow immediately named Palmeri as the triggerman. The cops swarmed in, started the investigation, and would uncover a damning motive for the murder. Gnazzo had taken out a hefty loan and was behind on payments. His creditor was none other than Angelo Palmeri, which meant Palmeri's luck had run out.

But fate and the Mafia worked in mysterious ways. As the case finally made its way to trial, Gnazzo's wife, the key witness for the prosecution's case, vanished. The woman was nowhere to be found, and without a single piece of corroborating evidence or another witness to come forward, the case was a wash. Palmeri had once again slipped through the grasp of the law. While he walked free, there was still a dark cloud over him; perhaps the proof that he wouldn't be fit to take over DiCarlo's spot when the time came.

Meanwhile, back down in Buffalo, the time for Giuseppe DiCarlo was coming fast as his world began to unravel. Tuberculosis was running rampant at the time and had taken hold of the boss, siphoning his energy and leaving behind a shell of the once vibrant leader. As if that wasn't enough of a shot to the DiCarlo family, death would come calling for his brother, claimed by the same disease that would kill Giuseppe. Then, to deal the biggest blow to him, his wife Vicenza lost her battle with cancer. The cool, calculated leader of the Buffalo Crime Family had no will to keep going.

With everything happening with Giuseppe, coupled with the run of bad luck that constantly found Palmeri, one thing had become abundantly clear: A power shift was imminent in Buffalo, and there was one up-and-comer that outshined everyone, Stefano Magaddino.

In July 1922, Giuseppe DiCarlo's reign had come to an end. The boss's death drew Angelo and his family back to the city of Buffalo, where he assumed temporary control of the family. Even Angelo knew that he wouldn't make for a good leader and that his control was a stop-gap measure until the family could decide on the next leader. The ruthless understudy Magaddino would soon get the vote of confidence. Palmeri, along with the likes of Filippo Mazzara and Giuseppe DiBenedetto—who were all Castellammarese Mafiosi held leadership roles under DiCarlo—simply transitioned their roles to the new regime. The changing of the guard had been completed, and the most successful chapter of the Buffalo Mafia's story would unfold.

The Palmeri-DiCarlo Legacy

Palmeri would continue for the next decade, even becoming a naturalized citizen of the United States in January 1925. Five years later Palmeri would support Salvatore Maranzano when the Castellammarese War broke out in 1930. However, toward the end of the bloody power struggle, Angelo faced increasingly severe health problems and died of a stroke in December 1932.

Although their years in power were brief, it was this partnership that was the turning point for the Buffalo Mafia. This period, while a far cry from the more sophisticated operations that the Mafia would later develop, was one of explosive growth. It was like the Wild West that Palmeri loved, full of brutal competition and rivalries settled by bullets and bloodshed.

But it wasn't all violence and money. No successful organization would survive without honor, and that was something that Angelo Palmeri and Giuseppe DiCarlo would display. Despite their contrasting styles, they shared a similar vision and remained loyal to each other. This would be a huge cornerstone in the family's code for decades to come, and their honor would also have a softer side. The often-violent Palmeri would use his influence within the Sicilian community to provide aid to the devastated family of a boy who had been slain by a drifter in 1925. Angelo, along with other underbosses, took donations from shopkeepers to fund the funeral expenses and offer other assistance to the family.

The legacy of Palmeri and DiCarlo lived on in the efficient and effective leadership of Stefano Magaddino and even in the leaders of today. But now the focus turns to that one up-and-comer who rose through the ranks and turned the Buffalo crime family into the Magaddino Crime Family.

PART II

THE MAGADDINO ERA

(1922-1980S)

CHAPTER 2

THE EARLY YEARS OF STEFANO MAGADDINO

Stefano "The Undertaker" Magaddino was born under a blanket of violence on October 10, 1891, in Castellammare del Golfo, Sicily. The streets of his hometown were buzzing with the sounds of a feud that had been spanning generations. Stefano was the third of Giovanni and Giuseppa Magaddino's eight children, and he was born at a time when the Magaddino family and their relatives were in an ongoing, bitter feud with the Buccellato clan. Violence wasn't a distant threat for a young Stefano; instead, it was a harsh reality that would influence his childhood.

While he would end up on the other side of this later, initially, he was privy to hushed conversations that were rooted in fear. That fear hung thick in the Sicilian air, but amidst the ever-present terror, the seeds of loyalty would flourish. Stefano witnessed the price some paid for their unwavering, misplaced alliance, which was often collected in blood. He also learned about the chilling chess game of revenge, a lesson he would become very familiar with. This "baptism by violence" was brutal, but it would forever shape the person Magaddino would become.

His formative years would be steeped in the shadowy structure of the Sicilian underworld, where Stefano would experiment with some low-level crimes. Every lesson and every brutal encounter during this time would be a brick laid in the Magaddino foundation. In 1909, right as he was on the edge of manhood and falling into deeper trouble, an 18-year-old Stefano left Castellammare for the quickly growing Mafia landscape in New York City.

He found himself surrounded by familiarity, though, in Brooklyn's Williamsburg. This wasn't a chance landing either; it was a Castellammarese hotspot, an area controlled by the Bonannos, another Castellammare clan, to whom the Magaddinos were bound by blood. There would be no time for late-teenage awkwardness, as Stefano found himself knee-deep in the New York Mafia scene.

He was already sharp and displayed immense loyalty, which caught the eye of Giuseppe "Joe Bananas" Bonanno. Stefano quickly carved out his own place as an advisor and a street enforcer. The combination of fists and cunning would help the Bonannos solidify their empire in the city. This was still in the "Wild West" years of the mafia, which were some of the most violent years, and Stefano was in the middle of it all, proving to be a rising star.

While it was a rush of chaos, Stefano would find a bit of normalcy in 1913 when he married Carmela Caroddo. His brother Gaspare followed suit soon after, marrying Carmela's sister. It was a slight reminder that loyalty went well beyond blood ties for the Mafia.

That normalcy would likely help Stefano keep a level head because at this time the Mafia presence in New York City was a fractured mess. There were various competing factions all trying to assert their dominance. It was because of this that Stefano would find another group, one that was feared and ruthless. They were known simply as the "Good Killers," and they weren't the average Mafia muscle. These were almost like the hitmen's hitmen, the ones that families called on for delicate matters and permanent solutions. Stefano, equipped with his growing reputation for efficiency and cold resolve, caught their eye. This crew was the embodiment of everything the Mafia was, and it was where Stefano thrived.

It was within this group that Stefano Magaddino developed his skills until they were razor-sharp. He learned the criminal art of the silent takedown, which is when a victim would disappear before the bullet left the chamber. Of all the defining moments in his younger years, this was the period that made the man who would go on to become "The Undertaker," the figure that was seen as the king of the Buffalo underworld. He wouldn't know it yet, but something was brewing in his former home, which would be the catalyst that put him on the path to Buffalo.

The Good Killers' Case

The following is a rare piece of evidence that the Good Killers existed in the history of the Mafia, and it paints a truly chilling picture of the underworld, where anything but fierce loyalty comes with the most severe consequences. In the end, Stefano Magaddino was still well on his way to being the head of the Buffalo Crime Family. However, this brush with the law could have severely altered the course of Mafia history.

The Murder of Pietro Magaddino

Around 1916, the atmosphere in Sicily was packed with tension. It was as if a dense fog of uncertainty and mistrust had fallen over a landscape that was already ready to become a violent storm. This storm would be one of a brutal battle, which would change the life of the future leader of the Buffalo Crime Family forever. It was in this violent skirmish that the life of Stefano's brother, Pietro Magaddino, would be claimed. Shockwaves were sent through Stefano's expanding world.

Stefano was naturally consumed by immense grief in the beginning. While it came with the territory of the mafioso lifestyle, he still devastatingly lost his brother. So, more than the loss, it was the nature of Pietro's death that was even more unbearable. However, as time moved forward, Stefano's mourning turned into something else—rage and an extremely loud cry for retribution. It wasn't an uncommon reaction in the criminal underworld or for anyone who lost a family member like that. It was almost expected, but Stefano didn't know who deserved his wrath. There were rumors, discussions, and a vast number of accusations thrown around about who could have killed Pietro.

It wouldn't take long for a solid lead to emerge from the chaos, and that came in the form of Camillo Caiozzo. Camillo was a low-level thug in the Sicilian Mafia, but he would become infamous when he was named as an accomplice in Pietro's murder. News of Stefano's retribution had already reached Camillo, which immediately put him in a state of fear. He knew what awaited him in Sicily for even being involved in Pietro Magaddino's murder. Vengeance was essentially a Sicilian birthright, and it was a shadow that would hang over his head until someone made the move to strike.

The fear was too much for Caiozzo to bear, so he decided to take his chances on fleeing. He needed refuge, and the only place where he could think of laying low was in the hustle and bustle of New York City. Perhaps Caiozzo thought that Buffalo and New York City were far enough apart, or maybe he thought that he could maintain a level of anonymity among the throngs of people. No matter what his thinking, the wheels were already in motion and Camillo Caiozzo's life was on contract. It was just a matter of time.

Stefano's Vengeance

In the aftermath of Pietro's death, Stefano Magaddino was hellbent on vengeance. He was a man possessed, consumed by a singular desire to avenge his brother's murder. Word had gotten back to him that Camillo Caiozzo was in America, likely walking the streets of New York City, waiting for things to die down. Stefano could have struck quickly, but he was patient. He would hold back, biding his time until the moment was just right.

The year was 1921, and New York City was a bustling place where a person really could disappear into a crowd. It was also a city where a secret could be made, except this wouldn't be a secret for long. In the most mafioso, unassuming way, Caiozzo met his bloody end. The execution was silent and effective. Stefano Magaddino had gotten his revenge, and he had just sent a clear message to anyone who dared cross him or the Good Killers. As long as no one spoke of what happened, it would be a done deal.

Time passed, allowing the memory of Caiozzo's disappearance (likely murder) to fade into the background. However, fate would have a way of bringing misdeeds to light. In the secluded cove of Shark River in New Jersey, a gruesome discovery was made. Lying with the driftwood that washed ashore was the lifeless body of Camillo Caiozzo. The chilling discovery served as a stern reminder that the Mafia's code of conduct wasn't a myth but a brutal reality. It was an eye for an eye.

The discovery of the body wasn't surprising. It's what came after that sent shockwaves through the underworld. This was a twist that no one saw coming.

A New Jersey barber named Bartolo Fontana walked into a police station, ready to tell them everything that he knew and had done. He confessed to being the triggerman who carried out the hit on Caiozzo, only two weeks before the body was found in the cove. The police were already accustomed to the inner workings of the Mafia, but they weren't ready for what Fontana would do next.

Fontana didn't stop at just confessing his role in the murder. He took it a step further by selling out the Good Killers. He admitted that while he did act alone in the murder, he had done so following the orders passed to him by the Magaddino-led criminal outfit. He pinned Stefano as the person who had been the mastermind behind the killing. This revelation would send a shockwave through the criminal underworld, and things were about to turn upside down.

The Sting and the Trial

Bartolo Fontana was highly aware of the dangerous path he had chosen to take. He, like many, knew all too well that anyone who dared to sell out a mafioso wouldn't live to tell the tale. The knowledge that his being cooperative with law enforcement would paint a massive target on his back that would eat at the barber. It was a jail sentence or a death sentence—Bartolo was between a rock and a hard place. But the looming threat of retaliation (and sure death) from the Good Killers that hung over Bartolo led him to choose to take a deal with the police. The deal would come in the form of a sting operation in which Fontana would act as the bait that would lure Stefano and the rest of the crew into a well-placed trap. The police saw it as a golden opportunity to unveil the Good Killers, and it could have rewritten the entire story of Stefano Magaddino and the Buffalo Crime Family.

The stage had been set for the sting operation. It would happen at the famed Grand Central Station, where Fontana would play the role of a terrified hitman looking to skip town and lay low. It was a legitimate front, as a killer would be terrified that their target's body had been found floating in the New Jersey water. He arranged the meeting with Stefano, looking for any help in fleeing. It was a tense exchange, with Fontana hoping that he wouldn't raise any of Magaddino's suspicion. The only thing Stefano saw, though, was someone desperate for help. He was so convinced of the barber's fear that he offered him $30 to leave town. As the bills exchanged hands, undercover cops swooped in and nabbed Stefano. Subsequently, four other members of the good killers were arrested, effectively bringing the group's activity to a screeching halt.

The threat of retaliation was a distant memory for Fontana, which emboldened him to reveal even more about the Good Killers. He gave the court as many details of the outfit and their activities as he could recall, including a hit previously executed on Detroit mafioso Felive Buccellato that took place in 1917. Again, he pinned Stefano Magaddino as the man who orchestrated the hit. Law enforcement, prosecutors, and even Bartolo Fontana himself all believed that they had done everything they needed to do to put Stefano and his crew away for good. However, justice had many different plans.

For reasons unknown—and those that favored the future crime boss—the state of New Jersey decided against pressing charges in the murder of Camillo Caiozzo. It was a resounding decision that left even the New York Police, who had meticulously organized the sting operation, stunned. Stefano and the other members of the Good Killers walked scot-free. Meanwhile, Bartolo Fontana was the only one to suffer any real consequences from the ordeal, as he was sentenced to 20 years in prison for Camillo's murder.

Becoming the Undertaker

The legacy of the Good Killers as a Sicilian secret society would fade from the minds of the public because there was much more activity from the criminal underworld to focus on. Magaddino narrowly slipped through the fingers of the law, and now with the taste of freedom, he left the New York courtroom a changed man. While he was already a strong leader, he was still naive. Stefano was still a young immigrant looking to cement his place in the United States. But now, he was more of a cunning operator who wanted more than just an underboss role, like he had a score to settle.

He spent some of his time after the trial traveling across the US, but it wouldn't be long before he found himself back in New York. Except, he found his place in the northwest corner, close to the

Canadian border. Stefano found Buffalo—a city that was booming while still rough around the edges, much like Magaddino.

Magaddino would set up shop in nearby Niagara Falls, which would ultimately be the Buffalo family's most lucrative move. Nestled among the industrial smokestacks and the harbors, Stefano opened the Magaddino Memorial Chapel. It was a symbol of death, but it was also a symbol of Magaddino's fresh start. This building would earn him the nickname "The Undertaker," which seemed to serve as a reminder of the line that he toed throughout his life. The funeral home wasn't a facade though. Like several operations, it was a legitimate front, but death wouldn't be the only business booming in the 1920s. Prohibition was now on the tip of everyone's tongue, and although there were many supporters, there were just as many people willing to break the law to quench this newfound thirst. Magaddino, ever the strategist, saw a tremendous opportunity.

Magaddino's funeral home was positioned so close to the Canadian border that it made for the perfect place for a much more prosperous endeavor. With Prohibition stopping at the US border, Magaddino saw his chance to enter the bootlegging racket. The booze that was high in demand made a slow but steady flow into the United States. Canadian affiliates would load crates of alcohol onto rickety boats and sail under the cover of darkness. Once the boats were safely on American soil, the crates were swiftly moved to warehouses, back alleys, or funeral homes. The alcohol would then make it to the speakeasies in the area. Jazz clubs and piano bars served as a front for Magaddino's biggest steps in the criminal underworld. With every clinking glass, Stefano Magaddino became that much more of an influence on the region.

It was more than just about lining his pockets and finding a piece of the "good life," although that was a great perk. The bootlegging racket was just a foot in the door, a way to get deeper into the underbelly of organized crime. He found that way in by working up through the ranks of the DiCarlo family. Magaddino took his already exceptional skills and honed them. While he was a great underboss who knew the delicate dance of loyalty and betrayal, he would prove to the rest of the DiCarlo-Palmeri family that he was ready for more. That ruthlessness and cunning nature kept him well ahead of his enemies and saw him quickly seated at the top of potential successors of the Buffalo family when the time was right.

Magaddino wouldn't have to wait long. DiCarlo's health was already in rapid decline, and his death would create that opening for Magaddino. There was no question that the role of boss would fall on Magaddino's shoulders. It was time for the DiCarlo-Palmeri Family to shed its old skin and emerge as the Magaddino Crime Family, a name that would become synonymous with power and influence in the city of Buffalo.

Once a sleepy town in the northwest corner of New York, Buffalo would soon become a hub of the American Mafia. Now, under the iron fist of Magaddino, the family was ready to grow and diversify. Bootlegging would remain a cornerstone, like with many families, but Stefano knew that they would need to dip into other rackets to remain on top. With a new leader, the family wouldn't just be out to make money. They were out of control, ready to tighten their grip and interweave themselves into every aspect of life in Buffalo.

CHAPTER 3

THE REIGN OF THE MAGADDINO CRIME FAMILY

In the expansive history of the American criminal underworld, few names have the same type of power as that of Stefano Magaddino—despite his name not being mentioned alongside your typical Mafia bosses. That said, Magaddino wasn't your typical Mafia boss. He was a man who had already taken on leadership roles, exhibiting an icy ruthlessness that set him apart from other figures in the mafia. While other bosses were characterized by flamboyance and living in the glitz and glamor of it all, Stefano was molded by a lifetime of experience, making him a quiet cunning force.

Taking control of the Buffalo family was an easy decision for the underbosses to make, and it was one that would have effects that were felt even outside the region. This wasn't a simple change in leadership, it was a shift that would propel the organization to unforeseen heights. The Buffalo Crime Family had a solid beginning under the control of Giuseppe DiCarlo, but they were about to enter the Magaddino era.

The next decade for the Buffalo—now the Magaddino—Crime Family would be a blur of cunning, strategic maneuvers. This period would be marked by bloody alliances and shattered loyalty, and it was all done in the pursuit of prosperity. That pursuit would leave behind a lot of enemies and those who couldn't adapt in its wake. There were triumphs and setbacks, but this would be the era that defined the Buffalo underworld.

Expansion and Power Plays

Again, Magaddino was a man of quiet authority, so he wasn't one to flaunt his power around. However, his actions spoke volumes about his leadership and his vision for the future. In 1923, after securing the mantle of leadership, he made a significant move that helped define the direction in which the organization would go. This was done by bringing in his brother Antonio over from their Sicilian breeding grounds of Castellammare. Antonio quickly became a valuable asset to the organization, and he would take his place as a trusted confidante and advisor to Stefano.

Together, the Magaddino brothers set up their headquarters in Niagara Falls. This maneuver was far more than just about Stefano staying close to home; it was a clear declaration of intent. The Magaddino family was staking its claim on the prime location for the booming bootlegging racket. As control was solidified in Niagara Falls, their underbosses (Angelo Palmeri, Filippo Mazzara, and the others from the DiCarlo days) fortified the hold in Buffalo. It was a coordinated effort that ensured that the family's grip wasn't on just a city but on the entire northwest region of New York.

While power struggles were a common thing in New York City, the Magaddino Crime Family took control over the area. Their strategic positioning and meticulous planning helped them curb a lot of the chaos and focus on the expansion of their operations.

An extremely calculative move followed soon after when Stefano became a naturalized citizen of the US in 1923. The act, while a natural event for many immigrants, would work well in favor of Stefano's reign. For many of the lower-ranking members of the Mafia, brushes with authorities would result in deportation. Deportation caused delays in operations, and that spelled trouble if you were in any type of leadership role. However, Stefano's citizenship gave him a secure base, allowing him to operate without that particular fear.

This newfound security allowed Stefano to expand into more legitimate businesses, all of which served as a smokescreen for his criminal empire. He worked under the radar while expanding his empire. It seemed everything Stefano was doing was a testament to his genius, especially as the family's image and revenue were significantly boosted.

The Magaddino family's rise to power wasn't chance or luck. There were no meetings of fate. This was the result of careful planning, strategic moves, and Stefano's shrewd decision-making. The boss's leadership, coupled with the support of strong underbosses, allowed the organization to establish a tight grip. What followed was an explosion of underworld success.

Bootlegging Gold

The 18th Amendment

Any look at the golden age of the American Mafia would point you right toward the Prohibition era and the days of bootlegging. The 18th Amendment, which banned the manufacture, sale, and transportation of alcohol inadvertently created the perfect environment for the criminal underworld, including the American Mafia to thrive. While there were plenty of people who were pro-18th Amendment, there were also those who had a demand for alcohol.

The Mafia, with its well-structured hierarchy and incredible efficiency, established sophisticated bootlegging operations. They brought in alcohol from places like Canada and the Caribbean, and they would then distribute it through networks of speakeasies and illegal bars, often touted as jazz clubs and other legitimate establishments. It was a time of great wealth, influence, and power for any crime family. It was also a time for power struggles and gang wars.

Moreover, the Prohibition era exposed widespread corruption in law enforcement and politicians during this time. Many would be "in the pockets" of the crime families, turning a blind eye in exchange for bribes (be it cash or other favors). This allowed the organizations to operate with impunity, and many would use these figures to rid themselves of any potential threats to their profits.

It was a chaotic period in American history, and the city of Buffalo was no exception either.

Magaddino's Role in the Alcohol Racket

In these early days of the Prohibition Era, luck (probably in the form of some well-greased wheels) smiled on the Magaddino Crime Family. While the United States was dried out, the sale and consumption of alcohol was still very much legal across the Canadian border. The geographical advantage made Buffalo a haven for anyone wanting to get into the lucrative bootlegging game. DiCarlo and Palmeri recognized that and had already exploited the positioning, but now with a new leader, things were about to grow exponentially.

Not one to overlook a golden opportunity, Magaddino exploited their advantage as much as he could. The family became the gatekeepers of the liquor coming in from Canada, deciding which cities received the precious booze and which were cut off. Control like this not only made the local speakeasies conform to the rules set by the Magaddino family, but it also ensured the surrounding areas followed suit. The Magaddino organization's influence spread rapidly, and their power was felt well outside their territory.

Stefano's cold, calculated nature played a huge role in this expansion. He ruled with an iron fist, ensuring that the family ran efficiently. If DiCarlo was a great strategist, it would make Magaddino a master of the craft given his ability to make tough decisions when necessary. Under Stefano's leadership, the Buffalo region had money and power that would rival any of the notorious gangsters.

That power would also be a deterrent for anyone who dared to cross into Magaddino territory. The family had a reputation for ruthlessness and the way they would show their control over the liquor racket made them a formidable force. Magaddino and his underbosses, especially Palmeri, would swiftly deal with anyone who tried to challenge them or attempt to operate in their territory.

The Magaddino Family's rise to prominence during the chaotic prohibition years was a testament to superb leadership, strategic planning, and no hesitation to execute those plans (along with a few foes too). They could spot the opportunities presented to them, just like the geographical positioning of Buffalo, and use them to their fullest advantage. Buffalo would become one of the strongholds in the liquor trade, which was one of the most lucrative trades for the Mafia. Not everyone would appreciate the Magaddino family's newfound prosperity though.

The result of that displeasure, combined with growing tensions within the families of New York City, would lead the way for the Castellammarese War. Named after the Sicilian town where Magaddino and many other members of the American Mafia were born, this war was a bloody power struggle for control of the American Mafia. Lasting for just over a year, it would be the very catalyst needed for a major change in the landscape of the criminal underworld.

Castellammarese War and the Commission

By the late 1920s, the American Mafia was controlled by Giuseppe "Joe the Boss" Masseria. His faction consisted of gangsters from Sicily, Calabria, and Campania, and while there were power struggles within the Mafia, things ran largely uninterrupted. That was until bootlegging was winding down, meaning that competition was becoming more intense over the smuggling racket. Masseria looked at the Magaddino family and other Castellammarese mafiosos as a growing threat. To him, their operations were acts of rebellion; therefore, he summoned family leaders, including Magaddino, to New York City. This was a not-so-subtle power move, and Stefano knew it as such. The intimidating Buffalo leader never took kindly to being intimidated by anyone else, and he wasn't about to start now. He refused to make the trip to New York City for the meeting, which only enraged Masseria. This refusal led Masseria to call for the murder of Magaddino.

The Landscape of the War

Don Vito Ferro, a powerful Sicilian Don, looked to take control of the American Mafia operations, so he sent Castellammare native Salvatore Maranzano to do so. Stefano Magaddino was a key figure in the Castellammarese faction, which meant he had an alliance with Maranzano. This would also mean that his alliances and refusal to meet with Masseria would be a significant contributor to the war.

However, jumping back just slightly, the Castellammarese War wasn't just a Mafia power struggle between Joe the Boss and Maranzano. The war itself was the culmination of a generational conflict between the older Sicilian leadership, known as the "Mustache Petes" and the "Young Turks," a younger, diverse group of Italian-Americans. The Mustache Petes were traditionalists; they wanted to hold on to the things they brought from Sicily and refused to conduct business with non-Italians. But the Young Turks, under the leadership of one Charles "Lucky" Luciano, wanted to modernize the mob. They also wanted to put an end to the constant in-fighting and resume their businesses.

Tensions finally boiled over when Masseria called for the murder of Gaspar Milazzo, a Castellammarese native who had not shown his support during one of many disputes. This common act, though, marked the beginning of the war. Things escalated more when Masseria also ordered a hit on ally Gaetano Reina, which would protect Masseria's secret allies. However, this betrayal of the Reina family saw their support move from Masseria to Maranzano.

The war became increasingly violent with blood spilling out on the streets of New York City. It seemed that things would wind down, though, when Joe the Boss was assassinated in April 1931. Salvatore Maranzano saw the opening and took over Masseria's position. Maranzano would create the Five Families of New York, giving each family a territory and a structured hierarchy. It was an overall beneficial move for the Mafia, but there were already issues with the new capo.

Maranzano's leadership was overshadowed by his arrogance, greed, and paranoia. What really drove the other families over the edge, though, was when he demanded that the Five Families pay him tribute. A rebellion was ignited and under orders from Lucky Luciano, a hit was put out on Maranzano. Five months after his reign as capo began, Maranzano was assassinated similarly to his predecessor.

It was clear as the Castellammarese War progressed that the old ways of the Mafia were no longer sustainable. That became even more obvious when Maranzano took control. The Young Turks saw a need for change and were going to take drastic steps to achieve it. Lucky Luciano's vision of the mob was an attractive one to many followers, especially those who saw many glaring faults with Masseria's leadership. The War would see fluid factions and several members switching sides or killing allies.

The war had finally ended with the assassination of Maranzano, which meant that change could come to fruition. That change transformed the American Mafia from the rough and tumble era to the syndicate that we know today.

Aftermath and the Commission

In the aftermath of the bloody war, Lucky Luciano, the visionary of the American Mafia, also realized that there were inherent dangers in having one unchallenged leader. It needed to be addressed, so Luciano called for a meeting in Chicago with the most influential figures of the Mafia, including Stefano Magaddino. The attendees made the journey with the expectation that Luciano would claim the role of Capo. While there would have been little to no disagreement about the move, those in attendance were shocked when Luciano eliminated the position. Instead, he proposed a radically different structure that would be known as the Commission.

The Commission would be much akin to a Mafia board of directors, a governing body that would oversee all Mafia activity across the country. There would be seven seats on this board, five seats held by the leaders of the Five Families, Chicago's Al Capone, and Buffalo's Stefano Magaddino. Putting this structure in place would democratize power within the entire Mafia, and the members of the Commission would become mediators in any disputes. They would also get to have the final say in leadership appointments.

Luciano drafted this proposal to be a power-sharing agreement, which would prevent future bloodshed and effectively resolve any internal conflict. While the role was abolished, Luciano was positioned as a silent capo. He would be more of a guiding hand instead of an arrogant leader. The bosses all agreed to the innovative approach, and so the Commission was born. The group agreed to meet every five years or whenever there were any important matters that needed to be addressed. And this was the turning point in the history of the American Mafia. The Commission brought organization and governance, something that was previously absent and something that would be needed for the future of the criminal underworld.

Triumphs and Setbacks

Despite the new structure for the American mafia with the Commission, tension within the New York families would continue. However, Magaddino wasn't going to back down from any challenge. He called on fear as his weapon. He had enforcers who were known for their brutality, which put a sense of terror into any potential rivals. If there were whispers of dissent, they would be met swiftly and with severe consequences. Stefano Magaddino wasn't just a one-trick pony though. He understood the power of "greasing the wheels." A little bribe here and a strategic relationship with a politician there were some common tactics that Magaddino used to ensure cooperation or a blind eye from people in positions of authority. He also knew how to infiltrate labor unions, which gave him even more of a hold on the region with power over key industries and their workforces.

Meanwhile, prohibition was becoming a double-edged sword, bringing great triumphs and crippling setbacks. While bootlegging was flourishing with the roaring '20s generating unheard-of profits for the Magaddino family, crackdowns from law enforcement began to ramp up. There was also a tremendous public backlash against the illegal liquor trade. Of course, the racket would take a much bigger blow when the 1929 stock market crash crippled the economy.

Magaddino, though, was a proactive strategist and had prepared for such challenges. The family had already started to diversify their portfolio by joining the gambling racket and other underworld activities. This may have been the foresight that would ensure the family would carry on, even as the sun began to set on the Prohibition Era and bootlegging.

By the end of the 1920s and the early 1930s, Stefano Magaddino took DiCarlo and Palmeri's foundation and built a powerful force in the criminal underworld. He navigated an explosive decade that was rife with family wars, political leveraging, and economic instability. With his effective combination of ruthlessness, cunning, and forged alliances, he didn't just set the family up for decades of success but also set himself up to be the head of the family during that success.

The abolishment of Prohibition in 1933 would bring in a new era, one that would bring its own set of challenges and new opportunities. However, for the Buffalo leader, whom they called the Undertaker, the 1930s were still just the beginning of the crime family's growth and stranglehold over Buffalo.

CHAPTER 4

THE MAGADDINO FAMILY AFTER PROHIBITION

The End of Prohibition

As the Prohibition Era wound down and finally came to a close with the repeal of the 18th Amendment in 1933, the Magaddino Crime family firmly established their dominance in the northwestern region of New York. The family successfully navigated the rough waters of this explosive time of bootlegging and violent infighting and capitalized on the opportunities that were presented, thereby expanding their criminal empire.

Stefano, the shrewd and efficient leader, managed to guide the Buffalo family through the yearlong Castellammarese War, and his effectiveness as a leader landed him a seat on the Commission. Being a part of the new governing body that oversaw the American Mafia was an incredible feat, allowing him to further influence Mafia activities across the US and not just in Buffalo.

During the days of Prohibition, the Magaddino family was well-positioned again and became heavily involved in bootlegging operations. However, as the era came to an end, the family quickly adapted and diversified their criminal activities. They would expand into other areas of crime, including gambling and racketeering, which allowed them to maintain their vice-like grip on the region, even as the lucrative days of alcohol smuggling faded into the night.

Gambling operations became a significant source of revenue for the family. The Magaddino organization operated numerous gambling dens and ran multiple bookmaking operations, some of which were even operating within horse racing tracks. It goes without question that the family had reach and influence. Their hold on the gambling world in northwest New York not only gave them income but also allowed them to influence the way the chips fell.

Racketeering was another major source of income for the family. This aspect of business involved collecting money from businesses and individuals in return for Magaddino's protection. Oftentimes, the dues were simply granting these businesses the ability to operate in what would otherwise be mafia territory. If sufficient dues were not paid, threats of violence would fall on those businesses or people. With Magaddino's rule, there would be no second warnings, ensuring that anyone living in the family's territory would pay up.

As the end of Prohibition loomed, there were also hints of the family venturing into drug trafficking. While it wasn't a major operation at this stage for much of the Mafia, it was clear that eyes fell on any potential source of revenue. With changes in politics later down the line, and the changes in American culture, drug trafficking became a significant part of criminal operations.

The end of Prohibition marked a major turning point for the Magaddino Crime Family. They had successfully navigated through some of the biggest challenges that were presented to the Mafia while also successfully expanding their operations. Stefano solidified their position, making them a dominant part of the Mafia as they pushed on to a new period of American history. It was his leadership and strategic foresight that allowed these changes to happen.

The Impact of the Magaddino Family

The operations of the Magaddino family had a huge impact on Buffalo, Niagara Falls, and the surrounding communities. While almost all of their activities were illicit, they still contributed to the local economy in several ways. The gambling dens and speakeasies they operated (even as Prohibition was repealed) employed several residents. Many of these establishments also served as places of entertainment, providing a brief moment of normalcy from the harsh realities of life during the Great Depression.

In addition to their typical Mafia operations, the Magaddino family also engaged in philanthropic endeavors. It's typically overlooked how much Mafia organizations positively contributed to their communities. While it doesn't negate the criminal aspect of their operations, they would donate to local charities and fund community projects—all aimed at improving public infrastructure and services. This philanthropy, along with other economic contributions would sway some public perception in their favor. This is particularly true when many families were struggling to just get by.

However, while some of these charitable actions were wholesome, these activities were often part of a bigger strategy put forth by the

Mafia families. They used their wealth to boost the local economy, which would gain them social capital and more influence throughout the communities they controlled. While specifics of the Magaddino contributions aren't clear, many families would sponsor local sports teams or provide scholarships for local students. Of course, many would donate to political campaigns, either gaining the influence of politicians in place or putting politicians that they favored into positions of power.

Again, while everything was seemingly harmless, their community outreach gave them leverage to maintain control over their territories and safeguard their criminal enterprise. By integrating themselves with the community, local authorities, and politicians, they could operate with little to no interference.

Yet not everyone celebrated the organization or even was on board with the long and ominous shadow that the Magaddino family cast over the northwestern region of New York. With their ruthless tactics and a blatant disregard for authority, they became a feared and often loathed presence in the community. Those who opposed the family or refused to fall in line with their demands would usually find themselves at the receiving end of Magaddino's wrath. These feelings were not unfounded, though, nor were they just a reaction to the proximity to the mafia. The Magaddino family was known for the brutal enforcement of their rules, and they were always willing to resort to violence to maintain their grip on the region.

However, the once-blind eye of the authorities toward the family's activities started to fade. With public outcry against the American Mafia beginning to swell across the country, law enforcement agencies, from local agencies to the FBI, were forced to take action against the families. This action also came from these agencies because further inaction would expose that they were complicit or, worse, had alliances with the crime families. So, for much of Stefano's reign, he and the rest of the Magaddino family found themselves as targets of multiple arrests, government investigations, and prosecutions.

The Apalachin Meeting

One such occurrence that showed that law enforcement was cracking down on organized crime came in the form of the Apalachin Meeting. On November 14, 1957, a historic summit of the American Mafia was held. It took place at the home of Joseph "Joe the Barber" Barbara in Apalachin, New York. This meeting would be a significant event in the timeline of organized crime, as it exposed the true existence of the criminal network that sprawled throughout the United States.

The purpose of the meeting was to discuss various topics, including loansharking, gambling, and even the trafficking of narcotics in the country. It was also held to discuss the division of operations that had been under the control of Albert Anastasia, who had been recently murdered. There would be an estimated 100 attendees from the United States, Italy, and even Cuba.

The meeting was originally set to take place in Chicago, but hoping that a change of scenery would ease tensions between families, Magaddino suggested that it be held in Barbara's home. Stefano also suggested the location because he believed the quiet country setting would help them avoid unwanted attention from the law.

However, it was hard for local and state officials to not be suspicious when numerous luxury cars, adorned with license plates from all across the US, began showing up in the normally tranquil Apalachin. Police sat in unmarked cars along the side of the road taking down those license plate numbers. Eventually, a roadblock was set up, and the police would strike, raiding the meeting. Many of the participants fled into the woods and other areas around the Barbara estate. More than 60 bosses were arrested and indicted following the raid.

Around 20 of those bosses who attended the meeting were charged with conspiring to obstruct justice. This came from lying about the nature of this meeting. All of the charged parties were found guilty in January 1959. They were all fined up to $10,000 and given a prison sentence of three to five years. It seemed like the criminal underworld had been dealt a major blow, except all convictions were overturned the following year on appeals.

Again, the most significant outcome of the events was that it confirmed the existence of a nationwide criminal organization. This was a fact that some, including J. Edgar Hoover (director of the Federal Bureau of Investigation), had refused to acknowledge until this point. The Apalachin Meeting also exposed the Mafia to the public that lived outside Mafia-controlled areas, which ramped up the pressure from law enforcement.

Despite the fallout from the Apalachin Meeting, which included the arrest of some of his own members, Stefano managed to maintain his position and avoid any severe consequences for his activity.

This fateful meeting was a game-changing event in the history of organized crime. The mafia and their activities were all exposed and now came under more scrutiny from the general public and law enforcement. However, some, like Magaddino, were still operating "business as usual," which made many wonder if anything could stop the criminal underworld.

The Sign of Descent

Despite the challenges that he faced, Stefano managed to keep a secure grip over the region. He also had the same type of control within the family, which led him to avoid any severe consequences for his criminal activities. It seemed like "The Undertaker" was always just out of reach of the law. However, by no means was this an easy feat. The Magaddino family was far from immune to the changing landscape of the criminal underworld. Like their contemporaries, the Magaddino family had to quickly adapt to increased pressure from law enforcement and the changing public attitude toward organized crime. This meant that every move the family made now would have to be made with the utmost care or everything could collapse on top of them.

Those lessons were proven well before the end of Prohibition when Al Capone was convicted of tax evasion in 1931 after the formation of the Commission. While Capone's position in the public eye didn't help matters, it showed just how quickly an organization could lose everything. This was also seen during the arrests made and the exposure of the Mafia during the Apalachin Meeting. While those flashier figures had exposed their activities, the Mafia as a whole was public knowledge after 1957.

In response to the challenges and threats to their livelihoods, the Magaddino family and other organizations within the American Mafia would look at other avenues to operate. This would lead to many expanding from just racketeering and gambling to loan sharking, extortion, and labor union control. They would also invest money into legitimate businesses in a more subtle way to launder their illegal earnings while maintaining and growing their influence.

From 1933 until around the 1960s, Stefano Magaddino, the effective leader of the Buffalo Crime Family, kept a firm grip on the organization that he had taken over after the death of Guiseppe DiCarlo in 1922. His leadership had spanned decades, and it was a testament to his strategic acumen, ruthless execution of plans, and his constant pursuit of power. It's also attributed to his ability to adapt to any changes that came his way. Magaddino's period of control is one of the longest regimes in the history of the criminal underworld, further cementing the absolute efficiency of his leadership.

However, like all reigns in the criminal underworld, there was an inevitable end. The landscape of the underworld was rapidly changing, especially after the exposure it received due to the massive raid. The 1960s, therefore, posed more challenges to the family's operations in the form of societal shifts, evolving tactics, and increased monitoring from law enforcement. There were even shifts in the internal dynamics of the Mafia and the Magaddino family that started to unravel the strings of control. However, even as these threats to power increased, the family's influence remained significant. This was a true testament to the foundation that was established by DiCarlo and Palmeri.

Stefano Magaddino's leadership style shouldn't be overlooked in the longevity of this reign. The lack of flamboyance, along with his strategic vision, foresight, and adaptability to change elevated him as a leader. He also surrounded himself with a crew of effective underbosses who were key factors in executing his plans and ensuring the family's operations ran smoothly.

While the knowledge of the Magaddino family is limited, this can be seen as just another attribute of their legacy. The reign of the Buffalo Crime Family under Stefano Magaddino is remarkable. Their influence stretched far beyond their bases in Buffalo and Niagara Falls, which helped shape the landscape of organized crime in New York City and beyond. That legacy was well known before the fall of it, but legacy didn't matter in the face of needed change. The world of organized crime in the United States was changing, just as it did in the early 1930s when the Commission took over. How much longer would the powerful Magaddino last as head of the family?

CHAPTER 5

INTERNAL STRIFE, DECLINE, AND THE POWER VACUUM

In the annals of organized crime, the Magaddino Family carved a powerful name for themselves, becoming the name people thought of when thinking about the Buffalo Crime Family. Their reign, however, would not last. The landscape of the criminal underworld was decisively altered in the wake of the infamous Apalachin Meeting. These changes weren't just coming from external rumblings either; they were echoing through the very core of the Magaddino family.

The aging leader of the organization found himself struggling to keep up with such large shifts. The once iron grip of Stefano Magaddino had started to slip away, strained further by the weight of rapidly evolving dynamics. Dissent was bubbling, and like many other families and regimes before, the call for change was becoming harder to ignore.

The twilight of the Magaddino era was riddled with complications, leaving the family staring at the potential for a power vacuum. The eventual death of the Magaddino patriarch would throw the entire organization into uncertainty and turmoil. This chapter serves as a look into the tumultuous last years of the Magaddino Crime Family, exploring those struggles for power, the changes in organized crime as a whole, Stefano's decline, and the absence of any leadership after Stefano's death.

Internal Conflicts and Power Struggles

The Magaddino family was a formidable force in the American Mafia landscape, but they were not immune to power struggles and other internal conflicts. Lower-level thugs and underbosses all had their own ambitions and visions for where they saw the family heading in the future. While unclear as to how many attempts there were to push Stefano off his throne, power struggles commonly led to assassination attempts. This led to more broken leadership and less loyalty within the family, and it would only grow after the failed Apalachin Meeting because of Stefano's ties to its downfall. As time passed by, these pushes were handled with less discipline, which served as a tell-tale sign of the external threats that the family was also facing.

Internal conflicts weren't just unique to the Buffalo Crime Family either. Many other families had the same internal strife as seen in the battles within the Five Families of New York. Some other families, like the Bonanno and Colombo families, experienced them as the landscape was changing from the 1930s to the 1960s. For example, the Bonanno family faced some of their most significant conflicts in the 1960s after Joseph Bonanno mysteriously disappeared. His disappearance led to more power struggles (more than what the families were accustomed to) and a period of instability and violence, as various factions within the family all looked to gain control.

As for the Colombo family, the power struggle began when Carmine Persico, who led the family for decades, was finally imprisoned for his criminal activities. His son Alphonse served as the boss, but without Carmine, his leadership was challenged immediately by other members of the family.

These internal conflicts were typically caused by disagreements over the distribution of power and resources within the family. One of the most notorious examples was the rise of John Gotti in the Gambino family. His ascension led to high tensions and several betrayals until Gotti was imprisoned.

Things were changing rapidly for the American Mafia, and it seemed to happen much faster during the height of the Cold War. Interestingly enough, these power struggles and conflicts seemed to occur at a much faster pace in other families than in the Magaddino family. A lot of this resilience could be attributed to the leadership style of Stefano Magaddino, who managed to keep a certain level of discipline within his family. Again, things wouldn't last as proven by the prominent Bonanno family. Their internal conflict, known as the "Banana War," proved that everything was about to change.

As time went by, the normal iron-fist discipline in the Magaddino family waned and the power struggles only increased.

Attempts on Stefano Magaddino's Life

Where there is smoke, there is fire, and when there are internal conflicts in a Mafia family, that fire is usually in the form of assassination attempts. While Stefano enjoyed a lengthy reign over the Buffalo Crime Family, his life wouldn't be without peril.

Assassination attempts were seemingly part of the territory as a crime boss, and Magaddino survived several attempts on his life. Two of those attempts stand out for their sheer audacity and the level of impact that they would have on Stefano and the rest of the family.

1936 Attempt

The first of the most notable attempts on Magaddino's life took place in 1936. While Stefano had been in control of the region for over a decade, others wanted a piece of the lucrative northwestern territory. Skirmishes and hits would break out, but this attempt on Magaddino involved the boss's home and a bomb. However, the plan had one fatal miscalculation. They believed that the bomb was planted in Magaddino's Niagara Falls home, but instead, they planted the bomb in his sister's home. That flaw claimed the life of Stefano's sister and injured his three young nieces.

This incident shook the criminal underworld, but it served as a crucial reminder that the life of a mafioso meant accepting that death lurked around every corner. No one, not even the powerful Magaddino, was immune to spontaneous attacks. The Magaddino organization felt the shockwaves that served as a testament to the collateral damage that came from violence.

The failed assassination was enough to rattle Magaddino, but the loss of his sister had even more of a profound impact on the boss. What followed her murder was a period of intense violence, fueled by his intense desire for revenge against whoever was responsible. Magaddino, known already for his calculated and cautious leadership, had unleashed a wave of retaliation that no one had seen before, as he was determined to also eliminate future threats.

The event marked a turning point for Stefano. While he had previously focused efforts on expanding the Buffalo family's operations, the assassination attempt instilled a heightened sense of paranoia and secrecy. Having something like that hitting so close to home forced him to tighten his grip on the family, which saw him become less trusting and more vigilant.

After Apalachin and the 1958 Attempt

By the time the Apalachin meeting took place, Stefano had been comfortably seated as the boss of the Buffalo crime family for nearly four decades, which was largely because he was a man with ambition who took calculated risks. It was his leadership skills that saw him play a pivotal role in where the large meeting of crime bosses was to take place. While he did have good intentions in mind to use the secluded location to evade the eyes of the law, the plan was a monumental failure. It was his miscalculation that exposed the entirety of the American Mafia network to the public. This brought unwanted attention that would have severe consequences for Magaddino.

In the aftermath of the Apalachin fiasco, there was an instant uptick in the number of assassination attempts made on Stefano. Those bosses who took the fall that day wanted their revenge, and violence was the answer. That violence would reach its boiling point when an assailant threw a hand grenade through the open kitchen window of Magaddino's home. Although the attacker had the right residence this time, fate stepped in. The grenade, a seemingly effective device to take out the Buffalo boss, was a dud. There was no detonation, and Magaddino was safe.

This near-death experience would establish Magaddino as a "Teflon Don," which was a moniker given to those who seemed to never go away. Despite the attempts from rivals and very powerful Mafia bosses, he remained unscathed. His leadership was untouchable, but the attack brought more than a stroke of luck for Stefano. It was a catalyst that spurred another period of ruthless aggression from the boss.

With the kindling of betrayal fueling the attacks, Magaddino grew even more paranoid after this attempt, and he used it to purge several members of the Magaddino Family. Not only was he suspicious of those who may have tipped off the other dons, but he was going for anyone he thought was after his position. Loyalty was the biggest concern, and if Stefano thought anyone was the slightest bit disloyal, they were removed from more than the organization.

The purge did serve Magaddino's other motives. He not only got to eliminate those he felt were disloyal but also potential threats that allowed him to consolidate his power. By weeding out those that he felt were traitors, he looked to prevent any further attempts while establishing himself as an unchallenged boss. He seemed untouchable, but this was only established by instilling fear into those around him.

The Apalachin fiasco was a huge turning point for Magaddino, and things wouldn't be the same during the rest of his time as boss. His remaining years would be a constant struggle, which inadvertently weakened the very thing he tried to fortify.

The Rise in Drug Trafficking and the Heroin Trade

Drug trafficking wasn't anything new to the Mafia, especially as this had been another lucrative venture for many families after the end of Prohibition. However, there would be one product in particular that impacted the power balances within the families, including the Magaddino family. That drug would be heroin, and it offered a huge opportunity for younger mafiosos and underbosses who were eager to gain more wealth and influence.

Again, it would be the younger members of the mafia who were instrumental in pushing for the involvement of heroin in their established trafficking. They saw large financial gains in this venture, and they often overlooked the tremendous risks that were associated with it. This was a slight contrast to the older leaders and underbosses who were a bit more conservative and hesitant. They understood the potential profits, but they also were wary about being associated with the highly addictive substance. This internal strife showed that newer members of the mafia could see the profits while the older family members saw the potential risks, with some being completely against the operation.

One example of this was the Lucchese Family. They were heavily involved in the heroin trade during the 1970s and the 1980s, which was largely driven by the younger members and underbosses. Older leaders were fearful of the increased scrutiny and backlash from the authorities, especially when their operations were going through another major shift and loss of power. The younger members, however, were willing to take the big risk for a bigger reward.

The Bonanno Family's "Banana War" and the power struggle within the family were also largely fueled by disagreements over involvement in the heroin trade. The Magaddinos were not immune to this shift in power and criminal activity either. It was a period of instability, and the drug trafficking racket would only make it worse. Things would also get worse in 1971 when then-President Nixon declared the War on Drugs.

Law Enforcement Efforts

The landscape of the American Mafia was shifting at a rapid rate, and the once dominant crime families across the United States started to lose their grip on the territories they controlled. But it wasn't just the dynamic shifts within the family; organizations lost their once powerful hold on law enforcement and the court system as well. Naturally, this would mean the same for Stefano and the Magaddino family.

Law enforcement, from local and state to federal agencies, was also in a seismic shift. Fearful of how the public would react to their complacency after the Mafia was exposed, they ramped up their efforts to take down the crime families. The Magaddino Family was no exception, with an increased focus on the infiltration and disruption of criminal activities. The number of informants increased exponentially during this period. While some informants were officers, many of these came from within the organization itself. With ambitions to move up or fear of punishment by the law, family members gave up valuable information. The insider knowledge of family activities gave law enforcement valuable insight, which allowed them to make more effective strikes to disrupt the family's operations.

Informant information led to a series of effective raids and arrests, and these actions dealt major blows to various operations. This disrupted activities and led to the arrest (and conviction) of lower-level thugs and underbosses. Once extensive and robust networks were either damaged or severed completely. The loss of key personnel and a large number of members quickly and significantly reduced the power and influence the crime family held over the regions.

The rest of the legal system would follow suit, as legal cases against the family significantly increased. Prosecutors were armed with a mountain of evidence thanks to various informants and the evidence gathered during raids. Strong cases were made against the defendants, which often resulted in long prison sentences, depleting the family's ranks.

The most notable of these moves from law enforcement was the Apalachin Meeting. Again, the suspicious activity led law enforcement to the conclusion that this was criminal activity. Many Mafia bosses were arrested, and while there was a relatively minor impact on the Magaddino Family, some of Magaddino's underbosses did go down in the raid. The most significant aspect of the raid was that law enforcement was no longer going to sit idly by and let the Mafia continue their operations.

Loss of Influence and Territory

The Magaddinos were no doubt a resilient force, but they began to experience a decline in their territory because of the internal and external factors that have been mentioned.

Internally, the family was trying to navigate through the fallout in the wake of the assassination attempts on Stefano. This led to a period of instability within the family, with members questioning each other and their loyalty to the Magaddino organization. With the constant threat of violence and fear of retaliation, a tense atmosphere spread across the family and impeded the smooth operation of their activities.

Externally, the decline of the Magaddino reign was spurred by public outcry and the sudden shift in how law enforcement handled the Mafia. With efforts now ramped up to combat organized crime, a sense of further distrust and paranoia was taking root in the family. While the consolidation of power would cut down on these betrayals, it would be a double-edged sword, as the family would find their grip loosening on the region.

Despite the contributions made to the local economy through their enterprises and philanthropy, the Magaddinos weren't protected. The call for justice against the American Mafia was spreading, which led to either rebranding or the shedding of some businesses to keep the heat off.

As the influence of the Magaddino Family waned, the door for rivals and other criminal organizations to capitalize on the territory opened. The groups moved in and attempted to take over. The family couldn't retaliate like they would have done, further weakening them and accelerating their loss of power.

The Final Years of the Magaddino Family

In the year following the Apalachin Meeting, the writing was on the wall that the Magaddino Crime Family would enter a period of great decline. The FBI gave Stefano the label of "top hoodlum" in the Buffalo region. This label was put in place by FBI Director Hoover, and it would come with heavy scrutiny from law enforcement. While the FBI had the boss under heavy surveillance, Magaddino managed to avoid questioning related to the Apalachin Meeting by the New York State Crime Commission in 1960 because he fell ill with a heart condition. Magaddino avoided dire consequences for his involvement in the meeting, but the authorities would not give up there.

In 1961, American *and* Canadian authorities would tear apart a narcotics ring that had Magaddino's approval. This was a strong point for the family, and Stefano took a share of the profits. It could have also been his undoing though.

Among the persons arrested were Alberto and Vito Agueci. The brothers were Magaddino underlings from Canada, and after their arrest, they expected protection and support from their boss. However, Stefano left them high and dry. Alberto was eventually freed on bail thanks to his wife borrowing money and selling their family home. His plan after release was to confront the Buffalo crime boss and demand the release of his brother. Furthermore, he planned on putting the squeeze on Stefano. Alberto would threaten to expose Magaddino's involvement in the drug ring if Vito wasn't released.

While not confirmed, Stefano likely didn't take kindly to the threat because, on November 23, 1961, Alberto's charred body was found in a cornfield near Rochester.

In 1962, the FBI would install eavesdropping equipment in the heart of the Magaddino empire. The Magaddino Memorial Chapel, which served as the meeting place for Stefano and his underbosses, was bugged. The equipment would gather enough damning information in less than three years, enough for the FBI to fill around 70,000 transcribed pages. There was even enough that in 1963, in front of the McClellan Senate Investigating Committee, Stefano Magaddino was identified as the Mafia boss of western New York and southern Ontario, Canada.

In 1964, after the disappearance of Joseph Bonanno, who was Magaddino's cousin, a newspaper columnist put out a report stating that Bonanno was being held by Magaddino in upstate New York. Stefano was subpoenaed in May 1965 to give his testimony to a special grand jury that was looking into Bonanno's disappearance. However, Magaddino, once again, didn't say a word as he developed coronary symptoms the very next day. He was hospitalized and wouldn't testify. It didn't go unnoticed though, as the press made sure to note that this was the second time that Magaddino's "health problems" seemed to go hand in hand with a government demand for him to testify.

Things from the government's side would ramp up in 1967, and federal law enforcement launched strikes against the western New

York Mafia's leadership. By December of that year, Magaddino lost Frederico Randaccio and Pasquale Natarelli (two of his top-ranking men) to prison sentences. Magaddino would quickly unravel under the pressure. He claimed that he was reaching poverty, so he demanded a higher share of family profits. Stefano also eliminated bonuses that had been previously handed out.

That move would be exposed a year later when Stefano, his son Peter, and several bookmakers and collectors were arrested after the FBI investigated a Buffalo sports betting ring. When federal agents searched Peter Magaddino's home, they found over $500,000 in cash. Leaders within the Buffalo Mafia were enraged that Stefano had lied to them about his finances, and a rebellion against the Magaddino administration was ignited.

By mid-year 1969, a rebel faction formed, with Sam Pieri as acting boss, Joseph Fino as acting underboss, and Joseph DiCarlo (son of Giuseppe) as consigliere. The group demanded that Stefano resign his position, which was refused. They then took their argument to the Commission, but the Commission took no action against the longtime member. They chose to await the death of the aging Magaddino.

It wasn't what the rebel faction wanted, but Stefano's time was coming quickly. His health problems made it nearly impossible to bring the long-reigning boss to trial. His arraignment in the bookmaking case was done in Magaddino's bedrooms when doctors deemed him too frail to appear in a courtroom. Despite his frailty, Stefano would slip through the fingers of the law one last time. In 1973, the FBI, having Magaddino dead to rights, refused to give up the identity of one of their informants who had been a part of the bookmaking investigation. Without that identity, the charges that Magaddino faced were dismissed.

Stefano "The Undertaker" Magaddino, a true Teflon Don, suffered a heart attack and died on July 19, 1974. He was buried in St. Joseph's Cemetery in Niagara Falls, where he had spent the better part of five decades as the face of the Mafia in the northwest part of New York.

The Power Vacuum and Power Struggles

Stefano Magaddino's death would leave a very noticeable hole in the leadership of the family. The once-powerful organization, which had already been weakened because of internal conflict, was now plunged into a period of instability. Several factions that sprang up in Magaddino's last days were all focused on power and control, which led to much more infighting. This internal drama left the Buffalo family fractured, desperate, and quickly losing precious territory.

The path to leadership wasn't clear either. Peter Magaddino, Stefano's son, looked to be the heir apparent to his father's position. However, he would step aside and leave the family after his involvement in his father's shady practices.

Sam Pieri, the leader of the faction that challenged Magaddino's authority the most in the years before his death, emerged as the strongest candidate. He did take the reins, giving some semblance of stability. However, that wouldn't last long, as Pieri's reign was short-lived. In 1978, he was hit with a prison sentence, which left the leadership role wide open yet again.

The Buffalo family was struggling to stay afloat. They needed a leader who could command respect the way that DiCarlo and Magaddino did. They needed someone ruthless to navigate them back to prominence, and they needed someone to navigate through one of the biggest shifts in the Mafia. The 1980s changed the landscape and threatened to snuff out the dim flame that was the Buffalo Crime Family.

PART III

THE TODARO FAMILY

(1980S-2020S-PRESENT)

CHAPTER 6

THE STATE OF THE MAFIA IN THE 1980S

The 1980s saw a major turning point in the American underworld. The vice grip that the Mafia had over their territories began to loosen, and its aging leadership had to come to terms with the perfect combination of internal and external pressures. The older leaders were either retiring, succumbing to old age, or finding themselves behind iron bars due to the increased pressure from law enforcement. Power vacuums were created in the absence of leaders, which would be true when looking at the disarray the Buffalo Crime Family was left in after Magaddino's death. Territories were shrinking every day and operations were under heavy scrutiny from the law. Moreover, there was a vast shift in the public perception of the Mafia. What had been one of the most powerful forces in the underworld was now struggling to hold on to some semblance of power.

When they weren't struggling with internal conflicts and external pressures, the families were trying to find new ways to maintain a steady flow of revenue. Traditional operations like gambling, racketeering, and loan sharking were still around, but they weren't nearly as profitable as they had once been. The new cash cow was narcotics trafficking, but that would come with its own heavy price in the form of increased attention from law enforcement. With a surge in arrests and convictions, the already rocky landscape was even more difficult to navigate.

Adding to the woes was the newfound fascination the media had with the criminal underworld. Gangster films like *The Godfather* and *Scarface*, television shows, and even news reports seemed to put more focus on the sensational aspects of the media. This not only skewed public perception, but it also potentially attracted newer members to the Mafia under the pretense of a lavish life.

Despite the changes, the American Mafia would still be able to hold a significant presence in the criminal underworld. However, their influence had waned. The late 1970s and the 1980s would be a crucial turning point that would see the once dominant American Mafia struggle to hang on to their influence. This chapter will look at the Mafia's struggle to adapt to an era defined by pressure from law enforcement, infighting, shifting public opinion, and the impact of the media.

The Changing Landscape of Organized Crime

The glamorous, powerful portrayal of the American Mafia in popular culture was a far cry from reality. What was fed to the general masses was a portrayal of an organization with a strict code of honor, with a refusal to get involved in drug trafficking because of the morality behind it. While there were some factions and older leaders that resisted, it was something that many would look past after they saw the allure of immense profits. Increased revenue amid shrinking territories that were under Mafia control was something they couldn't resist. This was certainly the case in the Buffalo Crime

Family's involvement in the drug trade under the leadership of Stefano Magaddino and eventually Joseph Todaro Sr. It also kept the family alive during the power vacuum that was created after Stefano's death.

Again, the choice to move into the narcotics trade wasn't driven by any sense of morality or lack thereof. It was driven by cold, hard economics. Traditional Mafia operations like gambling, racketeering, and loan sharking were losing their luster. However, the drug trade was booming, especially as the war on drugs actually increased the demand. However, the move toward drugs came with its own share of consequences. Mafia families found themselves in the middle of some violent turf wars, not just with rival families but also with a new breed of criminal organizations. Immigrant gangs from other places besides Sicily were spreading out, and there was also a rise in homegrown criminal outfits of various backgrounds. Everyone was looking for a piece of the pie, which led to increased conflict and resulted in a boon for law enforcement—the same law enforcement that had gained a wealth of resources to combat the escalating war on drugs. Therefore, every turf war and every drop of blood was open season for police scrutiny.

The move into narcotics would also deal a tremendous blow to the Mafia's already tarnished image. The impact that drugs had on communities and specific demographics was far more visible and destructive than anything that the Mafia had been tied to before. There was no longer an "invisible hand" that guided the underworld activity. It was now a very visible, destructive force, much like the very street gangs that the Mafia had once looked down upon.

For the Buffalo Crime Family, navigating through this shift was particularly difficult. After Magaddino died, he left behind no successor. So, while the rebel faction that rose against him took his position, there were increased internal conflicts. The organization was now caught between wanting to hang on to the traditions of the past and having to face the harsh realities that were tied to the world of drugs. This internal pressure, in conjunction with the external pressure from law enforcement and turf wars, threw the Buffalo family into further disarray. That itself led to further consequences, beyond internal strife and bad reputations. Violence had now taken control of the communities that they tried so hard to control.

The landscape was certainly not like the romanticized image that a lot of people had, and no one felt that more than the people who were still living in Mafia territory.

Increased Law Enforcement Efforts

The battle against the American Mafia wasn't a new phenomenon and had been going on well before the 1960s. The disaster known as the Apalachin Meeting in 1957 exposed the entire Mafia network in the United States. This raid by law enforcement served as a reminder that no one would be above the law forever and of the Mafia's growing vulnerability. However, the late 1970s and the 1980s would see a significant rise in efforts by law enforcement agencies across the country. Every Mafia family, including the once-powerful Buffalo family, was beginning to feel the squeeze.

This era saw a huge increase in not only awareness of Mafia activities but also a much more aggressive response from both federal agencies and local authorities. The Racketeer Influenced and

Corrupt Organizations (RICO) Act, passed in 1970, would be a game-changer for those agencies. It gave law enforcement more resources and powerful legal tools to go after and dismantle organized crime. RICO wasn't an act that would hand out more fines or short jail sentences; it was aimed to send mafiosos away for long stints in prison. They were also out to seize any assets acquired through illegal activities. Furthermore, the act let those agencies offer incentives for Mafia members (no matter their rank) to become witnesses of the state. Organizations would be weakened from within by encouraging betrayals of underbosses and other high-ranking members.

One of the most significant effects of this increased offensive was felt in Las Vegas, the city that was built on the back of the Mafia. For years, Sin City had been a lucrative hotspot that was very much under Mafia control. However, the FBI and local police forces teamed up and began to crack down on the Mafia. They used carefully planned efforts to take control of the casinos away from the embrace of the underworld. This move went hand-in-hand with efforts that would take Mafia influence out of the labor unions, which had been another significant source of revenue and power for the families. Buffalo and many other cities where the Mafia held significant power would feel the impact head-on.

These actions occurred toward the end of Stefano's reign, while there were internal struggles ignited by his deception. The organization couldn't escape the pressure, and again, Stefano himself faced two separate subpoenas and narrowly avoided imprisonment several times thanks to some well-timed illnesses. However, several key figures within the Magaddino family had fallen because of the increased scrutiny by law enforcement. This only made things more difficult for the family after Magaddino died. Even when Joseph Todaro Sr. took over, he had to deal with a weakened family while operating in an environment that was growing increasingly hostile.

Of course, despite the challenges, the Mafia wouldn't fully succumb to extinction. However, their power was significantly diminished. The aggression shown by law enforcement during these crucial years marked a turning point, and the once-untouchable Mafia now had to contend with a coordinated, supported, and well-resourced enemy. It was a far cry from the empire that had smuggled alcohol while the law turned a blind eye.

The Changing Dynamics Within the Mafia

By 1974, the cracks had already appeared in the decades-old foundation of the Magaddino Crime Family. Stefano, who had been the dominant leader, was facing dissent from outside of the family, especially after Apalachin. He also faced growing dissent within his own organization in the wake of his shady practices. Despite the loss of respect for the Buffalo boss in his final years, his death would still trigger a rough patch that led the family through even more chaos.

Magaddino's passing would cause a noticeable power vacuum. Underbosses and other members saw this as their opportunity to seize control, which ignited a ruthless internal war. It started as an attempt to gain influence to elevate their status; however, that boiled over into an open conflict. Factions, like the one that tried to remove Magaddino from his position, formed. The loyalties of these factions, however, were fueled by personal gain and long-standing grievances instead of the overall stability of the family. Eventually, the battles would be felt on the streets of Buffalo, mirroring the overall changing landscape of the Mafia.

The internal strife in the Buffalo organization wasn't an isolated phenomenon, as the 1980s bore witness to a surge of violence across the world of organized crime. America and Sicily saw body counts rise exponentially as rival families and inner factions clashed for control of operations and territory. While numerous events throughout their history shaped the direction of the Mafia, the 1980s would see its character significantly altered.

Despite the internal conflict, the Buffalo family would still hold onto some control in northwest New York. However, the influence that they had at this time paled in comparison to what it had been during the height of Magaddino's reign. The family was fractured, with unity being replaced by the struggle for leadership. There was now a level of uncertainty hanging in the air.

This period of instability would last for several years after 1974. There wouldn't be a period of calm until a formidable successor was chosen, which would be in the form of Joseph Todaro Sr. He would be the one to finally reconsolidate the family's power. It would be through his cunning strategy and ruthlessness that much of the infighting would stop and the family would be ushered into a new era.

However, the scars of these battles would linger throughout the Mafia. While the Buffalo family regained their grip on the region, they wouldn't be able to return to their former glory.

The Impact of Public Perception and Media

In the 1980s, there was another shift regarding the Mafia, and it was in the form of a public fascination that was continuously rising. This was no coincidence either. It was fueled by media coverage that transformed a once-secretive organization into a staple in pop culture. News reports, books, films, and television shows thrived on exposing the criminal underworld and their violence, rituals, and iconic leaders. While these expositions shed light on the illegal aspects of their operations, the Mafia was often glorified, even in news reports. Their lifestyle was seen by the public as glamorous and powerful. What the general population saw was a fictionalized image, which was a far cry from the brutal reality that those living in Mafia-controlled areas experienced.

The Buffalo family wasn't an exception to this trend. The real-world activities of extortion, loan sharking, gambling rackets, drug trafficking, and murder were just as sensationalized during this period. While the region wasn't as prominent as some of the more notorious regions, there was still a public eye on the family because of their involvement with the American Mafia. It only solidified their notorious reputation, but the focus on sensationalism came at a cost.

The fascination the media had with the flashier aspects like expensive suits, luxury cars, and lavish lifestyles never highlighted the destructive impact the Mafia had on individuals, businesses, and communities. Often left out of the narratives were the fear, intimidation, and violent tendencies that would drive operations. These were either downplayed or turned into elements of respect or a last resort (using violence because there was no other option).

Matters were also not helped thanks to films like *Scarface* and *The Godfather*. While mobster movies had existed since the 1930s, films like this rose in popularity during this time and contributed to the swaying of public perception. They would present the dramatized family dynamic while showing power, ruthlessness, and a strict code of honor.

Unless one was in proximity to Mafia-controlled regions, the embellished portrayal didn't just distort the truth but also put distance between people and the reality of the Mafia's influence. They included stylized violence, romanticized operations, and consequences that only felt like they existed in the mob world. When it all looked like a thrilling story, it was hard to see it as a dangerous reality.

With that said, even in the media frenzy of the 1980s, there were attempts to establish the actual narrative. Documentaries and investigative pieces attempted to shed light on the reality of Mafia life. These exposés were less prevalent and usually less popular, but they did offer a much-needed counterpoint to other portrayals.

The 1980s would shape a new perception of the Mafia, and it would only grow over time. While there were still popular characters on the fictional side of things, there were also reality shows based on families with Mafia ties. Furthermore, there were several books, podcasts, and other pieces that fueled interest in the Mafia. However, as the years have passed, many of these media pieces show the harsh reality of the Mafia. They shed light on the law enforcement agencies who are out to stop organized crime, and they also expose the very harsh realities of what life is really like within the mob.

A New Leader On The Rise

The 1980s proved to be a rough patch for the American Mafia. Power struggles only intensified as new leadership tried to push beyond the traditions set generations before. The Buffalo Crime Family, which had been mired in conflict (both internal and external), found itself especially vulnerable during this time.

The death of Stefano Magaddino left a void in the organization that was felt for years. Factions within the family, all hungry for ultimate power, clashed, fracturing what had been one of the quietest, most powerful families in New York. The streets of Buffalo and Niagara Falls became a battleground that mirrored the worldwide decline of the Mafia. A sense of desperation now hung over the region.

The Buffalo family severely needed a force to unify it again, a leader who was cunning and ruthless and wouldn't be afraid to navigate this new landscape. That leader was steadily rising up the ranks, and in the tumultuous atmosphere, Joseph Todaro Sr. emerged. He was the cunning individual who presented answers to the questions that had been lingering in the organization. But one very crucial question would arise with Todaro's ascension: Could he, amidst the instability, restore the once prominent Buffalo family to the glory they had been accustomed to? Only time, and Todaro's leadership skills, would tell.

CHAPTER 7

JOSEPH "PAPA JOE" TODARO SR.

In the history of organized crime, the Buffalo Crime Family long stood as a testament to the incredible dynamics of power and leadership. Yet after Stefano Magaddino's death, there was a scramble for control within the notorious family. That scramble would last nearly a decade, which proved to be enough time to establish a sense of uncertainty and instability in the organization.

Various figures would step up to fill the vacant seat. While each of them brought a unique approach and vision for the family, none of them could encapsulate the complex role of a leader, especially the leader of a criminal organization. That role did not ask for respect; it demanded it. A leader like this would need that, along with a cunning nature and an iron resolve.

This sticky situation was something the Buffalo family had never experienced to this point. The family's solid foundation was led by the short yet effective reign of DiCarlo and Palmeri. They established Buffalo's roots in the underworld and following them was the incredible reign of Stefano Magaddino. He took the helm and built on that foundation, guiding the organization to incredible levels of power and influence.

The world was changing for the Mafia, and the Buffalo family was standing at a crossroads. Everything that its previous leaders had accomplished was in danger of being lost to time, which meant that the family needed to change course. The need for a leader to get them through this tumultuous time was at its highest.

Enter Joseph Todaro Sr., a name that now resonates with power and influence in the history books of organized crime. Todaro's life in and out of the Mafia was one of controversy and intrigue, but he was just the man who could breathe new life into an organization that needed it. His leadership would mark a turning point for the Buffalo Crime Family, rejuvenating their operations and re-establishing its place in the criminal underworld.

This chapter dives into the rise of Joseph Todaro Sr., exploring his journey up to becoming the chosen leader of the Buffalo Crime Family. It will examine how he navigated the dynamics of power, stayed ahead of his rivals, and ensured that the family, now known as the Todaro family, would survive in the rapidly changing landscape.

The Early Years of Todaro

Joseph Todaro was born on September 18, 1923, to Anthony Todaro and Sarah Frangiamore. Call it "right place, right time" because Joe's life was deeply intertwined into the webs of organized crime.

Joe would later marry Josephine Santamauro, and the couple would have three children: Carol, Joseph Jr. who would follow in his father's footsteps into a life of crime, and Linda who would later marry Peter Gerace who was also involved in the Buffalo crime world.

Given the name "Lead Pipe Joe," and sometimes "Papa Joe," by his associates in crime, Todaro Sr. held the position of caporegime in the Buffalo family. This was a role that carried a lot of significance within the Mafia hierarchy, and it put him in charge of his own crew of soldiers. So, very early on, Todaro already had influence and control within the organization. As Joseph Todaro Jr. got older, he along with Papa Joe and his uncle Richard Todaro would control the family's bookmaking operations, which was still a very lucrative gambling racket.

By the early 1960s, after the infamous Apalachin meeting, Stefano Magaddino had started to delegate a lot of the daily activities of the family to one of his underbosses, Frederico Randaccio. While Stefano was still at the head of the table, Randaccio's assumption of power would mark the change in the Magaddino family and their dynamics. Randaccio's operations ran out of the Blue Banner Social Club during the 1960s and 1970s. That club, controlled by a Buffalo family soldier, Benny Spano, was a hub for a lot of the family's activities during this time, including the activities of Todaro Sr.

Todaro Sr. rightfully earned his position within the family as he was a significant money-maker for the Magaddino family. This would lead him to take part in more rackets, including card and dice games, loansharking, Las Vegas junkets, and even labor rackets. These activities brought in substantial profits for the family, which helped boost their financial power and influence in the underworld. A large portion of this could be attributed to Todaro's work; however, during those tumultuous years when Magaddino was taking money for himself, there wasn't much that Papa Joe could do.

Todaro Sr. didn't work without risks though, which was just part of life in the underworld. In May 1967, Todaro Sr. and 35 men were arrested at a party. The charge against Papa Joe was "consorting with known criminals," which was a very serious accusation that could have done a lot of damage to his operations and his reputation. Yet, Todaro, like the bosses before him, had a stroke of luck as the charges were dismissed in court, which allowed him to continue his activities unscathed.

Later, on the night of March 13, 1982, Papa Joe was in the middle of a huge brawl outside of the Buffalo Playboy Club. Not only was he caught in the violence, but he was an active participant, stepping in to help out Daniel Sansanese Jr. While he had been great at keeping his head down, the brawl was simply a reminder of how volatile and violent the criminal world was.

The Playboy Club is important here because FBI logs concerning Todaro Sr. revealed how skilled the caporegime was at conducting mob business away from attention. Papa Joe held meetings in hotel rooms and VIP rooms around the area. This kept prying eyes away, but it also added an air of exclusivity and secrecy around his businesses. His preferred venues, however, were the Executive Inn, the 747s disco, and the Playboy Club. These establishments, which were dotted conveniently around the Greater Buffalo International Airport in Cheektowaga, New York, all gave Todaro the perfect cover. Therefore, the brawl was actually one of the first big signs that something much bigger was happening behind the closed doors of the club.

From Caporegime to Boss

Again, there was no one to take up the mantle in Buffalo who could recapture even a bit of what the family had been in the past. However, the significant change that the family needed would come in 1984. Samuel Frangiamore, the man who took on the role of boss, decided to step down from the position. His retirement paved the way for Joseph Todaro Sr., who had been a hotshot caporegime, to transcend his previous role and become head of the Buffalo Crime Family. One of his first orders of business was to appoint his son, Joseph Todaro Jr. as one of his new underbosses, which marked the beginning of the Todaro Family.

1984-1990

Things had so far been working for Papa Joe, but his leadership would soon be put to the test. In 1985, not even a year after assuming the position, he was charged with federal tax evasion. Todaro Sr. had come under fire for underreporting his income for three years (1976, 1977, and 1978). These were severe charges, and they could have jeopardized the future of the Buffalo organization, but Joe Sr. managed to carefully navigate the legal proceedings. He would eventually be acquitted, and this matter would be the first example of his resilience and ability to endure anything that came his way. It was a welcome sign for the Buffalo family.

Things may have taken on an old familiar feeling of the bygone days of the Magaddino Crime Family, but this was a new landscape, and the authorities were consistently putting pressure on criminal organizations, which meant that Todaro would also be dealing with them while trying to re-solidify the Buffalo territory.

The pressure came on Todaro Sr. again in 1989 when the FBI filed a statement in connection with an investigation they were carrying out into gambling rings. The federal agency named Todaro Sr. and Todaro Jr. as leading figures of the Buffalo Mafia. This statement also named 45 made members of the organization. It was no longer a rumor, as the family was reported to control several criminal activities in the area, including labor racketeering, bookmaking, loansharking, and drug trafficking. This would also be one of the first times that Todaro Jr. would be named the boss of the family by federal agents. The statements in this investigation said that Jr. was running the family on behalf of Papa Joe, who had semi-retired from the criminal underworld, spending his time between his properties in Florida and New York.

That same investigation in 1989 also revealed that Leonard F. Falzone, a member of the Laborers' International Union of North America Local 210, was operating a loansharking operation for the Todaro Family. Also named were brothers Victor and Daniel Sansanese, who were members of Local 210. The brothers were reportedly in control of a bookmaking operation for the Todaros.

In the year before this FBI statement came to light, federal agents had bugged Falzone's union-owned car in an attempt to try and link the Todaros to the illegal gambling case. However, the bug failed to get agents the evidence they needed, which was more than a lucky break for the Todaros.

Despite the initial setback for the FBI, the bug planted in Falzone's car would also be a huge break for the authorities. The information taken from that surveillance operation gave them more than enough evidence to take down the Torina drug ring, a notorious operation that was responsible for millions of dollars in street sales of cocaine annually in the city of Buffalo. It would mark a significant victory for law enforcement agencies like the DEA and the FBI, who had been working tirelessly to find some sort of crack in the foundation of the criminal underworld.

As their investigation continued into the Torina drug ring, it shed light on the involvement of Papa Joe Todaro and Leonard Falzone in a Las Vegas-to-Buffalo pipeline for cocaine and other illegal operations. The revelation was huge as it exposed the extent of Mafia influence and just how far-reaching the Todaro Family operations still were, spanning across state lines and involving a complex web of illegal activities.

That investigation would come to fruition on March 20, 1990, when Mafia operations suffered a huge blow. Las Vegas police arrested Louis Giambrone, Joseph Amoia, and Lawrence Panero, who were all Buffalo natives and named as members of the Buffalo Crime Family. That alone was enough to tighten law enforcement's grip over the family's activities, but there would be more to it. Charles Torina, another Buffalo native, was identified as a key link in this drug pipeline from Las Vegas to Buffalo. Torina, who had previously worked as a pit boss in a Las Vegas casino, was now wrapped up in the Todaro Family's activities.

These events marked a turning point in the long-standing fight against organized crime, especially as fewer and fewer authorities were complicit in what was happening around them. This highlighted their new perspective and their relentless efforts to infiltrate and cause irrefutable damage to the Buffalo Crime Family and others like them. At the same time, however, this showed the resiliency and adaptability of Papa Joe. He continued to navigate the rougher waters of this criminal landscape, which showed that he was the right man for the job.

This wouldn't be the Todaro family's only brush with the law that year. Canadian police had conducted a large operation of their own, which resulted in the arrest of 14 suspects connected to a drug ring. As they learned more about these individuals, they unveiled deep-rooted connections to the organized crime units running out of Buffalo and Niagara Falls.

An anonymous agent tied to the investigation would also reveal that any activity in St. Catharines, Hamilton, Niagara Falls, and any surrounding communities required the approval of the Buffalo (Todaro) Crime Family, which further revealed the extent of their influence. This was the control established by DiCarlo, solidified by Magaddino, and resurrected by Todaro. Every mob family in the region answered to Buffalo.

Among those who were arrested were associates of John Anticoli. Anticoli was a businessman from Niagara Falls who, at the time, was serving a 10-year sentence in federal prison. Anticoli was a huge part of the Todaro network and was described by the FBI as one of the most significant drug dealers that had ever been apprehended in western New York. He would plead guilty to several of the charges brought on him, which included the possession of 270 pounds of marijuana, conspiracy to distribute cocaine, tax evasion, and failure to pay taxes on his drug profits.

Also, some of those arrested were Carmen Barillaro, Nicodemo Bruzzese, and Dominic Vaccaro, who were identified as "made men" of a crime family based in Hamilton, Ontario, which was operating under the indirect control of the Buffalo mob. This was even more proof for the FBI that the influence of the Todaro family was still just as wide as it had been under the leadership of Magaddino. However, the operation itself would be a significant step in the fight against organized crime that was happening across the nation.

The 1990s

Besides the two key breaks for federal agents against the Buffalo Crime Family, the Todaro family continued to grow. On September 6, 1993, Joseph Todaro III, married Dana Christine Panepinto, the daughter of Donald Panepinto, who had a large hand in Local 210, further extending the family's connections and influence into the labor unions of the area.

Things would ease a bit for the Todaro family, but calm waters wouldn't last. By 1996, the organization found itself under scrutiny yet again. Joseph Todaro Sr. and Joseph Todaro Jr. were listed with 24 other organized crime figures. All 24 figures were accused of having influence in the Laborers International Union of North America since the 1960s. The accusations only shed more light on the family's long-standing involvement in labor racketeering, which put the most lucrative and powerful portion of organized crime in jeopardy.

Despite yet another challenge placed before them, the Todaro family's operations would expand beyond Buffalo. Carmen Milano, an underboss of a Los Angeles crime outfit, reached out to Papa Joe about potentially joining forces. Together, the two organizations would take over a loan sharking and auto insurance fraud racket in Las Vegas. The operation's head was slated to be Herbert Blitztein, who was an associate of the Chicago outfit. Milano said that Todaro Sr. would get a piece of the profits that Blitztein's rackets brought in. This was going to be a significant expansion in the family's operations. The Buffalo and Los Angeles families arranged for Robert Panaro, who at the time was a foot soldier in the Buffalo family, to be the receiver for Blitztein's stolen jewelry. Everything seemed to be set on the right track until the entire plan took a dark turn.

On January 6, 1997, Antonio Davi and Richard Friedman, who were associates of the Los Angeles crime family shot and killed Herbert Blitztein in his own home. Peter Caruso, who was simply an associate of the L.A. family, had been behind the hit and took over the Las Vegas operations. The business partnership's operations had dried up, and the year would continue to dole out critical blows on the family.

The next upheaval in 1997 was when Johnny Papalia, the boss of the Buffalo family's Canadian faction, and Carmen Barillaro (Papalia's lieutenant) were assassinated by Kenneth Murdock. It would take nearly two years for federal agents to apprehend Murdock, and when they did, he decided to roll over and become a government witness. He confessed that he carried out the hit ordered by Pasquale "Pat" Musitano and his brother Angelo of the Musitano crew.

Murdock told the government that the brothers were no longer content with just being a "satellite crew" of the Buffalo family and paying them tribute money. Murdock would also reveal that the two assassinations were only the beginning and that he was awaiting the approval of orders to eliminate four members of the Luppino crew, another powerful Mafia family. These revelations shed new light on the complex dynamics and rivalries that were taking place in the new landscape of organized crime. However, as much as the government learned from Murdock, they would also learn a lot more.

Murdock told agents that Pat Musitano discussed with Vito Rizzuto (Quebec Marfia boss) and Gaetano Panepinto about Rizzuto investing money into Ontario. Canadian intelligence agencies had already been on their trail, but investigations ramped up after the double assassination of Papalia and Barillaro. They would go on to observe several meetings between Musitano and Rizzuto. It wouldn't take long before these agencies were convinced that the Musitano brothers were not acting alone in the hits.

In 1998, Lee Coppola, who was a veteran reporter of organized crime for *The Buffalo News*, wrote an article titled "The Withered Arm." In the piece, he discussed how the once-powerful Buffalo Crime Family was now in shambles, disorganized, and essentially broke, which was a far cry from the power and influence the family had during the Magaddino reign. The article also stated that the last bits of mob power had disappeared in Buffalo. It would have looked like the obituary of the Buffalo crime family, but Coppola's article was just a bit premature.

A year after said article, in 1999, Canadian intelligence found that a new crime lord had emerged, and this person was connected to the Todaro family, proving they still had just as much influence despite the setbacks. The figure would remain anonymous to public knowledge, but they had significant control in the region. They were the head of the Golden Horseshoe region of Ontario, which had a strong relationship with outlaw bikers. This was something that his predecessor, Johny Papalia, did not have. The unnamed boss and his new alliances led Peter Polcetti (Detective Sergeant of the CISC) to declare that the family was in firm control over Niagara, Hamilton, Toronto, and Montreal.

In that same year, Papa Joe, his son Joseph Todaro Jr., and 16 other individuals were named in a civil racketeering lawsuit. All 18 were accused of controlling Local 210 with various racketeering operations over the years. The significance of this lawsuit was how it identified Joseph Todaro Sr. as the boss and Joseph Todaro Jr. as the underboss of the Buffalo Crime Family. It also identified the father and son as owners of La Nova Pizzeria. While Papa Joe was never a member of the union, Todaro Jr had served as its business manager in 1990 before he resigned. The family was hard-pressed to work around the charges because they were based on the testimony of Ronald Fino, who had also served as a business manager of Local 210 before becoming an FBI informant.

The Final Years of Papa Joe Todaro

In June 2004, Todaro Sr. would once again find himself in the crosshairs of the law, as he became a person of interest in the unsolved murder of Charles Gerass in 1965. However, despite the serious nature of the accusations made, the investigation led nowhere, and there were no charges against Papa Joe or anyone else.

In 2006, Joseph Todaro Sr. retired as head of the Buffalo Crime Family, passing the role of boss (officially) to his son Joseph Todaro

Jr. Leonard Falzone was named the underboss of Todaro Jr., a position that he held until he passed away in 2016.

Throughout his reign, Papa Joe, his son, and the rest of the family faced numerous allegations from local agencies, the FBI, and the US Justice Department. They even came under fire for being the leaders of Buffalo's La Cosa Nostra family, but those allegations were never proven. Therefore, despite the tremendous pressure that the Mafia and the Todaro family faced during his reign, Papa Joe lived his entire life without ever being convicted of a felony crime.

Outside of the organized crime world, Papa Jope was also a successful businessman. He opened La Nova Pizzeria in 1957, a legitimate business that went from a small restaurant to a lucrative business. That business would thrive under one location until a second location of La Nova Pizzeria was opened in Amherst.

Joseph Todaro Sr. would have a lengthy battle with illness and succumb to it on December 26, 2012, at age 89. While he relinquished control six years prior, his death still marked the end of an era for the Buffalo Crime Family.

CHAPTER 8

JOSEPH "BIG JOE" TODARO JR.

While the history of the Buffalo family has always been a tale of power, ambition, and survival; for much of its existence, the leadership of the family wasn't determined by a blood tie. Angelo Palmeri stepped down and handed control over to Giuseppe DiCarlo. Although Joseph DiCarlo was Giuseppe's son, the family was handed over to Stefano Magaddino.

Magaddino was known for his very long reign over the family, and while his son Peter was part of the family, Peter would leave after his father's death. Salvatore "Sam the Farmer" Frangiamore held the family together during that tumultuous period. That transition of power would break the uncertain pattern after the rise of Joseph "Papa Joe" Todaro Sr. His son Joseph "Big Joe" Todaro Jr. was the underboss. This move set Big Joe up to take over the family's leadership after the death of Papa Joe in 2012.

For Big Joe, this chapter will take a step back to give more focus on the eventual leader of the Buffalo Crime Family.

The Early Years

Joseph A. Todaro Jr., later known as "Big Joe" in the Buffalo Crime Family was born in the mid-1940s into the world of power, influence, and illicit activities. He was, of course, the son of Joseph Todaro Sr. and Josephine Santamauro, the former being a key component in the Buffalo family. Big Joe later married Carol Ann, whom he affectionately calls "Cookie." The couple would have two children, Joesph E Todaro III and Carla, the latter would go on to marry Salvatore Pantano, which further cemented the Todaro family's roots within the criminal underworld.

Big Joe didn't have to wait long before following in his father's footsteps. His journey started when he became a business agent for the Laborers' International Union of North America Local 210. It was a position that gave him a legitimate front while also opening up opportunities to extend the family's influence within the labor sector. However, despite having the easy way in, his involvement in the family's illicit activities came with a fair share of challenges.

In 1976, Big Joe was accused of being involved in an unsuccessful attempt to eliminate Faust Novino. The alleged hit was claimed to be set up by a long-time associate and friend of Novino, Louis Pisa. Louis had come to Novino and proposed that the two commit burglary at a warehouse on the west side of Buffalo. Novino was under the assumption that it was just him and Pisa in the location, but he quickly noticed a large, heavyset man raising his arm to hit him. The man was later identified as John Sacco, but in response to the attempted attack, Novino pulled out his pistol and shot the attacker. Sacco wasn't the only one there, as stated by Novino. He heard footsteps behind him; so, he turned around and fired in that direction. He shot the second attacker, who would be identified as long-time Todaro family figure Leonard Falzone. Faust then saw two men, who he recognized as Todaro Jr. and Frank Billiteri, crouched on either side of him. He felt boxed in, so he shot back at the two previous attackers again. Falzone was shot at again, and Sacco was back on the attack. Novino tried shooting at the approaching Sacco's chest, but his gun jammed. He then made a break for it, finding refuge behind a large rolled-up rug. Eventually, he was able to get out of the warehouse through a door that led out to the streets. This incident was a major turning point in Big Joe's life, as it highlighted the dangers and explosiveness of the criminal underworld. This was an important lesson at this time because the constant threat of violence hung heavy over the entirety of organized crime, and it would highlight the lengths some would go to protect themselves or to get ahead.

In 1984, Big Joe transcended the business manager position that gave him a solid front for other activities. The younger Todaro now had a position of significant power within the Buffalo Crime Family. This came, of course, after the retirement of Sam Frangiamore and the ascension of Papa Joe to head of the now-Todaro Family. Todaro Jr. would take his place as the underboss, which was the first time in the family's decades-long history that leadership positions were held within a bloodline.

Todaro Jr. was now seated comfortably as second-in-command to his father, which gave him a significant amount of influence over the family's operations. It also established his positioning for his eventual ascent to the role of boss, which would continue everything that his father put into place while navigating the organization through a new era.

The Buffalo Crime Family and the 1990s

The landscape of organized crime was changing, and while it was difficult for Papa Joe to navigate that landscape as a boss, it was equally difficult for his underboss. Much of what happened during this period also involved Papa Joe, so this will review some of that with a focus on Todaro Jr.

Let's revisit 1989: This was when the FBI filed its statement in connection with a gambling investigation. They had identified both Todaro Sr. and Todaro Jr. leaders of the Buffalo Crime Family. Federal agents stated that the father-son duo was in charge of various underworld rackets. Their statements to the courts also mentioned that Todaro Jr. had more power at this time and that Todaro Sr. was semi-retired and splitting his time between his properties in Florida and New York.

In addition to Big Joe being identified as the de facto leader, those statements also identified Leonard Falzone as running loansharking operations and Victor and Daniel Sansanese as runners of a bookmaking operation for the Todaro Family. All of this information stemmed from when the FBI wiretapped Falzone's union-owned car to link the family to an illegal gambling case. While there were a few key statements made, the bug in Falzone's car failed to give any solid evidence to link the Todaros to the case.

In 1990, Todaro Jr. gave up his position as a business agent of the Laborers' International Union of North America after more investigations were done to uncover Local 210's ties to organized crime. Big Joe's resignation from the organization marked a huge turning point in his long career, as it highlighted the tremendous challenges that he faced because of his involvement in the crime family's operations.

In 1996, the Todaros were on the receiving end of scrutiny once again. The two were identified among 24 alleged figures in organized crime. Again, this was the group accused of influencing the Laborers' International Union of North America since the 1960s. While not much came from these accusations, it still underscored that the Buffalo Crime Family had long been tied to labor racketeering, which had been a very lucrative operation for the Mafia.

In 1999, Todaro Jr. along with Papa Joe and 16 others faced a civil racketeering lawsuit for their control of Local 210 through different acts of racketeering over the years. This all stemmed from the testimony of Ronald Fino, who was a former business manager of Local 210 and, again, a later informant for the FBI. The complaint filed in court identified Big Joe as the underboss of the Buffalo crime family. The father and son were also named as the owners of La Nova Pizzeria and Todaro's time serving as Local 210's business manager before resigning in 1990 was also brought up. This was important because although Todaro had resigned from that position, he still tried to maintain control over Local 210 with the help of Peter Gerace and Peter Capitano. These associates of Todaro's held positions in Local 210.

Todaro Sr.'s Retirement and Rumors

Joseph "Papa Joe" Todaro Sr., the well-tenured patriarch of the Todaro Crime Family, retired in 2006. There was now a scramble in law enforcement, as they were trying to identify the person that took over the role of the boss. The initial assumption was that Leonard Falzone had taken Todaro Sr.'s spot; however, others thought Falzone was simply acting as a "front boss" for the Todaro family. This was just an acting boss role that would let Big Joe transition into the role of leader for the family.

The FBI had charts of the Buffalo Crime Family's hierarchy, which lasted until Todaro Sr.'s retirement in 2006. These charts gave a look into the family's structure. This is how they came to the assumption that Falzone had taken over the top position of the family. However, when Papa Joe died in 2012, followed by the death of Ben "Sonny" Nicoletti in 2013, new rumors arose about the family's leadership.

These new speculations especially rose in 2012 when Matt Gryta (a crime reporter for The Buffalo News) claimed that the Buffalo family had spread its operations across the nation through telemarketing schemes, "pump-and-dump" stock market scams, and even internet pornography. While there wasn't much proof there to confirm Gryta's claims, it did highlight that the world of organized crime was changing with the times and making a significant shift away from the operations they had used before.

Another article came out that same year from Dan Herbeck. His article was about Ronald Fino, titled "Life After Local 210 for the FBI's Inside Guy" highlighted how Fino remained skeptical about claims from the US Justice Department that mob influences had been completely purged from not just Local 210 but the entirety of the Laborers' International Union of North America. Fino told Herbeck that while he believed that the government's initiative to clean up the unions had been a good start, they had not gone deep enough to really be free of Mafia control.

Those wouldn't be the only rumors launched against the Todaro Family. In 2013, The Toronto Star's organized crime reporter, Peter Edwards, made his claims that the family was trying to recover from their most recent downside by running loansharking operations out of the Casino Niagara in Canada. There was more than enough room to speculate. Had the family remained as resilient as they had been since the early 1900s? Were these articles just stabs in the dark? Even in the age of information, there was still so much uncertainty.

During the late 2000s, some news did come out about a homeowner association having ties to the Todaro family. A witness had come forward to the FBI, claiming that a company called Silver Lining Construction was involved in the scam and was part of the New York Mob. There was some weight to this claim though, as the company's owner, Leon Benzer, had a close association with attorney John Spilotro, who was the nephew of Vegas Mafia member Tony Spilotro. Those claims would progress after investigators disclosed the name of one of the key players in the homeowner association takeovers. They identified Paul Citelli who had already been known to have ties to the Buffalo Mob. Joseph Bravo, another defendant in the homeowner association scam, would be indicted with Citelli for their involvement in a cocaine trafficking ring run during the first decade of Todaro Sr.'s leadership. It would be during this period that the Buffalo mob was considered *the* family in control of the streets of Las Vegas.

The Canadian Connection

Nearly two decades after the Lee Coppola article, "The Withered Arm," in March 2017, Dan Herbeck—author of "Life After Local 210 for the FBI's Inside Guy"—penned a similar article to Coppola's called, "The Mafia is All But Dead in Western New York." By Herbeck's account, the FBI field office in Buffalo had said the once-powerful Buffalo Crime Family had become nothing more than scattered remnants. The article also claimed that those scatterings were either no longer active or lacked any real organization. It was a piece that strongly mirrored the 1998 Coppola article, with all the information leading to the conclusion that the Buffalo family had declined into a powerless organization.

However, much like Coppola's article, the events that took place following that report would say that doomsaying the Buffalo Crime Family was premature. In November of that year, there were a series of arrests made by the Royal Canadian Mounted Police. These were done in an operation known as Project OTremens, which negated yet another article. The family was still very active, and the evidence was backed up by FBI reports and Canadian newspapers.

Among those arrested during Project OTremens were Giuseppe (Joe) and Domenico Violi, both of whom had ties to the Buffalo family for years. The Violis were charged with trafficking narcotics, which hinted at the fact that the longstanding mafia drug trafficking ring that went from Ontario to Buffalo and Montreal to New York City was still very much alive. This was the same ring that had been established by The Undertaker, Stefano Magaddino, and Magaddino's cousin, Joseph Bonanno.

Michael McGarrity from the FBI said the operation had uncovered the roots of the decades-old partnership that formed the trafficking triangle. This revelation also showed that organized crime had evolved significantly from the days of neighborhood gangs and prominent figures. Things were moving back in the shadows and spreading across many figures, making it harder to track.

Peter Edwards, who was a seasoned journalist for the Toronto Star, would have another report come out in September 2018, which would make the proclamation that the Buffalo Crime Family was far from over, which had been the opposite of many of his contemporaries and other media reports. This explosive article claimed that the Todaro Family still had more than enough power to influence a recent mob war that was happening between several crime families in the Hamilton, Ontario, underworld.

Giving credit to Edwards' article were his sources, which included Paul Manning, a former undercover police officer in Hamilton, whose specialty was working on organized crime investigations. Manning was unsure of who would be standing tall after the dust settled from the war, but he was certain that the Buffalo family would always have the final word on the matter. It was this explosive statement that underscored the everlasting influence of the Buffalo mob and its Canadian connections that were established during the DiCarlo days and solidified during the reign of Magaddino.

That same article by Edwards would also go to state that the Todaro family had to give their approval for any high-level killings. This meant that any significant hits in the Canadian crime families had to go through Todaro and his underbosses. More of Edwards' sources stated that the leaders in Buffalo, at one point during the Canadian family dispute, turned their backs on one side of it and gave its approval to the other. While both sides of the feuding Ontario organizations were supposed to be under Buffalo's control, they only controlled aspects of the business, which underscored that their chosen side in the dispute was likely the one getting the least number of kickbacks for themselves.

In the same month that the Edwards article came out, Al Iavarone of Ancaster, Ontario, was murdered as an act of retaliation for the murder of Angelo Musitano, which had taken place in May 2017. It would be Angelo's hit though that spawned the most speculation. While revenge was one of the reasons given for Angelo's death, rumors began to circulate that the hit was ordered in relation to unpaid debts and rivalries between Mafia members in the Niagara region, along with the influence of the Todaro family. There was even further speculation that the hit didn't just come down from the Buffalo family but that it came from Domenico Violi, who hadn't yet been revealed as an underboss in the Todaro family. Violi was one of those arrested after the investigation into the drug trafficking ring but had since found his place of influence in the Buffalo family. An interesting aspect of this hit was that Angelo's murder happened 20 years to the month after Musitano hitman Kenneth Murdock killed Johnny Papalia, the long-time captain of the Buffalo family (and head of the Papalia Crime Family), and Carman Barillaro (soldier for both the Buffalo and Papalia families).

The news would continue to roll out from Canada, as the Toronto Sun would go on to claim that the mob war in Southern Ontario was rooted in a decades-old conflict that had eventually led to the murder of Paolo Violi, along with his brothers Francesco and Rocco, in Montreal during the late 1970s. The claim also named the Rizzuto family as the ones who ordered the hit. It was largely a theory, but it was suggested that there was a power struggle that was overwhelming the Rizzuto family. Their biggest threat was the

Calabrese family, which had a large base set up in Toronto while also being a big player in New York. The growth of the Calabreses after being pushed aside by the Rizzutos fueled the war between the Buffalo-controlled Canadian factions.

On December 3, 2018, Domenico Violi received an eight-year prison sentence for his involvement in the drug trafficking ring that Project OTremens had exposed. During an investigation as part of the project, police wiretapped conversations between a law enforcement agent and Dom Violi were released. These conversations revealed discussions about a variety of activities and other opportunities. Violi was exposed for trafficking large amounts of drugs, ranging from PCP and MDMA to meth. Furthermore, those drugs were moved to an undercover RCMP agent in exchange for nearly $500,000, with over $20,000 in profit for Violi.

Those same wiretaps also confirmed that Violi had been appointed in October 2017 as an underboss of the Todaro Family by the main boss Joseph Todaro Jr. during a meeting in Florida. This made Violi the first Canadian mafioso to hold the second-highest position in the American Mafia. Dom (through the wiretap revelations) was heard bragging that he had beaten out 30 other people for the title of underboss. This was damning, as it revealed that the Buffalo family had, at minimum, 30 made men. These made men included members like Violi's uncles Natale and Rocco Luppino.

In his new elevated role, Violi was expected to take over control of the operations of the Luppino-Violi crime family and further establish his power base. The expectation was also to do this through further and greater collaboration with the Mafia families based in New York. The wiretaps also revealed what The Commission had been up to. This was because Violi's promotion was unusual enough that Big Joe had to consult with the Mafia's governing body for permission to promote Violi as an underboss for the Buffalo family.

Current Standings of the Todaro Family

In the opening months of 2019, another significant event occurred in the world of organized crime, and it was one that directly affected the Todaro Family. Cece Luppino, the son of Rocco Luppino and grandson of Giacomo Luppino, was killed tragically at the Luppino family home in Hamilton, Ontario.

The wiretap evidence from the case built around the Violi brothers revealed that Giuseppe Violi had told an undercover agent back in 2015 that Cece was under consideration to be inducted as a "made" man. There were problems though, as Cece would express concern to his father that he would only be involved in the family if it was profitable. In short, he was concerned that there were too many problems throughout the family, which was not something that would have been pleasing to hear from the rest of the Todaro organization. In the wake of Cece Luppino's murder, the Hamilton Police would take the search for his killer across the Canadian border into US territory. Canadian agents requested that law enforcement and news outlets in the Buffalo area show the images of their suspect that were captured by surveillance cameras.

Another hit was ordered in April 2019 when an attempt was made on Pasquale "Pat" Musitano's life while he was outside of Joseph Irving's (Musitano's lawyer) office. The investigation of the attempt showed that Pat was shot four times—once in the head. The Buffalo News brought to light that Musitano had enemies in mafioso circles in Montreal and Buffalo. Once again, it would be Peter Edwards who asserted that he was more convinced at this point that the Buffalo Crime Family was involved in the shooting. This came after a source had made mention of the organization at the same time as talking about the shooting.

That claim by Edwards would be strengthened after a CBC News report came out of Canada, which stated that Domenico Violi was recorded in September 2017, saying that the murder of Angelo Musitano was committed to send a very clear message to Angelo's brother. Violi also told the same informant that Pat would be next, and he would be dead before the holidays, which would get rid of one more of the family's "headaches." The headache for the family would be gone by mid-2020. In July of that year, Pat Musitano would meet his gruesome end when he was shot and killed in Burlington.

In 2020, which proved to be a quiet year for most of the world mired in a pandemic, things were still changing for the Todaro family. Longtime member Frank BiFulco passed away, leaving a significant hole in the organization. Another revelation that year came when the FBI and the RCMP put out a report that Albert Iavarone's murder in September 2018 was in association with the ongoing turf war in Hamilton, Ontario. Their joint report also connected Iavarone to the bosses of the Musitano family. The investigation conducted by both agencies showed that the bosses from the New York families had gotten together with Tommy Gambino (boss in Los Angeles) to induct Iavarone into the L.A. family. It was the New

York families that wanted the inductee to be a liaison between the US and Ontario groups, but it was a move that had angered several members of the Todaro family, who were the overseers of underworld activity in the areas of Western New York and Southern Ontario.

The most recent news about the Buffalo Crime Family was that Domenico Violi had been granted day parole, which set rumors in motion that there was a significant development in the Todaro Family's future.

CHAPTER 9

THE CURRENT REGIME AND THE FUTURE OF ORGANIZED CRIME

As seen in the most recent years of the Todaro family, information is all but murky. Reporters make conflicting articles; in some, the family is alive and well, and in others, the family is dead and buried. There's even conflicting information about Big Joe. He denies any role or leadership position in the crime family, yet evidence still surfaces about activity that ties back to Buffalo. This chapter serves as a look at the current (alleged) hierarchy of the Buffalo Crime Family, and it will also provide a glimpse into what the future may hold for Buffalo and the American Mafia as a whole. Is the once-notorious underworld of America gone? Or have they mastered the art of blending into the shadows once again as they once did?

Administrators

Boss: Joseph A. "Big Joe" Todaro Jr.

Again, while Big Joe has said that he is not a part of the world of organized crime, things have been linked back to him since he took power in the mid-2000s. The Todaro name is one that still commands respect in the region and organized crime. While following in his father's footsteps with Mafia activities, he also took ownership of the La Nova Pizzeria in Buffalo, a legitimate, lucrative business in the area. Big Joe's journey to the top of the mountain wasn't easy, but it was marked with plenty of determination and resilience.

To recap, in the mid-1980s, Joseph Todaro Sr. claimed the top position of the Buffalo family, finally providing stability after the passing of Stefano Magaddino in 1974. He recognized his son's potential and promoted him to the position of Underboss. This was a significant move, not just for Big Joe but the entirety of the Buffalo organization.

Nearly a decade after becoming an underboss, Todaro Jr. along with Leonard Falzone, Frank BiFulco, and John and Joseph Pieri were forcefully removed from Local 210. It was a setback because labor racketeering was still lucrative, but it wouldn't deter Big Joe.

Finally, when Papa Joe Todaro retired in 2006, Big Joe would take over for his father, marking the first time the Buffalo family's head position was passed to a blood relative. His underboss would be longtime Buffalo member Leonard Falzone, and Falzone would keep that role until 2016 when he passed away. Around a year later, in a unique move for the Buffalo outfit, Big Joe made Canadian mafioso Domenico Violi his underboss. It was a strategic move for the family, and it needed the approval of the Mafia since Violi was Canadian.

Underboss: Domenico "Dom" Violi

Domenico Violi is the first underboss of the Buffalo family who operates from a Canadian faction. His journey to the top is one of tenacity and resilience, and it underscores why Todaro Jr. would choose him for the position.

His grandfather was Giacomo Luppino who was the boss of the Luppino Crime Family in Hamilton, Ontario. Dom's father, Paolo Violi, operated in the Cotroni family out of Montreal and served as a capo to the Bonanno crime family. However, Paolo's life was tragically cut short when he was murdered by a Sicilian faction of the Cotroni family. It would be this tragic event that would have the most impact on Dom, shaping the course of the rest of his life.

After Paolo's death, Domenico moved back to Hamilton with his mother and brother, Giuseppe "Joe" Violi. Joe Violi is also a member of the Luppino family. In January 2015, Domenico, after doing his share of work, became a made man in the Todaro Crime Family. It was a significant milestone in Domenico's journey, and it cemented his position in the world of organized crime.

In October 2017, over two years after becoming a made member of the Todaro family, Domenico met with Joeseph Todaro Jr. in Florida where Todaro promoted him to Underboss of the Todaro family. Again, this made Dom the first Canadian to hold the second-highest position in the American Mafia.

Domenico was arrested after a lengthy investigation, and he would be given eight years in prison after he pleaded guilty to drug trafficking charges. In November 2021 though, Dom was given day parole.

Consigliere: Unknown

This position in the Buffalo crime family is unknown at the moment. However, the consigliere is one of the key figures in a crime family, giving advice and guidance to both the boss and the underboss. Despite uncertainty about the position, someone is definitely still filling this role because it remains a crucial component of the family's structure and operations. The person in this position plays a huge part in shaping the family's future.

Caporegimes

Buffalo Faction

Like consigliere, the person currently serving as caporegime for Buffalo's operations is unknown. This move could be done intentionally to keep operations away from the eyes of the public and law enforcement.

Canadian Faction

On the Canadian side of things, Rocco Luppino fills the role of caporegime, leading the Luppino Crime Family in Hamilton, Ontario. Rocco comes from a long lineage of influential figures in the Mafia. His father was Giacomo Luppino, a powerful member of the Buffalo family who had a considerable amount of power and influence.

Rocco's brother, Natale "Nat" Luppino also serves on the crew as a soldier, which further strengthens the Luppinos' presence in the Buffalo Crime Family. But the Luppinos' have faced their share of tragedy too. The most recent tragedy was the brutal murder of Cece Luppino, Rocco's son, in front of Natale's home in Hamilton.

Soldiers

Buffalo Faction

Victor Sansanese

Victor Sansanese is a long-serving soldier in the Buffalo faction of the Todaro family. His lineage is also deeply intertwined in the fabric of organized crime. His father, Daniel G. Sansanese, and his brother, Daniel Sansanese Jr., have both dedicated their lives to the Buffalo family. Victor would follow suit, becoming a made man in the mid-1970s, which marked his official entrance into the family.

In 1989, both Victor and Daniel Sansanese Jr. were identified as officials in Local 210. Along with the identification came the accusations that the brothers were controlling bookmaking operations for the new Todaro family, which was one of their most significant operations at this time. However, things would end a few years later for Victor and Local 210 when he was removed from his position as a director of training. It was a pretty big shakeup that would send ripple effects throughout the Todaro family.

Robert "Bobby" Panaro

Bobby Panaro is a soldier for the Buffalo faction while stationed in Las Vegas, highlighting the reach of power the family still has in the criminal underworld. In Vegas, he runs a car dealership, which provides a legitimate front for any illegal activities. Panaro, as mentioned earlier, was indicted in 1997, along with members of the Los Angeles crime family, for murdering and robbing Herbert Blitzstein, who had been a Las Vegas associate of the Chicago organization. This was another event that caused a major ripple effect in the criminal underworld, especially in the Todaro family.

John A. Pieri

John Pieri was made to fill the role of soldier. His father, Joseph Pieri, and his uncle, Sam Pieri, were both high-ranking members of the family. In 1996, Pieri along with his brother Joseph Pieri Jr, Big Joe, Leonard Falzone, and Frank BiFulco were all pushed out of Local 210, seemingly ending the family's control over the operation.

Peter Gerace Sr.

Peter is a soldier with a high-ranking connection in the Buffalo family. His father-in-law was Joseph Todaro Sr., which made his brother-in-law Joseph Todaro Jr. Both of Gerace's sons, Peter Jr. and Anthony, serve as associates to the family as well. Before Gerace and other members of the Buffalo family were removed from Local 210, he had served as the union's president, business manager, and business agent. He would continue to hold his business manager position until he stepped down later on.

Donald "The Turtle" Panepinto

Donald is another soldier in the Buffalo family and a former member of Local 210 who has years of service under his belt. Donald's sons, Marc and Don, were both members of 210 and would go on to become lawyers. Donald's ties to the Buffalo Crime Family were cemented on September 6, 1993, when his daughter (Dana Christine Panepinto) married Joseph Todaro III, the son of future family boss Big Joe Todaro.

Things were quiet for Panepinto for a couple of years after the removal from Local 210 until in March 2000 when Donald and several other figures were indicted and charged with the illegal operation of a gambling business, which he had been running out of the Donato Social Club.

In 2014, Donald's oldest son, Marc, would win a seat on the New York State Senate, a position he only held until 2017. Marc would then plead guilty in 2018 to federal corruption charges that stemmed from unwanted advances on a Senate staff member. Marc would get two months in prison and lose his ability to practice law for a year.

Canadian Faction

Natale "Nat" Luppino

As mentioned before, Natale is a Luppino crew soldier operating in the Hamilton area. He is the son of the powerful Canadian Mafia member Giacomo Luppino, and his brother Rocco serves as a capo of the crew.

Giuseppe "Joe" Violi

Joe also operates out of Hamilton and has deep ties with the Mafia. His father was a capo for the Bonnano family's faction that was in Montreal. His ties are further cemented in the mafia through his brother, Domenico, who is the underboss of the Todaro family.

Associates

Buffalo Faction

Joseph Edward "Joey" Todaro III

Joey is Big Joe's son, which means that the youngest Todaro is a prominent figure in the Buffalo Crime Family. His lineage places him in a very precarious position to follow in his father's footsteps as the Mafia pushes forward into the future.

In October 1989, Joey was indicted for felony assault when he beat William Gorman with a baseball bat. Gorman had been a bouncer at Celebrities Nite Club in the Cheektowaga Ramada Renaissance Hotel, and the beating was certainly a blemish on the already-struggling family.

In June 1993, Joey Todaro, Frank BiFulco, Gaetano Miceli, John Catanzaro, Frank Tripi, Samuel Amoia Jr. (Sam Pieri's grandson), Michael A Muscarella, Larry Panaro, Steve Sacco, and Vincent Spano were all identified in their involvement in a telemarketing scam raided by the FBI.

Much like Big Joe, Joey Todaro III runs an offshoot location of La Nova Pizzeria. While this has come under scrutiny for both father and son, the business is legitimate and provides them with a large amount of credibility.

Peter "Pete" Gerace Jr. and Anthony Gerace

Pete runs Pharaoh's Gentleman's Club in Cheektowaga, which is owned by his father. Since Peter Sr. is married to Big Joe Todaro's sister, the Club has close ties (and likely acts as a front) for the underworld activities of the Buffalo Crime Family. Peter's brother Anthony is also a soldier, making the Gerace family a powerful force for the Todaro family.

In 2000, Gerace and Michael Geiger were indicted on one count each of wire fraud for their involvement in a telemarketing scheme. From around late 1992 until February 1995, the men would claim they worked for Advanced Distributing Company. Their setup was promising their victims that they could win a new car or large sums of money. Gerace eventually pleaded guilty to everything in 2005, after the hearings were delayed over a dispute about admissible evidence.

On December 17, 2019, Gerace's strip club was raided by Homeland Security following the indictment of Anthony and retired Buffalo DEA agent Joe Bongiovanni on drugs and weapons charges.

Peter Capitano Jr. and Sam Capitano

Peter and Sam are notable associates of the Buffalo family, as they are part of the Pizza Gang. The Capitanos were identified by undercover operative Ron Fino as being strong associates of both Victor Sansanese and Big Joe Todaro.

In 1996, the brothers would lead an opposing faction that would fight back against the federal trusteeship of Local 210. The trusteeship was to be put into place with the intention of getting rid of mob control and influence in the unions, and it would be the Capitanos' resistance that would lead to them being suspended for one year, with neither being able to hold a leadership role for the next five years.

Sam, in particular, let his fiery temper flare during the meetings. In one of these heated debates, he verbally attacked Gabe Rosetti, and on the next day, the two were involved in a fistfight. That fight would lead to Rosetti firing Sam Capitano from the board, which Sam would contest before the National Labor Relations Board.

Michael Masecchia

Masecchia is an associate of the Buffalo family and has a storied past with authority. In August 2019, the FBI and Homeland Security searched his home as part of an ongoing investigation into organized crime and public corruption. The agents uncovered homemade explosives, stolen firearms, and narcotics, but that would just be the beginning. A criminal complaint had also been made against Masecchia, which identified him as a drug dealer who had a long 20-year history of growing and distributing tremendous amounts of marijuana.

In September 2020, a grand jury indictment would name the associate as a part of Italian Organized Crime, and they would make note that law enforcement had already labeled him as such or possibly a made member of the Buffalo family. The heart of the indictment lies in the allegation that Michael Masecchia bribed then-DEA agent Joseph Bongiovanni to stop any investigations into himself and any others that were suspected of being associated with the local Mafia. The bribe worked because despite being investigated several times by the DEA between 2008 and 2019, Masecchia was never arrested or charged with any crimes while Bongiovanni was part of the DEA.

Michael also has more ties to the Buffalo family. He is married to Krista Mazzara, whose father Bart was alleged by prosecutors to be a made man in Buffalo. Krista also has ties to the Mafia, as her uncles are Dan and Victor Sansanese.

Utica Faction

Russell E. "Russ" Carcone

Russ is one of the most notable members of the Buffalo family that operates within the Utica region. Russ's journey to his position was a long one, starting in 1989 when Carcone, his father Benedetto, and several others were indicted on racketeering charges. This was a significant escalation in the Utica faction's conflict with the law, as it highlighted just how deeply they were tied to the criminal underworld.

In December 1990, Russ, Benedetto, Jack Minicone Jr., Anthony Inserra, and Jack Zogby were all convicted of running a criminal enterprise centered in Utica. This enterprise operated for nearly 20 years (1973 to 1989), and they were involved in multiple activities like extortion, loansharking, illegal gambling, the trafficking of stolen property, and murder. Backing this up was Benny's, Russ's father's, involvement. Benny ran the Swap Shop in Utica and used a large portion of his influence over local bookies, forcing them to make large, regular payments to him and his son.

In 2000, another indictment was brought down on 25 individuals for being involved in a Utica-based shoplifting and fencing ring. The group would steal items from various retail store chains like Walmart, K-Mart, CVS, and other stores around Oneida, Herkimer, Fulton, Madison, Montgomery, Albany, and various other counties in upstate New York. The shoplifting ring took a different approach. Instead of stealing and selling high-value items, they were focusing on items that would do quick resell like razors, batteries, and compact discs.

Russ lost his father in March 2004, and while Benny's death marked the end of an era for Utica, Russ was doing more than enough to carry the legacy. It's a role that he still fills today.

Allied Groups

Buffalo Chapter of the Outlaws

One of the Buffalo Crime Family's biggest allies is the Buffalo chapter of the Outlaws Motorcycle Club. Their connection in this alliance is through one John "Tommy O" Ermin, who coincidentally serves as the national president of the motorcycle club.

Before Ermin was promoted to this high-ranking position, he had served as president of the Buffalo chapter of the Outlaws, and during his time in that position, he established some strong ties with the Buffalo Mafia. He developed particularly strong ties to Joesph "Big Joe" Todaro Jr., and this connection between the two organizations played a huge role in strengthening their alliances while expanding both their influences.

In April 2021, Joseph Tripi (Assistant US Attorney) came out and revealed that Ermin, who was also holding a general manager position at Pharaoh's Gentleman's Club in Cheektowaga, had actually climbed higher and assumed the role of international president of the Outlaws. This was another significant milestone for all parties, as it reopened speculation about how far the Buffalo Crime Family's influence would reach.

Niagara Chapter of the Hells Angels (Canada)

Another notable ally for the Buffalo family is the Hells Angels Motorcycle Club in Canada. The president of the Canadian chapter is Gerald "Skinny" Ward, who started his association with the Buffalo organization in the late 1990s. His involvement started primarily with buying and distributing cocaine in the Hamilton, Ontario area, which contributed to the illicit drug ring that had become a significant part of the Buffalo family's activities.

Ward's alliance with the Hells Angels actually sprung up around the same time in 1998, and he and his smaller outfit joined the motorcycle gang in 2000. By 2008, police estimated that Ward and the Niagara chapter of the Hells Angels had nearly taken over the entire cocaine racket in the region. Not only did this underscore the extent of the Hells Angels' involvement in the Todaro family's drug ring, but it also showed that the Angels were just as big a part of the family as the family members themselves.

When the national president of Hells Angels Canada, Walter "Nurget" Stadnick, was taken in by police in 2001, Ward stepped in to become a co-leader. It was a tremendous shift, and as seen with the estimation taken by police, it was also an effective shift. Ward cemented his place in the Hells Angels and became a valuable asset to the Buffalo Crime Family.

The Future of Organized Crime and the Buffalo Crime Family

What the future holds for the Buffalo family is uncertain. While they, and other Mafia outfits, have held on to some sort of power, the landscape of organized crime is evolving at an unprecedented rate. The traditional structures and operations that have shaped the Mafia since it began have had to undergo incredible changes, reshaped by advancements in technology, globalization, and increased efforts from law enforcement.

Future Activities

We are rapidly moving into the digital age, which means the face of organized crime is evolving even faster and becoming even more sophisticated. Cybercrimes, for example, have seen a significant surge in recent years. These activities span a wide range of illegal operations including identity theft, online fraud, hacking and phishing schemes, and many others. Criminal organizations have found how to exploit the anonymity given to them by the internet, which allows them to carry these activities out with little risk of detection.

Then there is also the dark web, a hidden part of the internet that can only be accessed with specific software, which has long been a hotbed for illegal activities. It gives a platform for organized crime syndicates to do their business in a way that they have long been accustomed to—far from the sight and reach of law enforcement. From drug trafficking to arms deals, the dark web has become rife with all sorts of illegal goods and services.

In particular, human trafficking and modern slavery have emerged as areas of high concern for authorities across the world. These awful crimes are highly lucrative, making them attractive to any organization looking to maximize revenue. Organizations look to lure vulnerable people under pretenses and then exploit them, and many times those individuals disappear without a trace.

However, before we get into more details in the next section, we should note that while organized crime has found new avenues, thanks to technology, so has law enforcement. Law enforcement agencies across the globe are using the same resources to analyze data, find patterns, and stop criminal activity before it happens.

Law Enforcement Crackdown

The landscape of organized crime as we know it is changing rapidly. As criminal networks become more sophisticated and globalized, law enforcement agencies around the world are also stepping up their efforts to combat the growing threats. Authorities are investing in new technologies and tools, and they are making a shift toward international cooperation as they move away from traditional investigative strategies.

One of the most significant developments in their efforts is the use of artificial intelligence (AI) and machine learning in investigations. These technologies have changed the way these agencies operate. AI and machine learning algorithms can sift through vast amounts of data in a short amount of time, identifying patterns and connections that can easily get past human investigators. This is particularly helpful in cases involving organized crime, where criminal networks make the extra effort to keep their activities hidden. AI and machine learning will analyze everything, including financial records, phone records, surveillance footage, and even social media activity. Investigators will take those findings and piece together the intricate web of activity, leading them to more accurate conclusions.

Moreover, algorithms can be trained to identify specific types of activity, which allows law enforcement to identify specific threats from these networks. For example, machine learning algorithms can be trained to find behavior patterns associated with money laundering or human trafficking, which lets law enforcement take proactive measures.

However, the use of these tools comes with its own set of challenges. A large amount of data is needed for these tools to function effectively, and collecting this amount of data starts to raise concerns over privacy. Also, AI and machine learning are only as good as the data that they are trained on, so biases in data can lead to biases in results, which can lead to inaccuracies. Therefore, there has to be a greater level of care to ensure that these tools are used responsibly, ensuring that agencies aren't infringing on individual rights or creating biased algorithms that highlight existing inequality.

While they are using new technologies, law enforcement agencies have also discovered that international cooperation is just as important to combat organized crime. As these organizations become increasingly globalized, crimes spread to multiple jurisdictions, making it harder for one specific agency to fight them alone. To overcome that challenge, agencies now band together more than ever before, sharing intelligence and resources to go after these threats. This can come in various forms, from taking part in joint investigations and operations to exchanging agents and other resources. International organizations like Interpol also play a key role in ensuring this cooperation.

As criminal networks continue to evolve, the strategies used to fight them have to evolve too. When agencies can embrace new technologies and work together with other agencies, they can hope to keep pace with the criminal underworld's activities.

The Buffalo Crime Family

The Buffalo Crime Family, like any other organized crime outfit, isn't immune to these changing times. The family has shown a huge knack for adapting and evolving over the years, from the early days when Palmeri founded the family to its modern incarnation as the Todaro Crime Family under Big Joe Todaro. The organization has always navigated the changing landscape with resilience, and it has continued to exude just as much power and influence as it did before.

Looking ahead, and this is merely speculation based on what we've seen from the family in the last century, the Buffalo Crime Family will most likely continue to evolve and stay ahead of the curve in response to the changing dynamics. For example, they will see the rise of cybercrime as a threat and an opportunity. Increased activity online does open the door for law enforcement to track their activity, but it also lets the family find new opportunities to expand what they are doing and increase profits.

The increased efforts by law enforcement also pose a significant challenge for the family. As seen throughout this book, there has always been a great deal of invisibility and anonymity to their work. Even if the authorities have ever learned more than the public, it hasn't been much, at least based on the information that exists. However, with law enforcement's investments in new technologies and ramped-up efforts to crack down on the world of organized crime, the Buffalo family will find it far more difficult to keep their normal level of invisibility.

So, while the future of organized crime and the Buffalo Crime Family is uncertain, what we do know is that things are rapidly changing, and the criminal underworld has made tremendous strides to stay ahead of the changes. They are becoming more sophisticated and globalized, which makes them much harder to track, at least for just one law enforcement agency. As time passes by, their ability to adapt to changes will determine their survival. That said, if anyone can navigate these changes, it's the Buffalo organization. Only time will tell though if the saga continues.

CONCLUSION

As we reach the end of this book, we leave behind a world that is still just as fascinating as it is terrifying. This small piece of the world, known as the Buffalo Crime Family, as you now know, is one of power and ambition, much like the Mafia counterparts you are more familiar with.

In this book, we have met men of tremendous power and ambition, who have risen from a place of obscurity to rule an empire. We saw how they navigated the treacherous landscape of the criminal underworld, forged alliances, and eliminated enemies as they pursued power and respect. We have witnessed their rise and fall—their victories and defeats.

Take a moment to consider that amidst some of these stories of power and ambition lies a deeper narrative. At the heart of it all is the human condition that speaks of every person's capacity for good and evil and how the choices we make and the paths we choose all matter in the grand scheme of things. While learning interesting facts about mobsters, you also get to confront the darker parts of human nature and truly look at your own values and beliefs. Think about how thin the line between right and wrong is and how one decision you make can change the entire course of your life.

Curious, no doubt, but even as you place the Buffalo family pin into your timeline, you'll see that once you start looking at the entirety of the Mafia, the idea that a lot of these figures and families likely made their own history because of one crucial choice suddenly makes complete sense.

REFERENCES

Bruno, A. (n.d.). *The Banana War — Joe Bonanno: A man of honor. A crime family epic.* Crimelibrary.org. https://crimelibrary.org/gangsters_outlaws/family_epics/bonanno/3.html

Buffalo police then and now - Mob boss Stefano Magaddino cheats death, twice. (n.d.). Www.bpdthenandnow.com. https://www.bpdthenandnow.com/bombing1936.html

Cascio, J. (2022, November 1). *Apalachin, NY: 14 November 1957.* Mafia Genealogy. https://mafiagenealogy.com/2022/11/01/apalachin-ny-14-november-1957/

Daniele, G. (2023, January 27). *Modern mafia: Italy's organised crime machine has changed beyond recognition in 30 years.* The Conversation. https://theconversation.com/modern-mafia-italys-organised-crime-machine-has-changed-beyond-recognition-in-30-years-198352

Dickson, M. (2020, June 1). *Stefano "The Undertaker" Magaddino.* American Mafia History. https://americanmafiahistory.com/stefano-the-undertaker-magaddino/

Doyle, B. (2020, October 5). *The story of Willie Moretti — One of NJ's most infamous mobsters*. New Jersey 101.5. https://nj1015.com/the-story-of-willie-moretti-one-of-njs-most-infamous-mobsters/

Giuffrida, A. (2019, October 30). Italy mafia networks are more complex and powerful, says minister. *The Guardian*. https://www.theguardian.com/world/2019/oct/30/italy-mafia-networks-are-more-complex-and-powerful-says-minister

History.com Editors. (2019, June 7). *Mafia in the United States*. HISTORY; A&E Television Networks. https://www.history.com/topics/crime/mafia-in-the-united-states

Hunt, T. P., & Tona, M. A. (n.d.-a). *1921 confession revealed Good Killers gang*. Mafiahistory.us. https://mafiahistory.us/a014/f_goodkillers.html

Hunt, T. P., & Tona, M. A. (n.d.-b). *DiCarlo: Buffalo's first family of crime: Angelo Palmeri*. DiCarlo. https://buffalomob.blogspot.com/2013/10/angelo-palmeri-jan-12-1878-to-dec-21.html

Hunt, T. P., & Tona, M. A. (n.d.-c). *DiCarlo: Buffalo's first family of crime: Stefano Magaddino*. Buffalomob.blogspot.com. https://buffalomob.blogspot.com/search?q=stefano+magaddino

Hunt, T. P., & Tona, M. A. (n.d.-d). *Partial timeline of events in the book*. Buffalomob.com. https://buffalomob.com/p-tmline.html

Knight, M. (2021, April 17). *The commission trial lifted the lid on the New York mafia*. The Mob Museum.

https://themobmuseum.org/blog/the-commission-trial-lifted-the-lid-on-the-new-york-mafia/

Margaritoff, M. (2022, October 24). *He led A mafia family for 35 years, then wrote* a *tell-all book about it — and somehow lived to tell the tale.* All That's Interesting. https://allthatsinteresting.com/joe-bonanno

Marker, M. D. (2019). *Organized crime has gone high tech.* Policechiefmagazine.org. https://www.policechiefmagazine.org/organized-crime-has-gone-high-tech/

Musariri, D. (2018, August 9). *Rise of the cyber mafia: How organised crime went digital.* NS Business. https://www.ns-businesshub.com/technology/cyber-mafia-organised-crime-digital/

NCS. (2012, December 17). *What was the Castellammarese War?* National Crime Syndicate; National Crime Syndicate. https://www.nationalcrimesyndicate.com/castellammarese-war/

Peters, J. (2013, November 14). *On this day in 1957, the FBI finally had to admit that the Mafia existed.* Slate. https://slate.com/news-and-politics/2013/11/apalachin-meeting-on-this-day-in-1957-the-fbi-finally-had-to-admit-that-the-mafia-existed.html

Santolo, D. (2017, November 22). *Investigation spurs debate over Buffalo Mafia Family.* About the Mafia. https://aboutthemafia.com/investigation-spurs-renewed-debate-over-the-status-of-the-buffalo-mafia-family/

Staff. (2013, February 24). *"Mafia Summit" explores how Magaddino's bad call did in the mob*. Buffalo News. https://buffalonews.com/news/mafia-summit-explores-how-magaddino-s-bad-call-did-in-the-mob/article_3a19cf89-76e0-5cab-8323-75c77d9495c1.html

The Week Staff. (2019, April 21). *The mafia today*. The Week. https://theweek.com/articles/835970/mafia-today

Wikipedia Contributors. (n.d.-a). *Apalachin meeting*. Wikipedia. https://en.wikipedia.org/wiki/Apalachin_meeting

Wikipedia Contributors. (n.d.-b). *Buffalo crime family*. Wikipedia. https://en.wikipedia.org/wiki/Buffalo_crime_family#Early_origins

Wikipedia Contributors. (n.d.-c). *Castellammarese War*. Wikipedia. https://en.wikipedia.org/wiki/Castellammarese_War

Wikipedia Contributors. (n.d.-d). *Joseph Todaro Sr.* Wikipedia. https://en.wikipedia.org/wiki/Joseph_Todaro_Sr.

Wikipedia Contributors. (n.d.-e). *Stefano Magaddino*. Wikipedia. https://en.wikipedia.org/wiki/Stefano_Magaddino

Wikipedia Contributors. (n.d.-f). *The Commission (American Mafia)*. Wikipedia. https://en.wikipedia.org/wiki/The_Commission_(American_Mafia)

Wikipedia Contributors. (n.d.-g). *War on drugs*. Wikipedia. https://en.wikipedia.org/wiki/War_on_Drugs

THE BUFALINO
MAFIA CRIME FAMILY

MAFIA LIBRARY

INTRODUCTION

It would be very difficult to find a Mafia history reader or a person interested in organized crime who hasn't watched and loved Francis Ford Coppola's classic film *The Godfather* and its sequels. However, only a few know that legendary actor Marlon Brando's performance in the movie was in great part inspired by a real Mafia boss of those times: Russell Bufalino.

Marlon Brando actually met and hung out with Russell Bufalino during the making of *The Godfather*, and some of the actors who played in the film were real gangsters outside of the set. The real Mafia was similar to the set of the iconic movie that defined the way we imagine the Mafia, its leaders, and hitmen during its heyday in America during the 1950s, 1960s, and beyond.

But how did Russell Bufalino end up on *The Godfather*'s set with Francis Ford Coppola and Marlon Brando? And before that, how did he end up being one of the most prominent mob leaders in the United States?

The Bufalino crime family's history began before it was named the "Bufalino family" and even before Russell Bufalino came to the United States from his native land in Montedoro, Sicily. In fact, it began before he was born. The story presented in the following pages and chapters begins with the origins of American organized crime when the original and authentic Mafiosi came to the United States from Sicily and South Italy between the late 19th and the early 20th century. It goes on with the formation of Italian-American crime families in the various regions and cities of the United States. And it arrives at organized crime's golden era and its fall to our time.

We will begin this journey by studying and comprehending the broader historical, social, and economic context of Northeastern Pennsylvania and, more generally, of the early to mid-20th century United States. What was the industrial background, economic basis, and development of the Pennsylvania region inside the growing new superpower of the world? And how this growth made the United States and Northeastern Pennsylvania attractive to immigrants from Europe, and especially Italy and Sicily. We'll see how the cultural and social factors of the region, along with immigration, are related to the birth and rise of organized crime and how the latter varied by area in the United States.

With a clear historical vision, we'll continue entering the universe of the Italian-American Mafia, especially the Bufalino crime family, and its origins and roots: From the migration to the United States to the "Men of Montedoro" and the formation of organized crime in Northeastern Pennsylvania to the rise of Russell Bufalino. We'll meet Bufalino's mentors, like Stefano Magaddino, his competitors, and his rivals. We will learn about other rising mobsters and the fearless labor unionist Min Matheson, all while continuing to follow Bufalino's conquering of Northeastern Pennsylvania and beyond.

We will examine in detail the criminal enterprises and operations of the Bufalino family, from the majestic coasts of Havana in Cuba, that Las Vegas with the sea that didn't happen, to the brutal and raw typical activities of organized crime, such as loan-sharking, extortion, and infiltration in labor unions, to exploit businessmen and workers alike. We'll meet characteristic gangsters like Frank Sheeran and notorious events of Mafia history, such as the infamous Apalachin Meeting, with its origins and consequences.

No criminal organization can go on growing without being subject to the attention of law enforcement, and the Bufalino crime family was no exception. We will see the Federal Bureau of Investigations target and take on the Bufalino family, using all the modern techniques and methods of those years spent battling against organized crime—from wiretaps and surveillance to witness protection programs and informants. We will see the efforts of the law to put an end to criminal activity and the capacity to persist and invent new ways to prolong it from the tenacious Bufalino and his crime family.

We will delve into the interconnection between legitimate and criminal syndicates, labor union leaders collaborating with Mafia bosses, and government officials determined to destroy organized crime or to accept it as a de facto working partner and ally—from Batista's Cuba and World War II United States to the times of John and Robert Kennedy and Richard Nixon.

Learn how Russell Bufalino, who was quiet, calm, and uninterested in displaying wealth or detaining official power, enlarged the Bufalino family's reach far beyond Northeastern Pennsylvania, its bases in the Pittston, Scranton, and Wilkes-Barre area, obtaining national status, while its boss was the leader of two more crime families.

Finally, read intriguing and shocking stories and rumors that involved the Bufalino crime family—from the aforementioned making of *The Godfather* to the mystery of labor union leader Jimmy Hoffa to the assassination of JFK, as a last glimpse of fascination before the chapter dedicated to the eventual and inevitable disintegration. The sad but just demise of a criminal empire that was more efficient than spectacular, and it, fortunately, left its place to a more advanced society, which does not need criminal methods to satisfy needs and desires and be effective—or so we hope. Was it thanks to the combined efforts of law enforcement and the government, or because time ultimately beats everything and everyone? Were the protagonists of the story finally caught off guard by law and civilized society, or did they just grow old and leave with their consciences intact, like Russell Bufalino after turning 90 years old?

It could be a little bit of both. The fact is that the history of the Bufalino crime family is a narrative of a past we would want to be gone forever. It is a testament to the pursuit of success and personal and family growth that can sometimes surpass the limits of law and social peace. Yet, at the same time, it's also a testament to the need for justice, transparency, cohesion, and truth in human societies. Ultimately, it is a captivating mystery and crime story that continues to attract researchers and readers interested in organized crime.

CHAPTER 1

NORTHEASTERN PENNSYLVANIA'S UNIQUE HISTORY

The late 19th and early 20th centuries were pivotal for Northeastern Pennsylvania's industrialization, with coal mining at its center. The industrial growth attracted immigration waves, which created distinct and vibrant ethnic local communities across the region. At the same time, the challenging conditions of labor and life produced intense labor struggles and a working-class ethos. However, the fractured cultural and social environments and economic difficulties provided the best ground for organized crime. The Prohibition era and the Great Depression, along with weak law enforcement, completed the puzzle, creating very advantageous times for Mafia growth.

Industrial Background, Immigration History, and Economic Developments

Undoubtedly, the late 19th and early 20th centuries were critical periods in Northeastern Pennsylvania's economic and social histories and the most defining ones until the mid-20th century. That period determined the area's industrialization and its importance for the modern industrial economy in the United

States. As in earlier cases and the British historical model, what was crucial for the development of Northeastern Pennsylvania was its significant coal reserves. This natural advantage made the area one of the most noteworthy places for coal mining and central to the broader establishment and growth of the American industry.

The region's economy proliferated following the general boom of the American economy, which quickly became one of the most industrialized nations on earth, soon to be the most industrialized and rich. Northeastern Pennsylvania's mines played the role held by rivers and lakes in the pre-industrial economy, securing the flourishing of production and social growth around them. Since the population constantly increased, local communities were founded and filled with homes, churches, and schools.

The industrialization of the United States proceeded in extraordinary rhythm, and so did the importance of Northeastern Pennsylvania's coal mines, which became even more prominent. That situation brought a corresponding socioeconomic development in the region, attracting always more people who wanted to work in the mines. So, the cities and towns in the area increased and grew more prominent. At the same time, the population was always more diverse, as coal mining was one of the jobs new immigrants and unqualified workers more often tended to do to make a living, along with working in related factories.

Northeastern Pennsylvania became a multinational and multicultural region as soon as the early 20th century, as thousands of Irish, Italians, and Eastern Europeans, like Polish, arrived massively in the area and began working in the mines and the factories. That fact made the region what we would call a melting pot, which used to have a negative meaning and now has instead a positive one, with populations from different cultural backgrounds that had to find and form common grounds and values. Or that's the way we would see it today. Historically, what happened was the formation of closed and knit communities aligned with the national heritage of the population, even though they were all Europeans, Christians, and working-class people.

Even more challenging for the immigrants than getting along with each other was dealing with the working conditions in the mines and factories, which were definitely much harsher than we could understand, looking at historical eras closer to our lifestyles and working habits. On the contrary, the initial periods of industrialization were extremely tough and rough for workers. They responded with many labor struggles, claiming better working conditions and, of course, bigger salaries.

In any case, Northeastern Pennsylvania's social and economic fabric was shaped by its position in the US industrial growth as a major coal resource in the country. That brought economic, social, and demographic growth destined to be overthrown around the mid-20th century. By then, the coal industry declined heavily, and the region stopped being a central point in the American economic process. Many mines and factories simply ceased to exist, and ever-growing communities slipped and lost their potential. The new condition drastically changed the region's economic situation, and people had to find solutions and transform their society to adapt.

In this context, organized crime would appear in Northeastern Pennsylvania, where the tight and closed communities formed in the previous decades of the immigrant flows would make the perfect social basis for activities of that kind.

Cultural and Social Factors That Shaped the Region's Identity and Dynamism

Northeastern Pennsylvania is a blue-collar region, no doubt about that. As mentioned, industrialization and coal mines were the essential elements of its social fabric from the economic point of view. In that sense, the working-class ethos could not be anything but prevailing. Factory workers and coal miners were the population's bulk and heart. Working hard and being down-to-earth became the dominant anthropological model for the area's people. That condition also brought a sense of companionship among the working class, forged by the various shared, sometimes really hard, struggles about the working conditions. Struggles, strikes, and difficulties gave rise to narratives of resilience, perseverance, and working together to overcome aversion.

The harsh socioeconomic conditions and the not-so-many opportunities made life difficult but also created an attitude of collective activism against adversities that has since culturally characterized local society. Also, values such as family and religion were central to the region's cultural identity, with churches being central places of socialization and moral guidance for the communities of Northeastern Pennsylvania.

Yes, but that was pretty much it. What was even more crucial and determined heavily social dynamics was the fact of the different national heritages. Common grounds proved to be less influential than the predominant element of ethnic origins, and essentially, the immigrant working population formed closed and tight-knit communities based on ethnicity. The Italians constructed Italian-American blocks and neighborhoods; the Irish formed Irish-American blocks and communities; the Polish created Polish-American ones. Those ethnic-based communities were in great part culturally homogeneous and sometimes entirely homogeneous, as people continued to live according to the habits and customs of the country of origin, often spoke their national language instead of English, and had no intention of flowing and abandoning themselves into a multicultural melting pot.

Inside the national communities were shared cultural traditions but also the camaraderie of people who felt they had to deal with a quite strange or even hostile environment that did not conform with their own values and customs, or, to put it simpler, it did not speak their language.

The area's deindustrialization of the mid-20th century shocked the cultural and social format forged until then in Northeastern Pennsylvania. Historically and in the long term, it was not something terrible, as it led to a reshaping of local society, economy, and identity. The heavy landscape of the grey coal mines and factories of the first industrialization—forgive this caricatural image, just to make the point—gradually gave way to a more colorful landscape entering the era of advanced technology, better education and healthcare, and more opportunities. However, in the meantime, the osmosis of social, cultural, and economic conditions would produce social forms in the opposite historical direction, similar to those encountered in much older societies, such as mafia families.

The Historical Events and Eras That Led to the Rise of Organized Crime

We cannot escape evidence. Immigration was one of the principal historical factors of the United States' economic and social growth, but also one of the factors that led to the rise of organized crime in the United States in the early 20th century. As mentioned, the formation of totally inhomogeneous local societies, where different ethnicities had to coexist with their particular customs and traditions, resulted in a fractured cultural and social context. To make matters worse, economic difficulties, racism, and discrimination further increased the feeling of some communities that they had to find ways to survive and get more decadent on their own without integrating with the rest of society or without integrating wholly and harmoniously. That was an environment favorable to the development of groups living with norms outside official law, proposing themselves as forms of protection and support, especially to members of the same national community or, in other terms, minority.

However, the list of the historical events that led to the rise of organized crime is much longer. The rapid urbanization itself and, to be more precise, the inability of the state to create in a similarly quick manner law enforcement capable of dealing with the new dimensions of cities created a weakness in implementing the law and corruption. Often, law enforcement was not as strong as the situation demanded because there were insufficient resources, trained agents, organization, and coordination. The conditions were objectively very harsh, as a young state had to take care of an ever-growing and diverse population and social and cultural ambiance.

The young state was not totally innocent, though, as after thousands of years during which humans had used various alcoholic beverages, a US administration had the not-so-smart idea to prohibit alcohol in 1920. The Prohibition Era had a central role in the rise of organized crime, and we could say that it was the single most decisive event, as it created a very lucrative market, in that case, the black market, perfectly fit for rising criminal businesses or for the creation of new ones. On that occasion, notorious criminal organizations such as Chicago Outfit and the New York Five Families rose. They had the opportunity to take over the production and distribution of alcohol with illicit distilleries and bars and control the contraband. Finally, in 1933, the US administration canceled the Prohibition, eliminating the vast black market that had offered wealth to criminal groups, but dismantling them was not equally easy at that point.

Having established their organizations and expanded their activities in many other sections, criminal enterprises developed the ability to use political struggles and turmoil to their advantage, applying influence to politicians and labor unions, as well as exploiting other illegal activities, like illegal sports betting and gambling.

And then, there is another crucial historical event. The Great Depression, beginning in 1929, brought an economic and social earthquake with immeasurable consequences, which the criminal organizations were keen and able to use to their advantage. In desperate conditions, with difficulties making a living or even surviving, many people came close to organized crime in search of financial support. In that way, criminal organizations put down deeper roots in local societies, exploiting the favorable conditions offered by the abovementioned factors.

Socioeconomic Issues That Influenced Criminal Behavior

It's obvious, then, that socioeconomic issues had a critical influence on forming the social habitat in which criminal organizations found the opportunity to establish themselves and grow. If we want to take a closer look at them, we cannot omit the examination of the last factor mentioned in the previous paragraph, unemployment. The unemployment rates rose higher than ever after the Great Depression and before President Franklin D. Roosevelt's "New Deal." Still, in the case of Northeastern Pennsylvania, they were again at higher levels during the mid-20th century, as the coal industry declined, and many people lost what was, till then, their principal income source. Criminal organizations were eager to fill the gap before the growth of the normal economy could have by offering jobs in their illegal activities, like the ones already mentioned, or others like loan-sharking, forced protection, and raw blackmailing.

Also, the black markets formed during the failures of the regular economy or mistakes made by governments that alter the function of the market for the worse can be beneficial for organized crime to thrive. The aforementioned Era of Prohibition was an important example, but other market failures had similar results, such as the one imposed by the deindustrialization of Northeastern Pennsylvania. Not only unemployment but also the shrinking of the market itself, caused by the fall of the incomes and consumption of the population, created gaps in consumer goods that criminal organizations were able to cover through illegal channels. In that case, organized crime could also appear as welfare and earn the sympathy and social legalization of many people.

That kind of social legalization and sympathy was favored by another socioeconomic factor that played an important role in the rise of organized crime, which was economic inequality, especially in the Northeastern Pennsylvania region. Harsh working conditions of miners and low wages, in contrast with the wealth of the mine owners, created resentment and hate, as the working class felt it was a provocation and an injustice. Criminal organizations provided a sense of support and justice like law enforcement not controlled by the rich, whom poor workers often saw as the owners of the official law and the state. Related to this last factor was also the exploitation of labor struggles and disputes by criminal organizations, as they deftly infiltrated labor unions.

Unsurprisingly, these kinds of perceptions and activities empowered the roots and acceptance of criminal organizations in local and national close-knit communities that, since the beginning, were formed and came closer precisely in order to deal with substantial economic problems and insecurities. The result was that, in many cases, organized crime was perfectly integrated into the social fabric of communities and neighborhoods, justified and supported.

The Bigger Picture of Organized Crime in the United States and How It Varies by Area

The United States is a very big country and the biggest economy in the world for more than a century now. Organized crime in the United States could not be a simple and one-way thing. Complexity and differentiation between the various regions of the country are evident.

Wanting to paint the bigger picture of organized crime in the United States, we can begin with socioeconomic factors related to the previous paragraphs, such as the decline of the coal industry in Northeastern Pennsylvania. Similar evolution also intervened in many other Rust Belt regions, beginning in the 1950s. In many cases, the great industrial zone of the United States faced increasing difficulties and problems, such as unemployment, low wages, shortcomings, and poverty. In those regions, criminal organizations offered financial outlets by employing people in their illegal businesses.

Another theme already mentioned is the cultural and national background, which more precisely favored organized crime in cases where national communities had a heritage of similar social forms. It's not a secret that the Mafia was a thing in the Italian South decades before it immigrated to the United States and that other ethnic communities had their own traditions of organized crime, be it Hispanic, African, Asian, or anything else. Again, the fractured cultural and social fabric of the new country called the United States, combined with the material challenges and difficulties faced by the various communities, gave a hand to criminal traditions' rooting, at least in some of them.

There's no doubt, then, that organized crime varies between different local communities and regions. Yet, suppose we want to put things in relative order. In that case, we can locate and examine four mega-regions of the country, usually used for analysis, similar to those used by sports leagues' divisions: the East Coast, the Central or Midwest, the West Coast, and the South.

The East Coast, and especially the Northeastern part of it, where Pennsylvania is also located, is one of the most prominent candidates for the award of the region that has suffered most from organized crime. The Five Families in New York is a sharp reminder of the power that the Mafia had in the Big Apple, but other great cities on the East Coast, like the old NBA rivals Philadelphia and Boston, had their fair share. Drug distribution, raw extortion, and illegal gambling were some of the activities criminal organizations promoted in this deep urban area of the country, as elsewhere.

Then there is Chicago, in the central regions. "Chicago" had an almost mystical sense in the rest of the world, as it stood for something close to criminal utopia (or dystopia). Al Capone was a legendary name. Fortunately for the Windy City, the University of Chicago came with its famous School of Chicago in economics and social sciences. And, of course, Michael Jordan and the Chicago Bulls. However, during Prohibition, organized crime, especially the Chicago Outfit, had risen at an extraordinary rate in the city, influencing and corrupting politics and labor unions based on their profits from gambling, bootlegging, and more.

Moving to the West Coast, cinema has taken care of presenting the laundering and drug trafficking opportunities that criminal organizations can find in Los Angeles or the entertainment and gambling capital of the world, Las Vegas. The West Coast is not so related to classic Mafia, like Chicago and New York. Still, it has other types of organized crime, including Asian-American criminal organizations, cartels close to Latin American drug industries, and gangs.

Concluding the trip to the criminal side of the United States, the South, besides common activities like smuggling, bootlegging, drugs, motorcycle gangs, etc., is characterized by the presence of white-collar crime and elevated political corruption by organized crime.

Formation and Collaboration of Northeastern Pennsylvania's Criminal Networks and Organizations

Northeastern Pennsylvania summarized all the socioeconomic factors and the historical events that, as we saw, prepared the rise of organized crime in the United States. This region is the best example of the consequences of sudden economic holes, such as the unemployment and market shrinking caused by the Great Depression or the deindustrialization after the end of the coal industry era that we have mentioned on more occasions. It's also an excellent example of the role of ethnic differentiation in the formation of organized crime in the United States and the exploitation of labor struggles and unions.

But the most important and exciting is discovering the particular factors that made the region of Northeastern Pennsylvania a hub for organized criminal activities in the first place. That happened first during the 1920s and Prohibition because the area was perfect for contraband to supply New York, Philadelphia, and other nearby big cities with alcohol. Another geographical reason that made Northeastern Pennsylvania appealing to criminal organizations was the fact that the region offered opportunities to hide and escape more than others. There are rough terrains and woods where one can hide illegal operations and find ways out of law enforcement. That last one was not the strongest in the world in the early 20th century in the region, so we have another valid reason for criminal masterminds to set up their business, or departments of their business, in Northeastern Pennsylvania.

Geographical considerations are not finished yet, as the region presented another critical advantage, which was its nearness to some of the most important transportation arteries—a real treasure to criminal organizations and networks that looked for ways to enter or expand bootlegging enterprises. Obviously, the coal mining industry was in itself a very attractive element, as criminal organizations could and indeed did exploit part of the wealth produced, thereby infiltrating or racketeering labor unions or mine owners.

After organized crime was stabilized in the region thanks to all those geographical assets and took root in local communities, criminal organizations began to create networks with similar entities in nearby areas. The growing organizations, always having more resources and people at their disposal, now expanded in multiple communities, could then gain influence in bigger domains, like towns and also big cities. Collaboration with criminal organizations of other communities or cities multiplied the power of each of them, as they secured access to more resources, information, influence, and people in various sectors and professions. In that way, they were no longer locally limited organizations.

In this way, the criminal organizations made extended networks and alliances, could diversify their operations and businesses, and evolve in every aspect, rendering it more difficult for the authorities to confront and neutralize them. On the other hand, and even worse, the criminal networks had the ability to influence or control legitimate local businessmen, labor syndicates, and politicians.

The possibility of huge profits, offered by geography, natural resources, and position in the industrial and productive process, natural advantages. Those were the reasons for the formation and collaboration of criminal organizations and networks in Northeastern Pennsylvania. Gambling, drugs, contraband, controlling the black market and labor unions, loan-sharking, and raw extortion were all easier to think about and accomplish in Northeastern Pennsylvania's cultural, socioeconomic, and natural landscape.

CHAPTER 2

THE BUFALINO FAMILY'S ORIGINS

Russell Bufalino's family arrived in the United States, and he gained a reputation in local gangs in Buffalo, New York, as a teenager. A few years earlier, the Northeastern Pennsylvania crime family had been founded by the "Men of Montedoro." We'll see how the Northeastern Pennsylvania crime family's power and reach expanded with gangsters like John Sciandra and Joseph Barbara in leading roles as Bufalino began his criminal career. This chapter closes with a glimpse into the Lucky Luciano-Vito Genovese-Frank Costello alliance at the top of organized crime in the United States.

Roots and Migration to the United States

The Bufalino family was an Italian-American family from Sicily, the most oversized island of the Mediterranean, located in the Southern part of the Italian peninsula. Angelo Bufalino emigrated to the United States on July 9, 1903, to work as a coal miner. He settled in Pittston, Pennsylvania, where a broad Italian-American community was already sited. His wife Cristina Buccoleri and his kids would follow a few months later, arriving at New York's port in December 1903. Angelo Bufalino was the family's patriarch, but his role in our story is minimal. The founder of one of the most notorious crime families of the American 1900s was to become his son Russell.

Russell Alfred Bufalino was born Rosario Alfredo Bufalino on September 29, 1903, in Montedoro, Sicily, and that means he traveled to America with his mother and siblings when he was just two or three months old. This initial settlement would not last for long, though, as just a few months later, his father Angelo tragically died in a mine accident, like the ones that happened far more often than today in those harsh days of industrialization's first eras. Russell Bufalino's mother brought her children back to Sicily. Still, soon, she apparently understood that America offered more opportunities even without her husband, and she returned to the United States in January 1906.

The back and forth was not yet over for baby Russell, or better still, Rosario, as just four years later, he also lost his mother. Seven-year-old Buffalino was back in Sicily in 1910, only to finally return and settle in the United States on February 15, 1914. It was already a big tragic and adventurous story for a little boy, but what happened next would enter the books of organized crime's history.

When he was just 14 years old, Russell Bufalino left Pittston for Buffalo, New York. There, he would quickly follow the path of his criminal career, entering the local gangs of the Italian-American community as a teenager. He gained a growing reputation thanks to his ability to go unnoticed by the police and, in general, to his low profile, not attracting unwanted attention, attitude, and way of doing things. We can understand that he was really good at what he did, as around ten years later, on August 9, 1928, we find him getting married to the daughter of a traditional Mafia family from

Sicily, Carolyn Sciandra. His fellow collaborators were often capable, too. Many later became leaders of powerful Mafia families of the East Coast and the Buffalo crime family.

The Bufalino family story, before it became the Bufalino crime family, is typical for the numerous Italians and other immigrants who flowed to the United States between the late 19th century and the early 20th century. Some of them worked hard for some years, then returned to their countries with packages full of money and founded their businesses back home (who knows if they were successful). Others stayed forever and became Americans. Their descendants are the Americans of today. A few of them were involved in crime and organized crime or brought it with them from their country of origin, and if we want to talk about the original Mafia, from Italy, South Italy.

The typical Italian immigrant, like Angelo Bufalino, settled in industrial areas of the United States to work in manual labor, as a worker in factories, construction jobs, and, in this case, mining. It's easy to understand that people in Italian communities, like in other immigrant communities, faced difficulties and challenges of every kind, from financial to cultural and social, and in some cases, discrimination, contempt, and racism. That, along with objective limits, such as not knowing the English language, made the immigrants form close-knit communities and neighborhoods, where they supported one another and lived according to their own cultural costumes and social norms. Mafia was one of them, in the case of Southern Italians and Sicilians.

The Bufalino family may have been exposed to the Mafia world back in Sicily before emigrating to America. Still, they had nothing to do with that when Angelo Bufalino decided to emigrate to the United States to work as a coal miner. Yet, others were traditional Mafia families all along, and they had a crucial role in the criminal careers of young immigrants with no support, parents, or future, like Rosario Bufalino, Americanized as Russell. Mafia's loyalty and support code, the sense of belonging to an organization, a hierarchical structure that would be by your side in any case if you were loyal to it, the feeling of being part of a *familia*, a family, could be attractive for many young Italian immigrants. Knowing the story of Russell Bufalino's family, with the death of both his parents when he was just a little boy, understanding the Mafia's appeal to him may become even more accessible.

The Bufalino Crime Family Before Bufalino

The Men From Montedoro

The criminal organization, often called the "Bufalino crime family," was founded long before Russell Bufalino was involved with organized crime. In fact, its history began when Bufalino was a baby and had just arrived for the first time in the United States. That's why the same crime family is also called by other names: Pittston crime family, Scranton and Wilkes-Barre crime family, Northeastern Pennsylvania Mafia, and more. The point is that it's not about a family in the biological sense of the word but about a criminal syndicate formed in those locations, which Russell Bufalino would lead only decades later.

Our story begins again in 1903, but this time, it's not about the Bufalinos from Montedoro in Sicily, who emigrate to the United

States. This time is about people who were there already, and in those years began their criminal activity, Mafia style.

Tomasso Petto, "The Ox," was around 26 years old when he was murdered on October 21, 1905, in Browntown, a village near Pittston and Wilkes-Barre in Pennsylvania. He had been the best hitman of the Morello crime family. The Morello family was a criminal clan from Sicily, located in the early 1900s Manhattan, and Petto lived in Brooklyn. The Morellos were ruthless and used the most brutal methods of Cosa Nostra. They used to kill members of rival families without hesitation, put them in barrels, and leave them near the streets in order to shock and show who's the boss in the neighborhood.

Petto became notorious to the authorities, and on April 15, 1903, detectives from the New York Police Department arrested him for murder only after he put up a gunfight. They transferred him to the New York Central Jail, but he was released after an incredible mistake made by jail officials. And, of course, he left New York immediately, thanking his good luck. He went as far as he could, settling down where he could find people who could understand him and work together. That was Scranton in Pennsylvania, where he became a member of a local gang that operated in the extortion sector. A typical Mafia and Camorra mode, *Mano Nera*, Black Hand, meant extortion through intimidation, threatening kidnapping or violence, and life threats. Black Hand originated from the Kingdom of Naples back in the 1750s and entered the United States in the 1880s, next to Italian immigrants. But make no mistake, the victims of Black Hand were almost always other Italian immigrants, the non-criminal great majority, and especially the most successful and affluent ones.

Petto was finally killed in 1905, allegedly by a relative of one of his victims, but that didn't stop the crime family of Northeastern Pennsylvania from growing. The central figures were Steven Joseph La Torre, born Stefano, and Santo Volpe, who both came from Montedoro in Sicily, the home of the Bufalinos. La Torre founded what would later take the name "Bufalino crime family."

Born on March 12, 1886, La Torre emigrated to the United States and precisely in Pennsylvania in May 1903. In the immediate next years, the young Sicilian established criminal activities and soon saved enough money to cover the cost of his brother-in-law Mafia boss Santo Volpe's travel to America in 1906. This is a clear case of Mafia export, in which the criminal activity is transported to the United States from where it already existed and not created in the United States. Next, La Torre and Volpe founded an organization called "The Men from Montedoro," but in April 1907, they were arrested together with twenty other persons after they tried to sell protection to miners. One of the men who got arrested with the two young bosses from Montedoro was Charles Bufalino, uncle of Russell Bufalino, who by that time was still enjoying his soon-to-be lost mom's hugs as a three-year-old boy.

In 1908, Volpe became the boss of the newborn Italian-American criminal organization in Pittston, with La Torre's agreement, perhaps because he was more experienced. Born in 1880, he was a little bit older and had also been nurtured at the original Mafia school in Sicily. Known as the King of the Night, Volpe directed the crime family in Northeastern Pennsylvania successfully, as it got more prominent over time. The fact that he was a capable manager can be seen in that he somehow also became president of a coal company in the then-leading mining region of the United States. The intersection between the Mafia, coal industry, and labor unions is beginning to emerge while we try to examine those initial decades of organized crime.

The Volpe years as leader of the Northeastern Pennsylvania Mafia include the Prohibition Era, during which, as more times mentioned, those kinds of criminal organizations had the golden opportunity to expand their businesses. However, by the end of Prohibition in 1933, we can see Volpe appointed as the new boss of the family John Sciandra after Volpe was suspected of murder. Wanting to protect the family, Volpe chose to operate from the background from now on, as, like said before, he had a very important legitimate occupation, too. From that position, behind the scenes, the "King of the Night" would have the role of advisor and mentor, also expanded until Russell's Bufalino rise, which we'll see later.

The Rise of John Sciandra

John Sciandra, born Giovanni Sciandra, arrived with his parents and siblings in the United States in 1908 when he was nine years old. He, too, was from Montedoro in Sicily. His criminal career began in the early 1920s after he moved to Pittston from Buffalo, New York, the place his family had settled when they first came. Sciandra went to Pennsylvania to work as a miner in the coal industry; no surprise there. But soon, he met the local crime family run by Volpe. He felt that bootlegging, bullying, and threatening were a better fit for his talents and interests than working buried inside the earth with his face choked in dust, and during the following years, he became one of the top executives of the local Italian Mafia.

BY 1933, Sciandra was the organization's leader, after Santo Volpe and next to Angelo Polizzi and Joseph Barbara. Then Volpe decided to retire to the background and appointed him the new boss. At the same time, Polizzi became the *consigliere*—the chief advisor of the family, as the Italian-Americans kept calling them.

During Sciandra's leadership in the 1930s, the Northeastern Pennsylvania crime family related closer to the more prominent Luciano-Genovese family of New York and operated under the latter's guidance. Sciandra remained the boss in Pittston until September 11, 1949, when he died of natural causes at the age of 50. It was then that Russell Bufalino became the boss of the soon-to-be-called Bufalino crime family after him.

We should talk more about the role of Joseph Barbara, who was born Giuseppe Barbara in Sicily in 1905. As said, he was one of the four leaders of the crime family in the Pittston and Scranton region. Some historians believe Barbara became the boss around 1940 after Sciandra was murdered. In fact, evidence shows that Sciandra was not murdered, and he maintained his leadership until his natural death in 1949. Barbara was *capodecina*—leader of a fraction of a family in the Buffalo crime family under the boss Stefano Maggadino, and he was close to the Pittston and Scranton crime family. His role was presumably overestimated because he hosted the infamous Apalachin meeting in 1957, which we will talk about later, and other meetings between members of the Italian Mafia in 1956-57 on his estate in Apalachin country. But that happened because Magaddino ordered him to host them because of the convenient location, not because Barbara was the boss.

The "Men from Montedoro," or more straightforward, the Italian-American criminal organization of the Pittston, Scranton, and Wilkes-Barre area, is what later evolved in the "Bufalino crime family." We do not have every detail on the succession, the structure, or the unfolding of the early events, and, of course, every criminal act. We must not forget we are talking about criminal actions that their protagonists, even many decades later, are unwilling to communicate with precision, as it can always be dangerous for them or members of their families and their businesses. Moreover, that kind of organization seldom has written documents and archives, as everybody can easily understand, and facts are transmitted through time in their internal circles and, generally, the broader communities by voice. However, we can suppose with certainty that the "Men from Montedoro" were involved in a lot of extortion, loan-sharking, and contraband of alcohol during Prohibition, as well as illegal gambling and other criminal activities.

It is also evident that over time, the organization's operations developed and enlarged to include broader areas and activities. The initial small group of young Sicilian immigrants grew and came in contact with other Italian-American crime families from other cities, like Buffalo.

During the Same Years: A Glimpse to the Mafia Central Luciano-Genovese-Costello Alliance

In the early 1920s, Lucky Luciano, Vito Genovese, and Frank Costello had formed an alliance that grew considerably in power during Prohibition and had the opportunity to develop various other activities, like illegal gambling and prostitution. Their power increased, and they had precise roles between them, as for what each of them contributed to the group. Luciano became the leader of the Commission, and Genovese was his second in command, while Costello was his consigliere. Luciano and Genovese were the classic charismatic and ruthless mob leaders, while Costello was able to secure political and judicial cover, contacting and bribing with a lot of money politicians and judges, as well as police officials. Others had more operational roles, like Albert Anastasia, who became the leader of the "Murder Incorporated." That was the name of the brutal homicidal group that executed many killings ordered by the Commission.

Lucky Luciano had named Vito Genovese the boss of one of the five families of New York. When Luciano was convicted for pandering in 1936, he appointed Genovese as the leader of the Commission, although temporarily. Lucky Luciano had not considered that Genovese had his own problems with the law and that his condition was equally precarious because of a murder in 1934, for which he was indicted.

Genovese went to Italy to be sure that he'd avoid getting into jail and found his motherland in an interesting situation. Those were the years of Benito Mussolini and Fascism's peak, and Genovese did leave the opportunity to go away from his hands. He became a Mussolini supporter and got every advantage he could. However, things didn't turn out very well for the Duce and Fascism, as we know. Genovese, with the admirable opportunism that a real gangster must always have, remembered his American patriotism and became an interpreter of the Allies after they landed in Italy in 1943. At the same time, exploiting his proximity to the US Army, he was stealing supplies and food from the army's trucks to sell them in the black market to the American and British soldiers. We know he did so because the Military Police arrested him. But the army had more important things to do than spending time with little thieves, so they didn't put him on trial.

That wasn't the case sometime later when he returned to the United States. Finally, he was about to be tried by the court for the murder that had happened in 1934. But the trial never happened, as the key witness died poisoned while taking medication.

Meanwhile, Frank Costello had risen to become the undisputed boss, as his more flexible and political way of doing things proved to be very efficient and earned him and the family a lot of money.

CHAPTER 3
THE RISE OF RUSSELL BUFALINO

Russell Bufalino rose from a local low-level gangster to a high-ranking Mafia boss on a national level. Bufalino's mentor, Stefano Magaddino, the historical boss of the Buffalo crime family, was a central figure in this rise. We'll see Bufalino learning a lot from Magaddino and becoming a respected member of the Magaddino family, for then marries Carolyn "Carrie" Sciandra, sister of the soon-to-be boss of the Northeastern Pennsylvania boss John Sciandra. The two bosses moved him to Northeastern Pennsylvania, where he grew more as a mobster, and he focused on labor racketeering and the garment industry. At the beginning of the 1950s, Bufalino was the most powerful boss in the region, so the FBI had to prepare its first report dedicated to him. Meanwhile, though, the fearless figure of labor unionist Miss Min Matheson gave problems to the Bufalino crime family

Russell Bufalino's Mentor: Stefano Magaddino

During the 1920s, Russell Bufalino learned much about being a successful gangster from one of the best, Stefano Magaddino. And just like every talented individual who's also intelligent enough to carefully attend the example of experienced mentors and learn from them, he always became more prominent. His rise began in the Magaddino family's internal, as the boss appreciated his skills and attitude. Dealing successfully with the crime family's enemies, Bufalino gained Magaddino's respect, making his way as a new official member of the clan.

Stefano Magaddino historically led the Italian-American crime family in Buffalo, which, for that reason, is also called the Magaddino crime family. Magaddino was born in Sicily, in Castellammare del Golfo, on October 10, 1891. He immigrated to the United States when he was still very young, ten or eleven years old, and settled in Buffalo, in the western part of the state of New York. There, he was quickly involved in illegal activities and gradually elevated his status as a mobster in the area, gaining positions in the organized crime hierarchy in New York and nationally.

By the early 1900s, Magaddino entered and soon became the leader of the Italian-American criminal clan in the area. The clan, similarly to the "men from Montedoro" clan, was formed by men who originated from Castellammare del Golfo. Magaddino partnered with another clan, that of the Bonnano brothers, Giuseppe and Stefano, and soon after, they entered into a conflict with the Buccellato Mafia family, which was already established in the area. Stefano and Giuseppe were murdered, and their younger brother avenged their deaths by killing members of the Buccellato clan. Magaddino participated in that gang war, and in March 1917, he was the mastermind behind the killing of Felice Buccellato, the boss of the Buccellatos, based in Detroit.

In the early 1920s, Magaddino became the boss of the Italian-American crime family in Buffalo and would stay in that role for circa 40 years. How he ended the boss in Buffalo is worth mentioning.

Bartolo Fontana was a barber and also a gangster, apparently not of the highest level, who in August 1921 turned himself in and confessed the murder of Camillo Caiozzo, who five years earlier in Sicily was involved in the murder of Magaddino's brother Pietro. According to Fontana, he had acted to avenge that killing as a member of a clan called "Good Killers," whose members originated from Castellammare del Golfo, and the clan had been responsible for other murders as well. For whatever reason, Fontana was convinced that he was about to be killed by the clan, and he not only turned himself in to the New York police but also agreed to participate in a covered operation. He came in contact with Magaddino, telling him he needed some money to leave New York—he had killed Caiozzo in Avon, New Jersey. Magaddino agreed and met him at Grand Central Station. He gave him $30, but right after that, a team of undercover policemen came out and arrested him. In the following days, four more mobsters were arrested.

Yet, the charges against Magaddino could not be supported, so he was released, and he immediately left New York and settled in Buffalo. There, he came in contact and entered the pre-existent Buffalo crime family, whose boss was Joseph DiCarlo. Already in the following year, 1922, DiCarlo died, and Magaddino, who had made his reputation as an elite gangster, was elevated to the post of the new Buffalo crime family.

As a Mafia boss, Magaddino is known for the caution with which he used to approach his criminal businesses, guiding his crime family in a careful and even conservative manner, preferring a low-profile style. At the same time, in the metropolis of New York City and Chicago, the Italian-American Mafia was anything but low-profile, with a bombastic approach that made the crime families of the big cities notorious in the United States and globally. On the contrary, with his cautious approach, Magaddino managed to keep law enforcement relatively away from his activities and crime family, on which he was also careful to have a tight grasp and control rigorously every operation and action. This is how he remained boss for three decades, without excessive pressure from the authorities and the law in that period or afterward. Magaddino was accused of involvement in numerous criminal acts and activities, but there was never enough legal evidence to be convicted.

That's although he was also a member of the Commission. That was kind of a confederation of Mafia families in the United States. The organization was created to coordinate the illegal activities of Italian-American crime families in order to avoid or diminish conflicts between them—something like the United Nations or the World Trade Organization of Organized Crime. Also, the Commission helped crime families join forces in various issues and activities, giving them national dimensions, like controlling or influencing labor unions or cooperating in the sector of gambling.

Magaddino was a constant factor in organized crime after Prohibition, just like during it. He was a permanent member of the Commission for all those years, and his organization continued to have interests in various places and sectors. The area of Scranton was a source of earnings for Magaddino, as he received tributes from there. Bufalino had a pivotal role in defending and promoting Magaddino's interests in the area, as he was responsible for the collection and deposit of the tributes to Magaddino.

One of the things Bufalino learned from Magaddino was not to show off and provoke with his wealth. He used to wear simple clothes, the car with which he used to go around was old, and he didn't live in a palace but in a nearly ordinary American home, a little ranch he had bought for $22,000. Another important thing Bufalino learned from Magaddino, as we saw, was to be tough and merciless with the enemies. Having around him a group of experienced killers was his way of dealing with the enemies.

Moving on to his 70s, Stefano Magaddino decided that after 30 years, it was time to retire as boss of the Buffalo crime family. In the early 1960s, he appointed as new boss his brother Peter and, consequently, his son Joseph Magaddino.

Bufalino Begins the Northeastern Pennsylvania Conquest

Russell Bufalino's resolve and capacity to quickly analyze situations and find solutions elevated his status inside the Magaddino crime family and in Buffalo's outlaw underworld in general, as he secured his position as Stefano Magaddino's trusted protégé. Magaddino's respect was crucial for Bufalino to grow as a mobster and get married. In fact, the family brought him close to the daughter of another known family from back home in Sicily. The bride was

Carolyn Sciandra, whom Russell Bufalino married in 1928. Sciandra was the sister of John Sciandra, whom we met in the previous chapter, the soon-to-be boss of the Pittston and Scranton crime family, the one that originated from Montedoro, which by coincidence was the hometown of Bufalino too.

This last fact, along with his parenthood with Charles Bufalino, his uncle, and of course, his marriage to John Sciandra's sister, made the two bosses, Magaddino and Sciandra himself, move Russell Bufalino to Northeastern Pennsylvania, to be Sciandra's second in command. That happened in 1938, five years after Sciandra had become Northeastern Pennsylvania's don, as we saw in the previous chapter. The facade job of Bufalino would be auto mechanic at a bottling plant whose owner was Joseph Barbara, Canada Dry.

By 1940, Bufalino was focused on understanding and operating better in the infiltrating and racketeering labor unions sector of Mafia activities and also in expanding his businesses in the garment industry. By the end of World War II, he had indeed grown and was doing serious business in New York as well. He owned a restaurant on West 48th Street. The name of the restaurant was "Vesuvio," the name of the volcano near Napoli that had destroyed Pompey in 67 CE. He also owned many dress shops as well as jewelry shops, alone or in common with others. His jewelry shops were in the "Diamond District" in Manhattan, a very famous place at the time, on West 47th Street. Bufalino's businesses in Pennsylvania were much more extensive but fundamentally of the same nature as he was operating with success in the garment industry. And just like in his early mob years, Bufalino had no real problems with the authorities or the police. He could grow his activities with relative peace, away from great tensions.

That was about to change in 1945. In that year, she came to the Pittston and Wilkes-Barre area for the first time as a representative of the International Ladies' Garment Workers Union. Her name was Min Matheson, and her arrival would be a game-changer.

The Fearless Min Matheson Puts Bufalino in Trouble

Before that, very few shops in Pittston and surrounding areas were aligned with the Union, but by 1946, Matheson had made sensibility on the garments industry workers' rights, and the courage of the ladies who worked as sewing-machine operators increased exponentially. In that year, for the first time, a protest against a shop owned by Bufalino took place. Thirty workers participated, prompted by the energetic Matheson. It didn't go so well for Matheson and the protesters, as a number of people in the neighborhood attacked them with insults. Of course, mobsters of the Bufalino crime family threatened them Mafia-style, hanging guns. Nevertheless, Matheson and the women who decided to follow her in this struggle against the horrible working conditions of the garment industry in the region were tenacious. They held their ground, continuing the protests outside Bufalino's store for eight straight months.

Watching his bully tactics fail in this case, Bufalino adopted a more elaborate approach against this unexpected disruption. He put up another labor union, the Anthracite Needle Workers Association, controlled by himself. Of course, that didn't mean that the good old bully Mafia approach would not be helpful, too. As the initial number of workers who chose to become members of the Bufalino-held union was comprehensibly low, Bufalino's men made them recall that not so many years before, the crime family had dealt with the competition of Lori Dress in a resolute and efficient way: They smashed its two hundred sewing machines accompanying the firm out of the market. Note that the police and judiciary knew very well what had happened and that the Bufalino organization was responsible for the attack, yet nobody could touch Bufalino or his men.

The combined tactics of Bufalino succeeded in bringing far more workers into his puppet union as members. However, Matheson was unbent. She kept visiting workplaces, shops, and crafts, trying to convince women workers to enter the International Ladies' Garment Workers Union.

Bufalino was not the only gangster boss who was worried about Matheson's actions and saw their profits diminishing because of them. In 1949, there were forty-plus factories in union contracts thanks to Matheson, and that was nothing good for a number of Mafia bosses who held shops and factories in the region. Bosses like Albert Anastasia, besides Bufalino, were exposed to profit losses in their garment industry businesses because of Matheson's game-changing operations in Northeastern Pennsylvania. Things became even more uncomfortable for him after Matheson started working to unionize Anastasia's employees, who worked in a show he owned near Hazleton. At the same time, Matheson's brother, Will Lurye, was leading protests in a factory owned in part by Anastasia in New York, as he was connected to shops and factories both in Pennsylvania and New York.

That was too much for the Mafia boss. His clan's response was ruthless and bloody. Two of Anastasia's men blocked Lurye while he was talking in a public telephone booth and stabbed him many times with knives, killing him at the post. The victim of this horrible crime was a father of four, and he had followed his sister's occupation, joining as an organizer of the Union, although they paid him only $80, and his previous job as a presser earned him almost double the money. Both of them had followed their father's example and career, who was a union organizer himself. At the time of his son's murder, he was in hospital, and he died a week later.

But Anastasia did not achieve what he had hoped for. Matheson did not abandon her mission, but on the contrary, she was more galvanized after her brother's murder, as instead of frightening her, it convinced her more. Thus, she continued organizing in the Union, always more poor paid women who were working in inadequate conditions in factories and stores such as the ones belonging to Bufalino and Anastasia. Matheson did so, although even her superiors in the Union, back in New York, warned her repeatedly to be careful and let go. And, of course, despite the continuous threats of the crime family. Until 1953, she had brought sixty more shops into the Union, with 700 workers.

In doing so, Matheson had stood against another intimidating tactic from Bufalino's part, who had his brother-in-law Angelo Sciandra running the Northeastern Pennsylvania Needle Worker's Association: Another puppet union of his. To convince employees to become members of that Union, they would say: "Sign with us, or you'll be sorry." Matheson did not let go and continued her work in Pittston, where suddenly, one night, as she was walking in the street, a man came and told her that the Bufalino's men had told him to close his shop, threatening him that they would harm his family if he didn't.

Again, other than being intimidated, Matheson used this fact to make the situation public, promoting her struggle with interviews to newspapers and radio, saying that "to live by permission of goons is worse than death. Gentlemen, hoodlums, I don't scare easily." Another characteristic similar event happened in 1955. Matheson and members of the Union protested in front of a store that belonged to Bufalino, and his men ironized them, telling them that they should bring their husbands too. Then, Matheson, having seen that Bufalino himself was in front of the shop, went straight to his face and said: "I don't need my husband to protect me. I'm twice the man you'll ever be, Russ Bufalino."

Bufalino's Grasp on the Teamsters Union

Nevertheless, the problems given to him by Matheson's determination did not mean that Bufalino's position in relation to labor unions was that bad. In 1946, Bufalino moved his cousin William Bufalino to Detroit, where the latter was appointed as leader of Detroit Teamsters Local 985, which was controlled by Jimmy Hoffa. This fact gave more opportunities to Bufalino and strengthened his position as he came closer to a rising union leader.

Bufalino became increasingly influential in the Teamsters Union during the late 1940s and early 1950s, and that, by the mid-1950s, earned him 5% of every loan friends and collaborators took thanks to the facilitations he was able to offer. His influence in the Union was due in great part to his cousins William Bufalino and Jimmy Hoffa.

However, in 1953, the U.S. House subcommittee with chairman Representative Clare E. Hoffman was formed. The new subcommittee's mission would be to investigate cases of racketeering in Detroit, following the work of the Kefauver Committee and the interest it had brought to the Mafia issue. Soon, the Hoffman Committee managed to discover what was happening in Hoffa's 985 Detroit local, paying attention to the activity of William Bufalino.

The committee's report mentioned that in Detroit, not only the unorganized workers but also the workers who were members of unions, businessmen who were independent, and even sometimes the Federal Government were victims of a "gigantic, wicked conspiracy," which used to extort and accumulate millions of dollars through force, threats, and economic pressure. The report made it clear that the "principal offender and perpetrator of the racketeering, extortion, and gangsterism" was the Local 985 Teamsters Union through its president, William Bufalino.

However, the committee was proven incapable of practically diminishing the Mafia's grasp on the Union. Having Hoffa on his part, Bufalino continued to control the Teamsters Union efficiently and profitably for him. But a tangible effect came through. The FBI, which had for a long questioned and rejected the very existence of the Mafia, was obliged to accept it. The next step was the beginning of the Top Hoodlum Program, ordered by J. Edgar Hoover. The goal of the project was to document in detail the most powerful leaders of organized crime in the United States and their businesses and operations. Many agents participated, following and taking notice of the Mafia bosses' activities. One of the latter was obviously Russell Bufalino.

Bufalino Keeps Rising

From the beginning of the 1950s, Russell Bufalino was undoubtedly a very powerful boss of the Pittston Mafia. Fundamental to his rise had been the fact that he had the opportunity to have as advisors and mentors gangsters like Santo Volpe and Charles Bufalino, his uncle, and above all, Stefano Magaddino. Years before, the former had a durable impact on the Wyoming Valley, using the typical Mafia instruments of murdering and bribing the right people. For his part, Magaddino was always the leader of the Buffalo crime family, where Russell Bufalino had grown up and began his mobster career.

Bufalino was not active only in the Pittston and Scranton area or in New York. He had interests in Philadelphia, too, where Angelo Bruno, a good friend of his, was a big deal in the organized crime world, as his father was the boss of the Philadelphia Mafia. In 1946, his father died, and Angelo Bruno became the new boss, gaining the nickname of "Gentle Don," as his way of doing business was based more on negotiation, even though he regularly used violence. The point is he was more prompt to act diplomatically than his friend Russ, who was also skillful with working in the background but more prone to conflict and violent resolution of issues.

In 1954, the first FBI report on Bufalino was ready in the Philadelphia Top Hoodlum file. According to the report, by the early to mid-1950s, Russell Bufalino had become one of the two most powerful Mafia leaders in Pittston. He was the active boss of the local crime family, while Santo Vole and his uncle Charles Bufalino acted as silent partners. The report mentioned that Bufalino worked as a mechanic in a bottling factory run by Joseph Barbara during World War II, which was located in Binghamton, New York. But by the time of the report, Bufalino reportedly had seven dress factories in the area of Pittston. Also, he controlled the gambling activities in the area, as everybody who was involved in them had to pay him a "cut."

In 1953, Bufalino reportedly controlled around twenty of the dress factories existing in Pittston, directly or through members of the family. Moreover, to enter the garment industry in the region, someone had to come to an agreement with Bufalino, who earned money from the clothes manufactured by producers who had a contract with him. Apart from what is mentioned in the FBI report, we know that Bufalino also owned banks, jewelry shops, hotels, and restaurants. The report talked about Bufalino's contacts and collaborations with other gangsters, like Angelo Bruno. The agents followed him and registered everything. On his trips to New York every week, he stayed more often at the Hotel Forrester and a few times at the Hotel New Yorker and the Hotel Lexington. In Pittston, Bufalino often visited the Imperial Poolroom, while in Scranton, he had an office near the Martz bus terminal.

Also, the report mentioned that Bufalino controlled all gambling in the area. If you wanted to bet on baseball, football, or basketball games, you earned him money. His best friend was William Medico, who was a businessman and owned the Medico Electric Company. But he had also passed from illegal businesses during

Prohibition, operating in the bootlegging sector before turning to be a respectable entrepreneur and respectful toward the law. That explains his close friendship with Bufalino and the fact that Medico was considered a leader in the inner circles of the Northeastern Pennsylvania crime family, which we can now begin to call the Bufalino crime family. There were also suspicions that the real owner of Medico Electric Company was Bufalino himself and that Medico was a facade.

Every Wednesday, Bufalino usually returned to Scranton from New York and had dinner with his wife Carolyn and friends, often in some of his own restaurants. He typically enjoyed red wine, pasta, and chicken or fish. He was also a good cook, as he liked and relaxed by cooking sometimes and eating with friends and collaborators, talking about fun things or business. In New York, he used to go on Monday mornings taking flights from an airport near Scranton, the airport of Avoca, Pennsylvania. Bufalino was also competent with what mattered most, that is, the politicians and the police. He was very attentive to their needs and desires to keep them happy with their lives in the way that was more suitable in every case, from doing favors to passing them money.

Another important characteristic of Russell Bufalino was his friendly attitude toward people who had nothing to do with his criminal activities and businesses. He was kind and respectful, and not surprisingly, he was often seen in a positive way. A telling anecdote they say about this aspect of Bufalino was when one day he saw a man doing work on the roof of his house. It was a scorching summer day, and it was noon, so he told his men to go to the roof and do the work for the man, saving him from the scorching sun.

In 1956, Bufalino, accompanied by his second in command, James Osticco and Medico, traveled to Cuba and stayed there for a month in Havana amidst casinos and dazzling nightclubs. That wasn't his first trip to Cuba, but it was the first that the FBI was watching him. On that occasion to Cuba, Bufalino met Santo Trafficante Jr., with whom he was co-owner of a nightclub called Sans Souci. Trafficante was the boss of the South Florida crime family.

CHAPTER 4

CRIMINAL ENTERPRISES TAKE SHAPE

This chapter examines the Mafia's massive investment in Cuba during the years of Fulgencio Batista, whose policy was to attract investment from solid economic actors from the United States without distinctions between legal and illegal. We will see how it all began after a summit legendary gangster Lucky Luciano called in Havana in 1946 to discuss and organize the entrance of heroin to the American market and how Russell Bufalino was one of the bosses who collaborated closer with Batista, gaining money, while excelled in criminal activities back home, such as loan-sharking and infiltrating labor unions. The Bufalino crime family also had legitimate businesses, but violence and intimidation were essential; that's why the chapter closes by introducing a characteristic gangster, Frank Sheeran.

Cuba Business

By the time the Second World War started, Lucky Luciano was convicted for pandering and put in jail. Though the emergency condition of those bloody days for the world was a bit of great luck for him, the validation of his name, as the need for the American government to control the East Coast docks and also the waterfronts, preventing German agents from causing sabotage, gave Luciano a precious opportunity. He came to an agreement with the authorities, according to which he positioned his men in the area as counter-espionage and counter-sabotage in service of the government. In this way, when the war was over victoriously for the Allies, the New York governor, Thomas E. Dewey, gave Luciano a pardon as a reward for his help.

However, the deal was on under the condition that Luciano would leave the United States. Indeed, he went to Italy and found a way to make his permanence there promising from an organized crime point of view. In Italy, he learned about and understood how profitable the new drug named heroin could be. So, he called for a meeting of all the Mafia families' bosses in Cuba, who gathered in a meeting that had historic proportions for organized crime. Names of powerful Mafia bosses we have seen, like Stefano Magaddino, Frank Costello, and Albert Anastasia, participated in the Havana meeting in 1946. There, Lucky Luciano explained what a great opportunity and immense potential introducing heroin in a huge, new market like the one of the United States would have, and they talked of how the drug flows from Italy to the United States could be organized.

In the background, but rising and growing in status, Russell Bufalino was present at the 1946 Italian-American Mafia summit of Havana, as Magaddino had his lieutenants from Buffalo and Scranton coming with him in Cuba. Bufalino was not a factor in this meeting, which decided the heroin to come to Cuba first and then be transported to the United States. Not a factor, but growing, and also in his first trip to a country that will occupy a crucial role in his future operations as a Mafia boss.

Beginning in the late 1940s and then much more during the 1950s, Bufalino was a close friend of the Cuban dictator and president, Fulgencio Batista. In power essentially from 1933, after a revolt through controlled presidents, the former military sergeant became officially president of Cuba in 1940, winning the elections.

The US government had recognized the new Cuban governments controlled by Batista from 1934, as he was very attentive to securing the favor of the Americans. Not only the politicians and diplomats. Also, the gangsters. During his years as the leader of Cuba, Batista collaborated tightly with organized crime based in the United States, buying and building hotels and casinos on the island, which was becoming a resort for American and European tourists, almost something like a Las Vegas in the middle of the sea, developed in parallel with the actual Las Vegas.

Batista expanded and grew his business even more after he lost the elections of 1944—which was kind of strange and maybe shows that, at that point, he was sincere about wanting to make Cuba a democratic country. Anyway, Batista made the most of his year out of the presidency by often visiting his houses in Florida and New York and mostly making friends.

Obviously, democracy soon became very boring to Batista, who in 1952 preferred to return to power with a coup instead of elections. President Dwight Eisenhower recognized the new Cuban government, which maybe wasn't democratic but was certainly friendly to the United States and American investment. Indeed,

Batista quickly stipulated agreements with many American companies, and with the sector of the economy, he knew even better that of organized crime. The Cuban Las Vegas project gained new momentum as Batista made anything he could to attire investments in hotels and casinos. And he did it. In the next years, almost all big Mafia bosses in the United States invested in Cuban hotels and casinos, like Sans Souci, Plaza, Sevilla-Biltmore, Nacional, and Commodoro. The mastermind of the US crime families' contacts and agreements with Batista was always Lucky Luciano. Their coordinator and representative was one of his close collaborators, the Jewish mobster Meyer Lansky.

We must say that the project seemed to work well. Those choices brought huge amounts of money to Cuba, with many American rich seeing it as a good opportunity to invest. The Cuban economy grew, and some Cubans began to create considerable wealth. First of all, Batista himself got bribes from construction companies that wanted to get deals for work in the country, like highways and airports. Plus, Batista had 10-30% of the casinos' revenues, which offered earnings of more than one million dollars per day to the crime families in the USA. It was a win-win situation, wonderful also for Russell Bufalino.

Bufalino was not just one of the gangsters who did business with Batista in Cuba. He was also a really close friend of the corrupted Cuban president. It's telling that Batista's kids used to take vacations in Northeastern Pennsylvania, guarded and protected by Bufalino.

So, by 1956, Russell Bufalino had amassed a large fortune from his control of the wealth on the island of Cuba, his influence in the Teamsters Union, particularly its Central States pension funds, as well as from his grasp over the garment industry, and numerous other companies in Pennsylvania and New York. Bufalino was also involved in a number of other businesses in both of these states. After John Sciandra died and Bufalino took over as the head of the family in Northeastern Pennsylvania in 1949, he was also recognized as one of the most important Mafia bosses in the United States. Meanwhile, Joseph Barbara still held the reins of the southern tier of New York despite having suffered two heart attacks within one calendar year and being in bad health.

So, by the time he reached his mid-fifties, Bufalino had earned the respect of his peers in the criminal underworld as one of the most powerful criminals in the nation. Nevertheless, very few people outside of organized crime circles knew or heard of him, and those who did have a difficult time comprehending how a crime boss from Northeastern Pennsylvania could wield more authority than a crime leader from New York or Chicago. But this is exactly what he managed to do.

A series of criminal activities executed with precision and efficiency by his crime family, which followed the lead and the example of its quiet, cool, and not cocky boss, brought Bufalino to that elevated position among American organized crime. The most important of them are examined in the following paragraphs.

Loan-Sharking

One of the criminal enterprises the Bufalino crime family was definitely involved with was loan-sharking, which means that they provided loans at very high, usurious text rates. The usual rate they asked for was 20% per week, thus around a 1000% annual rate.

Although the terms of the repayment could vary and consist of sometimes unorthodox arrangements, there is no doubt that this kind of rate was illegal and violated Pennsylvania's laws on loans, a criminal act.

Loan sharks were attracted by desperate people who couldn't provide collateral to obtain a loan from a bank in a legitimate way. Those borrowers had often defaulted and failed to cover earlier debts. They were eager to find a way to get cash quickly, putting themselves in an extremely precarious and dangerous situation, as the Mafia loan sharks didn't hesitate to collect debts in a forceful manner, creating fear and using intimidation, a very useful atmosphere to them. There were many examples of assaults or at least threats against borrowers.

On the other side, sometimes borrowers would resort to loan sharks out of an unfair inability to have access to legitimate loans because they were erroneously characterized as "high risk." Loan sharks, in those cases, appeared as a way out of the deadlock. The problem is that, more often, they proved to be a far worse and more dangerous deadlock than a way out of it.

There were loan sharks and their associates who ended up arrested and convicted after legal recourses by borrowers. However, the Bufalino family was not one of them.

Infiltration Into Labor Unions

It was typical routine for families implicated in organized crime to try to establish friends and relatives of theirs in roles of authority inside labor unions. This way, they had the opportunity to exert leverage and supervision over the functions and finances of the labor unions. To force union the leaders and the members of unions into conceding to the directives of the criminal organizations, the criminal syndicates employed a combination of actions, including menaces and intimidation. In case the union officials stood up to those demands, they could enter at risk of being attacked physically.

Operations of racketeering were carried out by Mafia families using labor unions as their instruments. That kind of operation could be a variety of unlawful things in any precise case, such as loan-sharking, appropriation of union money, and illegal gambling, to name just a few.

The effects labor union infiltration by crime families like the Bufalino one had on labor relations, particular industries, and local economies were wide and heavily influenced local societies, business, and their everyday lives and work.

The infiltration of unions often created good examples of corruption, of course, and also of nepotism inside these institutions. All of that had the unsurprising effect of influencing labor relations in a deeply negative way. Corporations linked in one way or another to organized crime often profited from union contracts, which resulted in treating employees not in a just way. It's obvious that often, the workers' rights and interests, like salaries, job security, and safety in work, were at risk when union officials were more focused on helping criminal organizations profit and expand their influence and reach than on the needs and desires of the unions' members. The Bufalino crime family and other Mafia families often orchestrated strikes, stoppages, or slowdowns of the productions not to promote the interests of the employees but to make employers concede to the family's demands and extortion.

The Bufalino crime family tried to gain economic power over lawful companies by controlling labor unions, using them as leverage instruments. Influence over unions meant influence on legitimate businesses as well, by implication. In order to obtain a direct and easy way to the treasuries of the unions, funds for pensions. It was also a method to extort businessmen, as mentioned, and at the same time to get workers to spend money on gambling or get loans with the huge loan shark interest rates we've seen.

The goal to control labor unions, in the beginning, was achieved mostly by using brutal violence, such as killings and destroying facilities. Over time, the Mafia's operating mode on this issue went from raw violence to a more businesslike, indirect approach, with the use of strikes and slowdowns from the workers or by just threatening the employers that they would have the workers doing them. Of course, violence was not abandoned altogether—intimidation and coercion were always in the game.

Another tactic was the so-called "sweetheart contracts." Union officials were given money illegally to keep the workplace in peace from the labor point of view, keeping the workers calm.

A lot of people who were involved in racketeering of this kind, between labor leaders and management, met prosecution by the federal government, and some were sentenced. With those prosecutions, the state aimed to stop the criminal operations of corruption in the internal labor unions, whose reason for existing should be the protection and promotion of the employees' rights and interests.

The entry of organized crime in labor unions and companies provoked greater costs for the industries impacted by it, as the corrupt practices diminished efficiency and damaged the function of those industries. That was bad news for companies and consumers alike, as it meant lower profits for the former and higher expenses for the latter.

It was also sometimes feasible for criminal organizations to corrupt competition in sectors of the economy where they had control over labor unions or companies by favoring economic actors with whom they collaborated at the expense of others. Moreover, unions and enterprises under organized crime are certainly more prone to illegal and unethical acts themselves, such as exploiting the employees, acting like cartels that fix prices, and manipulating bids for public works.

All those practices probably resulted in the loss of jobs for people. Although this is not a measurable effect, we can consider that organized crime corruption damaged companies or forced them to relocate to other regions, with employment losses. Moreover, the crime families influence over companies, markets, and labor unions comprehensibly canceled or made much more difficult and discouraged companies and corporations that had plans of investing in certain areas and local industries.

And the negative consequences were not strictly economic but also social. Corrupted labor unions with criminal presence, influence, or total control profoundly damaged communities that now lived in an atmosphere of intimidation, fear, and lack of trust. Fascinating as they may seem to many people, those mobsters provoked great problems in human relationships and the cohesion and joy of everyday life of local communities under their violent and bullying supervision or control.

Members of criminal organizations can infiltrate legitimate businesses for various reasons. At times, they could do it to obtain a source of income that will function as a cover for their true criminal professional activities, as well as facilitate money laundering operations.

The appropriation of legal companies by criminal organizations can happen through many different strategies: violence, threats, and seizure of debt to grab the rate of a company. Over time, the criminal organizations expand their grasp and operate in order to impose their monopoly on the sector they put under pressure, expelling in one way or another all the previous actors.

When that finally happened, the criminal organization could use its political connections and alliances to gain protection and tax breaks. Don't forget the cheap and quiet labor power thanks to the crime family's leverage or control on labor unions. Illegal operations in legitimate businesses typically followed, including evading taxes, cheating insurance companies, and false bankrupting, in a chain of lawless and criminal actions.

A very simple example could be that money gained from debts on gambling was an excellent capital for loan-sharking operations. Another example could be that declaring false bankruptcy defrauded creditors, and then assets were hidden and sold in the black market illegally.

Criminal organization members could be owners or co-owners of numerous and very different, and as we've already seen, the Bufalino crime family had its hands on hotels, casinos, the garment industry, restaurants, construction companies, and more.

Extortion

Crime families like the Bufalino one sold so-called protection to businesses, pretending that they would keep their clients safe from possible danger. To do this, they must be paid on a constant basis, of course. And that's where the trick is: if they don't get paid, they will cause themselves the damage they expect to be paid to prevent. It is a genius scheme, as, in fact, they aren't even lying: They indeed protect their "clients" from being harmed by themselves. The same genius strategy could be used in a slightly different way, by demanding money or a profitable attitude and management to offer favorable treatment or take care of issues that the crime family had created or fomented in the first place.

Another method was contacting the owners of companies or properties and demanding that they accept members of the crime family as partners, threatening to use violence or disturb the function of the company if the owner refused. The violence and the threats were headed not only toward the counterpart of the negotiation but also their families, including their children, according to the most noble Mafia traditions. The same peaceful arguments were used to convince owners to sell their properties at lower prices than the actual ones.

Another method to extort people was acquiring sensitive information and then threatening that they would expose uncomfortable or embarrassing facts if the poor victims didn't concede to the demands of the Mafia boss.

Intimidation, blackmail, violence, and threats all aimed to foment fear and panic in order for the victims to succumb psychologically and become subdued subjects to the will of the crime family. On the other hand, the most typical way to deal with politicians and law enforcement in order to avoid their reaction to extortion was to bribe and affect them with any means necessary.

A Characteristic Gangster: The "Irishman"

One could ask oneself what kind of people could be capable of conducting those kinds of activities and actions in a profitable way without remorse. One of the best examples of the essential gangster of that time, who made possible all of the above at the operational everyday level, on the streets of the cities and the towns where the Mafia families put their tentacles, was definitely Frank Sheeran.

During the mid-1900s, when Russell Bufalino was rising to become a powerful Mafia boss in Northeastern Pennsylvania and at the national level, a key figure in the organized crime universe was Frank Sheeran, born Francis Joseph Sheeran in 1920. Known as the "Irishman," Sheeran and his criminal career were connected to Bufalino and thus with the Mafia.

Before that, Sheeran had served in the Army during World War II, where he took part in the Italian Campaign and had the experience of heavy combat. Apart from that, he participated in less honorable situations and, to be more precise, in executions of German prisoners of war, which, of course, violated the Geneva Convention.

All this should not be considered an excuse or explanation for the occupation Sheeran would choose to follow, though. Not only because millions of people have fought in bloody wars, which sometimes crossed the boundaries of international war law, without becoming criminals afterward. But also because Sheeran entered the world of organized crime ten years after the end of the war. It all started in 1955, when "The Irishman" met Russell Bufalino. Sheeran's truck, while he was working as a driver for a food company, was broken, and Bufalino, being the nice guy we saw he was in his non-gangster life, offered to get it fixed. In this case, the new friendship would evolve into doing some business together, first, with Sheeran being Bufalino's driver and delivery boy. Then, with less peaceful activities.

It seems that at the beginning, he started working for organized crime as a bully who intimidated people and smashed things. That's how he was hired by Whispers DiTullio, a mobster who needed somebody to smash the Cadillac Linen Service in Delaware for good and was willing to pay $10,000 for that. Sheeran tried to do the job, but he didn't know that Cadillac Linen Service's owner was Angelo Bruno. The latter's men caught Sheeran before he accomplished his mission and brought him to their boss. And he would be about to have the most serious trouble if it wasn't for Bufalino, who learned what happened and intervened to save him. They made a deal, though. Sheeran had to kill DiTullio. And so he did. As said in his autobiography, this was the first Mafia murder Sheeran committed.

Later, now a full associate of the crime family, Bualino introduced Sheeran to Jimmy Hoffa, the labor union leader of Teamsters International. Also, Hoffa thought that "The Irishman" could be a good friend and mostly a valuable option for carrying out a series of tough missions of intimidation and killing of union members who weren't loyal to him or killing members of competitor unions. Apparently, over time, Hoffa thought that Sheeran was good for other jobs, too, and he appointed him as acting president of Local 326 in Wilmington, Delaware, one of the departments of the Teamsters Union.

Sheeran would be imprisoned in October 1980, convicted for eleven cases of labor racketeering. The sentence was 32 years in jail, and he served 13. Before that, he had been accused or suspected of several murders, like the ones of Robert DeGeorge in 1967, Joe Gallo in 1972, Francis J. Marino in 1976, and Frederick John Gawronski again in 1976.

"The Irishman" died on December 14, 2003, at 83, nine years after the death of Russell Bufalino, his mentor and boss, who introduced him to organized crime half a century before. However, the most crucial chapter in the criminal career of Frank Sheeran was maybe one we haven't talked about yet. That's his role in the murder of Jimmy Hoffa.

CHAPTER 5
LAW ENFORCEMENT'S INVOLVEMENT

This chapter brings us to the biggest gathering of crime bosses in United States history, made in Apalachin in 1957. The arch-gangsters discussed business and the Lucky Luciano family succession. Russell Bufalino was there, and he was one of the bosses who got arrested after the surprise police operation. The event proved the existence of the Mafia and prompted law enforcement to use more sophisticated methods to battle organized crime, such as new technologies of surveillance and witness protection programs. After Apalachin, the FBI paid much more attention to the Bufalino crime family. Bufalino had severe problems with the law, as he was ordered to leave the U.S.

Becoming Nationwide Famous in the Wrong Way: The Apalachin Meeting

On November 14, 1957, Russell Bufalino was at 625 McFall Road in Apalachin, New York. He was anything but alone. Around a hundred other high-ranking gangsters were at the same place for what would go down in history as the Apalachin Meeting, the greatest gathering of the Italian-American Mafia bosses. The place was the house of Joseph Barbara, and the topics of discussion were loan-sharking, trafficking of drugs, illegal gambling, and other Mafia businesses, as well as splitting the activities of Albert Anastasia, who had been murdered a few time ago.

The meeting was at Barbara's residence in Apalachin, but the one who had called that nationwide organized crime conference was Vito Genovese. Genovese's goal was also to make official his assuming the leadership of the Lucky Luciano family after Frank Costello's forced backdown.

Origins of the Apalachin Meeting

That last phrase would need a more detailed explanation. Not only because the particularities of the Apalachin Meeting are interesting per se, but also, and most importantly, because they give us the opportunity to delve deeper into the secrets and mysteries of organized crime in the 20th century United States.

Indeed, this story goes back more than twenty years and includes some of the most famous (or infamous) Italian-American Mafiosi.

It was June 18, 1936, when legendary Mafia boss Lucky Luciano and others were convicted to the devastating sentence of 30-50 years in prison. Almost ten years later, on January 3, 1946, New York state governor Thomas E. Dewey grudgingly mitigated Luciano's sentence on the condition that he not oppose being deported to Italy. This mitigation was a putative reward for Luciano's purported wartime aid to the United States (we'll talk more about that later). Luciano happily took the offer but insisted that he was a citizen of the United States, thus not liable to be deported to Italy or another country. Nevertheless, he had to depart with a ship from the port of Brooklyn on February 10, 1946. That day was the last he ever stood on U.S. soil. After seventeen days, Luciano's ship entered the port of Naples. It was February 28, and he informed the journalists who awaited him upon his arrival that he would most likely live in Sicily.

The next year, 1937, the acting boss of the Luciano crime family, Vito Genovese, after the murder of Ferdinand Boccia and concerned about the possibility of being prosecuted, had to leave the U.S. too, and he went to Italy, taking with him $750,000. He would settle in Nola, near Naples, the hometown of the famous philosopher Giordano Bruno, who was burnt alive for heresy by the Sacred Inquisition of the Catholic Church back in 1600.

The problem was that after Genovese left the States, the Luciano family needed a new acting boss. That would be Frank Costello. The scheme functioned well for some years, but in the mid-1950s, Genovese felt it was time to take back control of the family. His ambition was so big, and perhaps his memory for the reason of Costello's rise so short, that he was determined to hit even against the very powerful ally on which Costello could count: The leader of the Anastasia crime family and firm member of the Commission, Albert Anastasia.

Luckily enough, his intentions found an unlikely ally, as Genovese managed to find a link and join forces with the underboss of the Anastasia crime family, Carlo Gambino. Seeking to become the top dog, Gambino met his opportunity in Genovese's intentions, and they both began planning to take Anastasia out for good. It must be noted, though, that apart from Gambino's goals, according to a theory, Anastasia's violent ways of acting had become frustrating not only for Gambino but also for many Commission members, who sanctioned or gave permission for his assassination, believing that it would be in Mafia's best interest as a whole.

At the beginning of 1957, Genovese felt the pieces were in place to make his move in collaboration with Gambino. He ordered a hitman named Vincent Gigante to kill Costello, and Gigante shot him on May 2, 1957, outside the building where Costello lived. Costello was not killed, and his wound was also not so serious. Nevertheless, this attack, and maybe the swift power he felt that happened, made him think that it would be better if he retired and gave back control of the Luciano family to Genovese. The fact that he wanted to stay out of trouble and that the whole balance of power inside the Mafia world was not in his favor can also be deducted from his refusing to recognize Gigante as the gunman who had shot him when the latter was put on trial. Thanks to Costello's omission, Gigante was free of charges.

Of course, that happened after the conclusion of the Anastasia removal, which was consumed on October 25, 1957. That day, Genovese and Gambino's plan was executed in perfection, as two gunmen with covered faces shot Anastasia to death in the Park Central Hotel barber shop in Manhattan. Genovese had heard that Costello was plotting with Anastasia to regain the Luciano crime family's leadership.

That was the long sequence of Mafia events that led to the infamous Apalachin Meeting, a focal point of organized crime's history in the United States. A few days after Anastasia's murder, seeking legitimation and wanting to secure and stabilize his grasp of the Luciano family, Genovese organized that big meeting, which was also an opportunity for American Cosa Nostra bosses to arrange a series of business staff. The initial idea was that the meeting be held in Chicago. Still, Stefano Magaddino, the powerful New York boss who was also a Commission member and the mentor of Russell Bufalino, insisted the meeting be held nearer to his base and appointed Joseph Barbara and Russell Bufalino to take care of everything. Barbara's estate in Apalachin, New York, along the southern side of the Susquehanna River, should be the perfect place, but it wasn't.

The Apalachin Meeting Fiasco and Its Consequences

On November 14, 1957, over 100 Mafia leaders, advisors, and bodyguards gathered at Barbara's estate in Apalachin. The meeting's goal was, as already explained, double. On the one hand, to discuss regular Cosa Nostra business, thus activities like illegal gambling, casinos, and narcotics deals. There were also garment industry discussions, particularly interesting for Russell Bufalino, as we can imagine.

On the other hand, the second goal was the division of criminal enterprises headed until then by Albert Anastasia, who was just assassinated. Before the Commission authorized his assassination, powerful family bosses and, among them, Bufalino, were concerned about Anastasia's attempts to wrest control of their Havana casino operations. Cuba was also discussed in Apalachin, specifically the island's gambling and drug smuggling activities.

Another essential item on the agenda was the worldwide drug trade. Recently, just before the meeting in Apalachin, some Italian-American Cosa Nostra leaders had visited Palermo, where they met with Sicilian gangsters to talk about the trafficking routes and methods.

Unluckily for the elite of organized crime, law enforcement had come to know about the meeting and the great opportunity to arrest and put charges on such a large number of Mafia bosses. The numerous luxury automobiles with license plates from all over the United States gathered in a quiet Apalachin residence did not help the mob leaders keep the eyes of the police away from them. State and local agency officials stormed the Barbara estate after erecting barricades to the streets in order to cut the way out of the area. With nothing else to do, many bosses ran and tried to hide in the surrounding woods.

Some managed to escape, but the majority, some sixty gangsters, including Russell Bufalino and his underboss James Osticco, were arrested and charged. Twenty of the participants at the gathering were put on trial and found guilty of "conspiring to obstruct justice by lying about the nature of the underworld meeting." They were convicted to three to five years in jail, plus fines of up to $10,000. However, one year later, all the sentences were overthrown in the appeal court.

Even more important than the arrests of so many top organized crime figures was the mere fact of the confirmation that the Mafia existed, that it was not a conspiracy theory but a real criminal organization at the national level, or better, a net of numerous interconnected criminal organizations. That was really crucial, as until the Apalachin meeting, even the director of the FBI, Edgar Hoover, had repeatedly rejected the notion that such a thing existed in the United States, at least officially.

The Bufalino Crime Family Targeted by Law Enforcement

As an immediate reaction to the growing power and involvement of the Bufalino crime family in an extensive range of illegal operations, the authorities got more active in their inquiries and efforts to tear down the criminal organization.

The fruit of this new tendency in law enforcement's acts was that authorities undertook several legal procedures against the crime family's structure.

Particularly from 1957, following the notorious Apalachin meeting that we covered in detail above, the Bufalino crime family became known to the public. The meeting and the intervention of the police were undoubtedly critical points in the evolution of the government's efforts to counter organized crime as law enforcement agents intervened, arresting many bosses. Some of them managed to escape prosecution and charges by making appeals. Nevertheless, this incursion revealed the volume of organized crime and prompted law enforcement to take even more intense action against it as public awareness elevated.

The authorities understood that they had to pay more attention to the Bufalino family, too. Then, they recruited people who could give information on that crime family. Some of those informants came from within the family and became witnesses under police protection. The witnesses gave very useful insights into the organization's system, operations, and leaders.

The law enforcement agents investigated the criminal activities of various Mafia families, including the Bufalino crime family, conducting surveillance, using wiretaps and other methods to collect proof against the organization's components and associates. They aimed to hurt the Bufalino crime family's finances, the point it would hurt the most, and they employed measures to seize the earnings of criminal operations, undermining the family's economic foundations. The authorities utilized financial documents, inspections, and accounting investigations in order to successfully trace the money movements and confiscate patrimonial assets when they had the chance.

Coordinating their efforts, law enforcement was able to comprehend deeply how the Bufalino crime family functioned and, above all, that its activities were not limited to Northeastern Pennsylvania but were nationwide. They also pursued collaboration with various communities that had contact with the family's activities in their local reality to put it smoothly. The local communities indeed often collaborated since the Bufalino effect on them was not the best thing that ever happened to them.

Local communities' cooperation and coordination among the authorities themselves gave fruits, as cases against gangsters were built based on the information gathered.

Techniques to Combat Organized Crime

The techniques used to combat organized crime with greater efficiency were multiple, like the creation of task forces, the use of new technologies, new surveillance methods, witness protection, and collaboration among law enforcement agencies we've already seen.

The task forces were specialized teams that enabled cooperative operations by bringing together the expertise and resources of authorities of different levels, from local to federal. The use of new technological advances like electronic spying and wiretapping made surveillance much more sophisticated and precise, and collecting evidence and clues much more feasible for monitoring suspects and getting to know Mafia family members' moves and plans. When this kind of technology wasn't available, the ability of law enforcement to penetrate criminal organizations was much smaller.

The witness protection programs also played a crucial role in X-ray criminal organizations and put their members behind bars. They encouraged witnesses to talk to the police and kept safe those who did, giving incentives also to members of crime families. Another method law enforcement used to get into Mafia structures and minds was covert informants. They weren't members of the organizations who decided to collaborate with the authorities but agents of law enforcement agencies who infiltrated criminal organizations, offering direct information from within.

All of the above could work better and give positive results if the general public was aware and willing to help law enforcement's efforts to counter organized crime. So, the operational techniques accompanied public awareness projects, with which the authorities encouraged and motivated people to report when they happened to see something suspicious that could be part of a criminal activity. Educating the communities about the Mafia and organized crime, the authorities also hoped to have more people willing to work with the police as informants and undercover agents.

The pressure applied by the authorities, thanks to those techniques, methods, and means, created a much less comfortable situation for organized crime and made the continuation of illegal activities, like the ones of the Bufalino crime family, harder.

Informants and Witnesses

The role of informants and witnesses was crucial in helping law enforcement face the Mafia challenge, as they offered precious inside information on the criminal organizations. Their contributions, which offered knowledge of the operations and internal structure otherwise not accessible, allowed the authorities to raise more solid and founded cases against members and leaders of criminal organizations like the Bufalino crime family.

Doing so was not easy for informants and witnesses since they could endure serious physical dangers and suffer stress and emotional pressure because of their choice to cooperate with the police. Cooperating could expose them or people close to them to retaliation. Informants often lived in a constant sense of threat and risk, fearing they could be discovered and under mental strain because of the continuous secrecy and pretending. On the other hand, witness protection programs were created to respond to the reality of danger and fear faced by witnesses, securing the lives and identities of people who choose to help the police. However, on the other hand, entering such a program could mean cutting oneself off friends and relatives and abandoning one's personal life altogether to begin a new, and at least initially lonely, path. To add to that, in some cases, informants and witnesses did not experience only external threat and danger but also internal struggle, remorse, hesitation, and a sense of guilt because of their decision to cooperate with law enforcement against what until then was their family, friends, and partners.

Nevertheless, there were many valid reasons for a crime family member to become an informant or witness and cooperate with law enforcement. Leaving behind the mobster's way of life and protecting their community from activities they had come to consider damaging and harmful, retaliating for wrongdoings against them, or seeking protection from an already existent threat to their life or those of their loved ones were some of the most important.

And often, their decision was a successful one. It wasn't easy, but the help offered by informants and witnesses was crucial for law enforcement agents to proceed with their investigations and deal with organized crime, dismantling Mafia families by bringing them to the court of law and convicting their leaders and members to be enclosed in jail or reducing the criminal organizations' reach and strength. The programs resulted in success in many cases and helped law enforcement, putting the Bufalino crime family in serious trouble.

Federal Bureau of Investigations Vs. Russell Bufalino

In 1958, after the Apalachin meeting and the arrest the previous year, Bufalino was ordered to leave the United States because he had lied about his citizenship, he had entered the country illegally in 1956 from the Bahamas, and his moral character did not appear to be that good. From that point and for several years on, avoiding deportation became one of the biggest concerns Bufalino had. That's why he hired a lawyer who was a known expert in immigration issues, Jack Wasserman. Wasserman had already managed with success a similar case, that of New Orleans Mafia boss Carlos Marcello. The latter was ordered to leave the country in 1952, initially in Italy. Wasserman delayed the deportation, getting from the Italian courts an injunction that prevented Marcello from going to Italy as he was not an Italian citizen. So, in 1959, they sent Marcello to Guatemala, but Wasserman found a way to make him return to New Orleans.

Bufalino hoped that Wasserman would save him from being deported, too. His case was also easier since it was determined that the whole issue came from a change in Bufalino's place of birth, made by someone in the Luzerne County Clerk Office, who had replaced "Montedoro, Sicily" with "Pittston, Pa." After a series decisions and appeals beginning in April 1958, two years later the U.S. Court of Appeals ordered Bufalino to leave the country, in April 1960. Bufalino and his lawyer filed one more appeal and accused the U.S. Immigration and Naturalization Service of having prejudiced him. That move gave him some time so he could stay in the country until a decision was taken on his appeal.

Since 1961, the new attorney general of the FBI was Robert F. Kennedy, who aimed to destroy organized crime. And he was the brother of the President of the United States, which made things even more complicated for the Mafia bosses. Kennedy did not want to waste any more time. He ordered the FBI agents to surveil every move of the Mafia bosses, each and every one of them, each and every day. Obviously, Bufalino was one of them.

The FBI agents began surveilling Bufalino on a 24-hour basis in March 1961, and the reports arrived at J. Edgar Hoover from the

Philadelphia bureau every Monday, Wednesday, and Friday. They soon had the information according to which Bufalino was sending to Cuba arms. The interesting part is that the informant claimed that Bufalino was collaborating with a secret organization. That secret organization was producing arms and passing them to Cuba. The goal was naturally overthrowing Castro. And the irony is that the "secret organization" the FBI didn't know about was simply the CIA. Or maybe that wasn't the case, and in fact, the FBI played ignorant, as their decision not to investigate further on the information may suggest. In any case, the FBI claimed that the issue was out of its jurisdiction. Instead, according to the FBI's decision, the matter was under the Department of Customs' jurisdiction.

However, the FBI kept surveilling Bufalino's activities and contacts. In Pittston, he used to go often to Club 82. In Scranton, he used to go to Preno's Restaurant, to the Sahara Bar, and to the former Medico Electric Company we have seen earlier, which now was called Medico Industries, and had successfully established a collaboration with the U.S. government, firming several contracts. When in New York, Bufalino used to stay in the Forrester Hotel and visit his Vesuvio restaurant, hanging out with notorious New York mobsters. The FBI agents were a little bit surprised to see that New York gangsters had great respect for Bufalino, something that pointed out his national and not just local status as Mafia boss.

In his travels, Bufalino usually had with him some of his closest associates from Northeastern Pennsylvania, like Anthony Guarnieri, who worked as capo regime in the drug traffic sector of the criminal organization; Casper Giumento, who was like the adjutant of the boss, from driver to payments collector; Al

Baldassari, the director of the gambling sector; James Plumeri, who was close to Bufalino and had a brilliant Mafia resume as he had worked for Lucky Luciano himself back in the 1930s.

Women and Sports

Probably, most readers will find more exciting Bufalino's relationships with attractive women, as he had many girlfriends in various cities while being happily married to his wife, Carrie, since 1928. In the early 1960s, this men's dream (let's be honest here) had taken the likes of Jane Collins, a rich divorced woman whose housemate was a prostitute named Judy McCarthy. Bufalino used to meet Collins in McCarthy's apartment when McCarthy was not in the city.

To tell the truth, at least in this particular case, Bufalino's motives and attraction to Collins were not only romantic. In fact, it was also his difficult financial state that brought him close to the wealthy divorcee after the disaster in Cuba and the continuous need to spend money on attorneys for the matter of his attempted deportation to Italy. Although definitely not poor or broke, Bufalino could use some of the financial prosperity Collins enjoyed as co-owner of the Wyoming Coal Company. Indeed, Collins obviously really liked Bufalino, and she began to pay his bills and bought him a Cadillac as a birthday present. Or she did so because, for her part, she could use some of Bufalino's muscle to spy on her ex-husband as truly happened.

In 1963, Bufalino and Collins separated, and she started a new relationship with another man. Bufalino was mad and tried to win her back, visiting her several times and yelling at her, but to no avail.

The last time he visited her, he talked to her about his deportation battle, and he offered her a New York Yankees-St. Louis Cardinals World Series ticket. Yet, she refused to come with him to New York. Things were way worse than Bufalino could think, as, in fact, Collins had begun to talk to the FBI, which obviously approached her because of her relationship with Bufalino and convinced her to help the immigration department and the law to get the job—that is, to deport Bufalino from the U.S.—done.

However, it could be entertaining to mention the initial approach of Bufalino to Collins. He had a friend call Collins to give her a tip on a horse race, thanks to which Collins bet and won $100. One week later, they gave her another tip, and she won $250. Then, $1000. At this point, Bufalino had to give her the money himself because that was what they used to do in gambling when the earnings were that big.

Sports and gambling were central to Bufalino's entertainment and activities, and he liked boxing particularly, as the FBI agents came to know. During that period, Bufalino also tried to get into the boxing industry by managing boxers and promoting fights. In those activities, Bufalino collaborated with Al Flora, who was a former boxer from Baltimore and also was his occasional bodyguard and driver. Undoubtedly, the most impressive involvement of Bufalino with the boxing and sports industry would come a few years later, in 1965, when he purchased the rights to the closed-circuit broadcast of the second heavyweight championship fight between Cassius Clay (later Mohammed Ali) and Sonny Liston for Washington, D.C.

Bufalino had a wide business circle, yet he kept almost everything in cash and had only a tiny checking account with a few hundred dollars in common with his wife. Maybe this helps to explain how, although he faced financial difficulties, that was never evident when he left Pittston and Scranton and traveled to big cities. The FBI agents noted that when he was in Philadelphia, he used to go out at the Penn Center Social Club with friends. There, he met luxury escorts he paid $600-800 cash each, provided by the choreographer Kay Carlton. He also had another girlfriend in parallel with Collins. Her name was Alberta Stocker, and she was a bartender.

CHAPTER 6

THE TENACITY AND ADAPTABILITY OF THE BUFALINO FAMILY

Russell Bufalino's agonizing efforts to avoid deportation and the struggle for power in the Teamsters union. Frank Fitzsimmons replaced imprisoned Jimmy Hoffa as leader of the Union, and he collaborated in a very profitable way with organized crime, being at the same time close to President Nixon. Thanks to the Union's pension funds, the Mafia had the opportunity to get credit flows and invest massively in the entertainment industry, making Las Vegas the entertainment capital. However, Hoffa was released in 1971 and was determined to get the Teamsters' control back. Bufalino advised him to retire and tried to protect him, but he turned hostile to him after a Time article we'll see. Hoffa mysteriously disappeared in 1975.

The Struggle for the Teamsters' Control

Having arrived in his mid-sixties, by the late 1960s, Russell Bufalino was still fighting against the government, which, on its part, was fighting to kick him out of the United States. In 1967, his attorney, Jack Wasserman, claimed that Bufalino was the victim of illegal wiretapping from the FBI, so the whole process was illegitimate and should be stopped or dismissed. He had added that by deporting his client to Italy, they could send him to his death, as Bufalino's life would be in danger in his country of origin. The Board of Immigration Appeals rejected those claims on June 5, 1967, and denied Bufalino's request, insisting on the deportation decision. Wasserman reacted with another appeal.

This deportation saga was long and, even worse, expensive, as Bufalino had to pay an army of lawyers to face his tough legal wars. That was the case also because the deportation case was not the only one. In 1969, he was indicted and charged for plotting to transport tens of television sets to Pittston from Buffalo. The televisions were color sets and cost $35,000; the problem was that they were stolen. Two more persons were accused with him, members of Stefano Magaddino's crime family. Bufalino had to deal with other charges, too, but he always got clean without severe consequences.

In the same years, Bufalino continued to be very present in criminal and legitimate businesses alike. Apart from his essential Mafia operations like extortion, gambling, prostitution, and loan-sharking, he earned a tribute of 10% from every aspiring entrepreneur in "his" area. And he owned legitimate car junkyards, hotels, and, of course, his dress shops and garment factories. Also, he facilitated many hotel owners in the Pocono Mountains to get loans, which is not clear if it was entirely legal.

But. Perhaps the main sector of the Bufalino crime family's business operations was, by this time, labor racketeering. Bufalino earned money off the loans that were made from the Teamsters Union pensions fund. That was serious business, so Bufalino and the family had to be very careful with Jimmy Hoffa and keep an eye on him.

Jimmy Hoffa had been convicted in 1964 and was finally brought to prison in 1967 at Lewisburg, Pennsylvania. So, in charge of the Teamsters union was now Frank Fitzsimmons, who was previously the chief lieutenant of Hoffa. Fitzsimmons had a different approach from Hoffa in managing the Union, as he was a conciliator and tried to find common grounds satisfying all parties and not confrontational like Hoffa. That means he was also more political and grasped that the Union had to be decentralized as an organization if it wanted to remain influential. Hoffa had maintained a kind of dictatorship in his way of making decisions. Fitzsimmons changed that, giving much more autonomy to local directors of the Union, the regional leaders.

That also brought changes in the way the Union contacted and collaborated with the mob. With Hoffa in charge, the rest of the Union's directors had a secondary role, to say the least. Hoffa himself was in direct contact with Mafia bosses and members and did everything by himself. On the contrary, Fitzsimmons's new decentralized structure collaborated with organized crime at the local levels. He determined that when a Mafia boss wanted a favor or money, he should just talk to the regional representative of the Teamsters union in his area; there was no need to contact the Teamster's national leadership.

Hoffa did not like these new arrangements made by Fitzsimmons. Actually, he was like really mad. However, Fitzsimmons got it right with the ones that mattered the most: the mob bosses. Organized crime leaders, in fact, liked the new direction given by Fitzsimmons, as access to funds would be easier and more direct. Bufalino was one of them. Indeed, thanks to Fitzsimmons's decentralizing reforms, the Teamsters Union began lending money to an unparalleled extent.

A lot of that money went to Las Vegas casinos owned and controlled by the mob, which, after the fall of Cuba to the Communists, concentrated the whole of entertainment investment to Las Vegas—strange twists of history. Without Fidel Castro's Communist revolution and then dictatorship, Havana would have become arguably more Las Vegas than Las Vegas, as it also had the beach. Castro's rise to power and the end of Mafia investment in Cuba brought all that money and investment in the casino industry exclusively toward Las Vegas, creating the entertainment capital of the United States and the world there.

There was one more reason for the Mafia's favor toward Fitzsimmons. That was the fact that he was working on creating links with President Richard Nixon, even though in 1968, the Teamsters Union had officially endorsed Hubert Humphrey, the candidate of the Democratic Party. President Nixon was a pragmatic and realist politician, so he understood that the Teamsters' support would be useful to him. He was open to forgetting their previous political preference and even, most importantly, giving Hoffa a pardon if they backed him up and came to his camp.

Fitzsimmons did not drop the opportunity and fueled Nixon and the attorney general, John Mitchell, with money flows. Under Nixon, Mitchell and the Justice Department focused on other issues. The Mafia investigations and prosecutions faded, and the mob had the chance to grow again fast, without big obstacles.

Nevertheless, on October 7, 1971, after years of appeals and a tactic of delaying deportation, the U.S. Court of Appeals rejected another Bufalino's appeal against his deportation and ordered him to leave the United States and go to Italy immediately. Yet, there was always another appeal in the law world, and Bufalino would, of course, use it together with every other possible option. He was definitely not going to give up.

Two and a half months later, as the 1971 Christmas was coming, and the cities' streets were full of decorations, Santa Clauses, and happy children, Hoffa was released from the Lewisburg jail after almost five years on December 23. President Nixon had reduced his initial sentence, which was thirteen years in prison, because Hoffa had been a model prisoner, and he needed to assist his wife, who meanwhile suffered a heart attack.

Of course, everything couldn't be so idyllic and magical for Hoffa. In order to set up a morally and legally supportable release, the government forbade Hoffa to engage in any kind of labor organization management, direct or indirect, until March 1980. That was more than eight years in the future, and Hoffa, by the end of 1971, was nearly 59 years old. So, the release was almost also a forced retirement. That should be good news to Hoffa, as he had told the parole board that if released, he would spend the rest of his days teaching and playing with his grandchildren. Naturally, that was a lie. Hoffa became furious with Fitzsimmons, as he learned about the forbidden clause of the deal only after he was released.

Hoffa thought that Fitzsimmons and the Teamsters leaders had betrayed him as rats that were devouring that which he himself had created. He was the one that made the Teamsters a national big deal, and now he was cut off in order for Fitzsimmons, the chief rodent, to take charge of the Union. Hoffa thought he was the owner of the Teamsters, the king, and that he had to be its leader for all his life. Also, he thought that without that deal, he would have been released by 1974 for good behavior anyway, and in that case, he could return to office as President of the Union in 1976. It was clear to him that Fitzsimmons made that deal only to neutralize him and grab the Teamsters' presidency. The fact that they kept the forbidding clause secret from him until he was released perhaps proves that his accusations toward Fitzsimmons weren't wrong or entirely wrong.

Fitzsimmons had grown strong on his own during the years Hoffa was imprisoned. He had also established a really close relationship with President Nixon, and that gave him all the momentum and power he could wish for. He did not want to be seen as the temporary replacement of Hoffa anymore, but become the official President of the Teamsters Union. Indeed, supported by the President, who even surprisingly visited the Teamsters 1971 convention in Fitzsimmons's support, Fitzsimmons won the Union's election. Then, in 1972, he repaid the favor by supporting Nixon's reelection with all the might the Teamsters could have. The partnership between the President and the labor union became even stronger, and Fitzsimmons's post and leadership were secure and consolidated even more.

Yet, Hoffa would not bow down so easily. He contacted Bufalino and told him that he had the intention to hit back at Fitzsimmons and get revenge for what he felt was his overthrowing from the leadership of the Teamsters. He was determined to get the Union back and become its President once more. But Hoffa's time has passed. Nobody needed him anymore, as Fitzsimmons, with his reforms and his friendship with the President of the United States, was a hell of a better option for being the leader of the big labor union instead of the ex-convict Hoffa, who was much tighter in the management of the Union's finances, and at this point couldn't even dream of being a close friend to the U.S. President either.

Bufalino was so happy to suck off the pension funds thanks to Fitzsimmons policies, so he responded to Hoffa that instead of planning his revenge and return to power, he should better take the $1.7 million of his Teamster pension and truly do what he had said to the judges that he was going to do if released by prison: play with his grandchildren and teach them for the rest of his life. It was a closed case. Bufalino had already years ago taken his cousin William away from Hoffa, as there was no business future there. He understood Hoffa's anger, but things were as they were, and everybody was winning with the new situation. Hoffa was not in a bad position, frankly. He could just take the money and have fun, free, away from stressful situations.

The problem for Russell Bufalino was definitely something entirely different: his deportation proceedings. His group of lawyers, guided by Wasseman, argued the last appeal Bufalino had the right to do on November 27, 1972. The decision of the Board of Immigration Appeals was again the same as on January 30, 1973, when it ordered him definitively to leave the United States. The judges added that his attorney had been in charge of the techniques that had kept the petitioner in the United States, although he purposefully and fraudulently claimed U.S. citizenship.

Yet, team Bufalino had another secret weapon. A suitcase containing one million dollars was sent to Italy, and perhaps it helped the Italian authorities to determine that Russell Bufalino had such a bad character that Italy couldn't accept him in the country. That decision made the U.S. court decision inapplicable, and Bufalino stayed in the United States.

Meanwhile, on July 16, 1972, Tommy Eboli, the boss of the Genovese family after Vito Genovese's death three years before, was shot to death while walking to get into his car on a street in Brooklyn. The Eboli assassination left the leadership of the Genovese family vacant, and Bufalino took control of this crime family, at least until the Commission came up with an official successor.

By the mid-1970s, Bufalino was more powerful than ever. In his 70s but still perfectly active, he had more power than even the FBI could imagine for a gangster who lived in the Scranton suburbs and wasn't a member of the Commission. The Bufalino crime family in Northeastern Pennsylvania had, by that time, more than fifty members and was ever-growing. But there was much more for him.

First, he had control of the Genovese family, and through this, he was in constant contact with the other four Mafia New York families. Then, in July 1974, Stefano Magaddino died at age eighty-two after a heart attack. With his mentor gone, who was also a member of the Commission and boss of his crime family in upstate New York for more than half a century, only Bufalino himself could maintain the Magaddino family united and secure their interests in Buffalo and in other regions.

In this way, Bufalino was essentially the boss of three Mafia families. His own in Pennsylvania, the Magaddino family in Buffalo, and the Genovese family in New York. A real crime empire that made him even stronger and bigger than other bosses and law enforcement agents could think. Bufalino liked that. He had no interest in becoming a bombastic capo, a leading member of the Commission. He preferred the role of the powerful man behind the scenes.

However, if someone thought that Bufalino's problems were over and he could finally enjoy his wealth and power, they would be completely wrong.

Hoffa Goes Out of Control

In April 1973, Jimmy Hoffa went public about his intention to get control of the Teamsters union back while he was at a banquet in Washington, D.C. He had already talked about that on other occasions in closed circles of supporters, like during the dinner for his 60th birthday in New Jersey at the Latin Casino in Cherry Hill. Old buddy Russell Bufalino was there, but Fitzsimmons was not, saying he already had another commitment.

By the spring of 1973, it was more than a year after Hoffa's release, and he had done everything he could to convince others about his social goodwill. Also, he vigorously supported Richard Nixon for the presidency, aligned with the position of the Teamsters. With all that, Hoffa hoped that he could challenge and remove the ban that forbade him to run for the Union's presidency or any other office.

He claimed that the secret clause in the deal for the President's pardon and his release was unconstitutional; the President didn't have the authority to put such clauses in order to give his pardon. Also, Hoffa suggested that the clause could have violated his right to freedom of speech, protected by the First Amendment, and he argued that it wasn't included in the sentence that had condemned him to prison in the first place.

In the same period, Hoffa played a strong card in obtaining an affidavit from John Mitchell, the attorney general and now director of the Committee to Reelect the President. A suitcase with around $300,000 delivered to Mitchell by Frank Sheeran obviously helped in that. After the delivery, Mitchell stated that Nixon had nothing to do with the clause that included the aforementioned restrictions for Hoffa and that no one in the Justice Department had initiated or suggested them as a term for the President's pardon of Hoffa.

A few months later, in February 1974, Hoffa began an all-out attack. Feeling again in shape and confident that he would have the permission to run for the Teamsters presidency, he said openly that Fitzsimmons was not the right leader for the Union. In March, he prepared his lawsuit arguing that since President Nixon and Attorney General Mitchell hadn't imposed the restrictions, as the affidavit stated, they were invalid because nobody else except for the two had the authority to impose them. Hoffa also declared that the restrictions clause had been kept secret by him and that if he had known, he would have disagreed. Nevertheless, in July 1974, a Washington D.C. federal judge rejected Hoffa's lawsuit on the grounds that the President had signed the pardon with the restrictions clause, so the restrictions couldn't be invalid. Hoffa naturally made an appeal.

After Nixon's resignation, in the autumn of 1974, Hoffa made the statement that after he won the election for the Teamsters residence in 1976, he would call in pension loans given by Fitzsimmons. That would be his revenge against his former friend and associate.

Many Mafia bosses were concerned and nervous to hear the news, as those loans were used for the construction of casinos in Las Vegas, and members of several crime families had majority interests in those casino projects. One of the bosses who was concerned about Hoffa's intentions was Bufalino. So, he told Sheeran to arrange a meeting between himself and Hoffa at the bar restaurant Broadway Eddie's in Philadelphia. Apart from him, Angelo Bruno would be there.

During the dinner, Bufalino told Hoffa that it would be better if he abandoned his plans to run again for the presidency of the Teamsters Union. However, Hoffa responded that he was determined to be a candidate, as he strongly desired revenge against Fitzsimmons, kicking him out of the Teamsters' leadership. We have seen earlier in the book that Bufalino used to make his point only once and then to hear the response from the other part, considering it final. In this particular case, he insisted, arguing for a second time that it would be better for everyone if Hoffa changed his decision and forgot about running for the Teamsters presidency. Hoffa did not accept Bufalino's suggestion.

In the following period, Bufalino, through Sheeran, tried his best to convince Hoffa to change his mind and then to protect him from the not-so-friendly intentions of many people in the mob, like Tony Provenzano, who hated Hoffa because of their previous beef. Bufalino had known Hoffa for thirty years and had collaborated profitably with him for a long time, and he believed that he was honest. He rejected the notions about Hoffa cooperating with law enforcement that some people, even during the Teamsters convention in April 1975, were spreading. Bufalino stood against these kinds of rumors and accusations. Nevertheless, Hoffa's position became always more precarious and dangerous, as gradually more mobsters considered him a pain in the ass, to say the least, or an all-out enemy to be eliminated without any more time wasting.

Time Magazine Convinces Bufalino He Has Had Enough

Bufalino changed his mind about Hoffa after, on June 9, 1975, Time magazine published an article in which Bufalino, along with James Plumeri and Salvatore Granello, were mentioned as cooperating with the CIA in 1961 as spies in Cuba, in preparation for the Bay of Pigs failed operation.

Bufalino and the others were mentioned literally as "Mafiosi," and Bufalino was pointed out as the mob boss in Scranton, while Plumeri and Granello as lesser fry. The article wrote that the three mobsters had left Cuba $450,000 and that they wanted Castro to be overthrown in order to get the money back and also return to profit from their Havana businesses that's why they had cooperated with the CIA to no avail.

That was too much for Bufalino, who had always been very careful in remaining away from the public eyes and was committed to playing behind the scenes. It was obvious to him that the source of the information given to the Time was Hoffa.

On the evening of July 30, Jimmy Hoffa went missing. Two hundred FBI agents would participate in the investigations of his disappearance. That afternoon, he was supposed to have a meeting with Tony Provenzano and another known mobster, Tony Giacalone, from Detroit. They were supposed to eat together near Bloomfield Township at the Machus Red Fox Restaurant. The 1974 Pontiac Grand DeVille of Hoffa, color green, was indeed there. But nobody knew anything about its owner. Provenzano and Giacalone denied that they had an appointment with Hoffa, claiming alibis.

The FBI formed a list in which Provenzano, Sheeran, and Bufalino were the most important suspects. Other names involved in the investigations were Charles O'Brien, who used to call himself Hoffa's foster son, and Salvatore "Sally Bugs" Briguglio, who was a business agent of the Teamsters in Detroit. And more. The FBI agents were certain that around 2:30 p.m. on July 30, Hoffa had entered a car with O'Brien, Briguglio, and others at that precise location. What happened next remained a mystery, and it would be so for almost 30 years, as we shall see in the next chapter.

Back in 1975, the authorities continued to press hard against Bufalino, trying to find evidence of his involvement in Hoffa's disappearance and, as the FBI agents believed, murder. Bufalino was called to testify in front of a grand jury in December of that year, just like the other names mentioned above and more. William Bufalino, their lawyer, told them to take the Fifth Amendment, that is, the right not to respond because they could say something that would incriminate them. So, nobody answered anything.

But the pressure continued, and in June 1976, New York law enforcement investigators called him to the Consulate Hotel in New York and interviewed him on his shops and plants in the garment industry, which were much less than in the past. Bufalino now was owner or co-owner in only six of them, instead of the tens he once had. The investigators had found a not-so-clear connection of Bufalino to Fair Frox Inc., which was on Fifth Avenue in New York. He responded that from 1972 onward, he was employed at Fair Frox and got a regular paycheck. In fact, there wasn't much to tell about Bufalino's garment business, and it was obvious to him that the whole investigation and interview were part of a plan orchestrated by the FBI to put more psychological pressure on him and break him in order to make him talk about the Hoffa case. Similar tactics were probably followed with other suspects as well.

CHAPTER 7
THE BUFALINO FAMILY IN INTRIGUING AND MYSTERY STORIES OF NATIONAL INTEREST (AND BEYOND)

We delve into the fascinating making of "The Godfather" and the real Mafia's role in this, especially how Russell Bufalino stopped the initial protests and supported the production, actively helping Marlon Brando interpret his classic family boss role under Francis Ford Coppola's direction. Second, we discuss the mystery of Jimmy Hoffa's disappearance, which was solved almost thirty years later. Last but not least, a brief look at the ultimate Mafia conspiracy theory: Frank Sheeran's notion that Bufalino was involved in the assassination of John F. Kennedy.

Russell Bufalino And *The Godfather*

While Russell Bufalino was locked in his battle with the government concerning his deportation from the United States, in 1969, Mario Puzo's "The Godfather" was published and had enormous success. The novel, which talked about a fictional Italian-American crime boss from Sicily named Vito Corleone, became a New York Times bestseller and stayed on the book list for sixty-seven straight weeks. Right away, Paramount Pictures started working to make a movie based on the novel with Francis Ford Coppola as director and Marlon Brando in the first role as Vito Corleone.

Of course, we all know this is a classic film, as well as its two sequels. And we can't even imagine the Mafia and that historical era of organized crime in the United States without bringing into mind the magical touch of Coppolla, Marlon Brando's (and Al Pacino's, and Robert De Niro's) brilliant performance, and Nino Rota's evocative music. But the first reaction of the Italian-American community and of the real Mafia toward Puzo's novel and the possibility of a movie based on it entering the 1970s was not so positive.

On the contrary, it was quickly formed the Italian-American Civil Rights League which accused the FBI of being discriminatory against Italian Americans. In June 1970, it rallied more than 100,000 people to protest in New York. Feeling that the film would be yet another chapter in the literature's and cinema's tendency to present the Italians in a negative and repulsive way, many Italian-Americans joined the league, which soon came to have branches in several cities. The founder and leader of the league was Joe Colombo, the boss of the New York Colombo crime family.

Soon, another rally was organized in New York at the Madison Square Garden, and Colombo claimed that the league would use the link with the Teamsters union to cancel the production of the film.

Also, Frank Sinatra was not happy with the novel and the movie's production. Probably, you'll remember the Johnny Fontaine character in "The Godfather," the famous singer loved by many girls, who was connected with the Corleone crime family and gained fame and wealth thanks to the family's promotion and support. Well, that character was inspired by Sinatra and his close relationship with Sam Giancana, the crime boss of Chicago. The famous singer did not like the prospect of a film and tried to cancel the production any way he could.

Colombo got something to go. The word "Mafia" was removed after he requested so, and then after he reviewed the script, he changed his mind and position toward the movie. The protests faded away. Russell Bufalino had very much something to do with it, as together with other Mafia bosses, they ordered the turmoil to stop and Colombo to make peace with the producers.

The bosses and, most of all, Bufalino saw that, in fact, the movie was not that defamatory for the Italians, but it could be seen as an immigrant Italian success story in the United States. The violent and gangster-like elements were secondary; the primary effect of the film would be the presentation of a family with humble immigrant origins that managed to become wealthy and powerful in America.

Coppola's version of "The Godfather" was not a vulgar film about the blind and brutal violence of ugly Italians who terrorized society and oppressed their families but a high-quality drama to be put among the great tragedies of theatrical and cinematographic history. Also, the Corleone family was not a gang of thieves and murderers but more of a corporation that sold entertainment, corrupting politicians and law enforcement agents just as part of the business. When Bufalino was informed about what that young director from Detroit named Coppola was working on, he was excited. He assumed an extremely positive attitude toward the production of the film.

The film gave for the first time a deeper view of what the Italian Mafia was, pointing out that that kind of organized crime corresponded with a form of social organization and rules. Of course, it was a primitive and underdeveloped social form with a lot of violence, something like a relic of past centuries that somehow had survived in the modern extended societies organized on the rule of law and not the rule of family blood and paternal hierarchy. Yet, that view gave back to the Mafiosi their humanity, and intelligent mob bosses like Bufalino understood that.

Bufalino's interest and support made him a factor in the production itself and, precisely, the casting. He was the one who promoted Al Lattieri for the role of Virgil "the Turk" Sollozzo, the crime boss who tries to have Vito Corleone assassinated in the film. Lettieri was a real gangster. He was associated with Tommy and Patsy Eboli, the two acting leaders of the Genovese crime family during the 1960s when Vito Genovese was in jail after the Apalachin fiasco; they became official bosses after Genovese died in 1969. Lettieri worked for his Eboli "uncles," and he also became an actor, playing in a television movie in 1964. Bufalino promoted him to a role in The Godfather, and Lettieri invited and hosted Marlon Brando, Al Pacino, and James Caan to the house of Patsy Eboli in Fort Lee, New Jersey. Later, Patsy Eboli himself helped the production as an advisor on the set near Coppola.

Lattieri, Eboli, and Bufalino were not the only real gangsters who were involved in the making of The Godfather. One of them, Lenny Montana, is Luca Brasi in the movie, a very brief but emblematic role.

Russell Bufalino visited the set several times, and he hung out particularly with Marlon Brando, also in his trailer in Little Italy in Manhattan. It was a rough time for him, as he was battling against his deportation, and we can imagine that The Godfather was a comfort for him. On the other hand, Marlon Brando had the chance to get many takeaways from a Mafia boss's thinking and acting, which helped him pull away his iconic performance, which gave him the Oscar for Best Actor, while the film won the Best Picture award. Marlon Brando's performance was inspired by Russell Bufalino's style, at least to a certain extent, a charismatic imitation of him. So, if someone wants to see Russell Bufalino in action, they can watch The Godfather again—just keep in mind that Marlon Brando was way more handsome.

There is another Bufalino-related story in the making of The Godfather. Coppola had chosen the singer Vic Damone for the role of Johnny Fontaine, but the singer Al Martino really wanted it. He tried so hard to get it that he organized a big party with showgirls and booze in Las Vegas, on which he spent approximately $25,000, where he invited Coppola and his collaborators in the production. Martino's partying attempt to get his hands on the role failed miserably, but he had another card in his pocket. He was connected to the real Mafia, and Bufalino was his godfather. Martino begged Bufalino to help him, and a few days later, Damone coincidentally quit the role, and Martino finally got it.

This story is ironic as Johnny Fountaine does exactly the same thing in the movie, asking his godfather, Vito Corleone, to convince a film producer to pick him for a movie. Fortunately, in the real story, the director was left out of that, and there was no cut horse head, at least as far as we know.

The Truth About Jimmy Hoffa's Disappearance

Jimmy Hoffa's disappearance and presumed death in 1975 were destined to be clarified only nearly thirty years later when, before dying, Frank Sheeran finally confessed that he had indeed killed Hoffa so many years before, as the FBI had always suspected. Sheeran made the confession when he was 83 years old to the author Charles Brandt, who wrote his biography titled "I Heard You Paint Houses," published in 2004, the year after Sheeran's death. The other suspects, who were thought to have collaborated with the murder, were Russell Bufalino, Tony Provenzano, Sally Briguglio, Anthony Giancala, and Steve and Tom Andretta. Law enforcement was right but always lacked evidence.

According to Sheeran's story, after Bufalino decided that Hoffa had to die joining his fellow gangsters on this matter, withdrawing his support for Hoffa because of the Time article we talked about, he put up a plan. On August 1, 1975, while Russell Bufalino and Frank Sheeran were in the latter's black Lincoln driving to Detroit for the wedding of Bill Bufalino's daughter, they stopped near Lake Erie in Port Clinton, Ohio, around a hundred miles from the city. They left their wives there at a diner for a break, saying that they had a job to take care of and they would return later to continue the trip. That didn't feel strange because Bufalino used to make similar stops and jump to quick works.

Then Bufalino and Sheeran drove to a small airport that had an airstrip with grass. Sheeran took a single-engine airplane that awaited him and flew to Detroit. Sheeran arrived at an airfield north of Detroit named Pontiac, and there he took a car that was left there for him with the keys under the mat, a gray Ford, and he went to a house in the city. There, he met Sally Briguglio and the two Andretta brothers, and Chuckie O'Brien was on his way to get there, too. Jimmy Hoffa raised the latter, and that would be his only role in the plan, making Hoffa feel comfortable and safe. O'Brien didn't know that the meeting with Hoffa would end with the death of him. Also, Sheeran would make Hoffa feel comfortable and safe.

After O'Brien arrived, he, Sheeran, and Briguglio left with a maroon Mercury car, and they went to meet Hoffa at a restaurant, where he reacted with anger as he waited for Provenzano and Giacalone for hours. O'Brien introduced him to Briguglio, and Briguglio told him that he was there with Provenzano. Then, Hoffa saw that Sheeran was also there, still inside the car. Sheeran told him he was with his "friend," meaning Bufalino, and explained that they were late because of some delays.

Hoffa indeed felt calmer because of O'Brien and Sheeran's presence, and he agreed to get into the car, dropping his guard. Soon, they were back at the brick house. O'Brien and Briguglio remained in the car and drove away. Sheeran was the only one who accompanied Hoffa to the house, where Hoffa expected to see Provenzano, Giacalone, and Bufalino. But there was neither of them. After they walked up the stairs and entered the house, Hoffa realized that the house was totally empty. Knowing what that meant, he tried to get out the fastest he could. But Sheeran was well prepared for the moment and an expert in those kinds of situations. His gun was already loaded, and he shot Hoffa in the back of the head two times before he could reach the door and get out.

Sheeran left with the gray Ford and returned directly to the Pontiac airstrip, where the pilot was waiting for him, and he boarded the same single-engine aircraft. After an hour, he was back to the airport of Port Clinton. He caught up with Bufalino, who was waiting for him in the car, and they returned to the diner to pick up their wives. Then, they finally drove to Detroit and went to Bill Bufalino's daughter's wedding.

Bufalino later said to Sheeran that the Andretta brothers had cleaned the house of Hoffa's body and blood and took his body to an incinerator. Hoffa's body was never found for the simple reason that it didn't exist, as it was cremated that same day.

Hoffa's murder is a cruel and raw example of the coldness and precision those gangsters used to act, capable of organizing a similar sequence of actions in the middle of a happy road trip to a wedding without anyone noticing anything strange.

Related to JFK's Assassination?

Closing this chapter with the most intriguing and mysterious stories of the Bufalino crime family on a national level and beyond, it's time to reveal that the most shocking information by the time the FBI was investigating Bufalino was not included in Chapter 5, where we saw in detail the battle between law enforcement and the Bufalino crime family during the 1960s. Instead, it is definitely one that relates to JFK's assassination.

The FBI came to know in September 1963, around two months before the shooting in Dallas that shocked the world, that Bufalino had some contacts with a person who was in Mexico, initially in Guadalajara. Later, in November 1963, he received many phone calls from Mexico City. The FBI didn't know, though, that in parallel, Jimmy Hoffa called Frank Sheeran, telling him to visit Bufalino at his house in Kingston, Pennsylvania.

Bufalino guided him to visit their Brooklyn pals, pick up a box there, and transport personally with his car to Baltimore. The Brooklyn pals were Genovese Mafia family members. Among them was Tony Provenzano, a captain of the family, who was also a Hoffa's colleague, as he managed a Teamster local in New Jersey.

When Sheeran got to Brooklyn and met him, Provenzano gave him a bag and told him to go to Baltimore and meet a pilot there. Sheeran never checked what the bag had inside, but he knew how guns in a bag felt, as he had earlier transported guns on other occasions. He was sure that inside the bag were three rifles.

Sheeran went to Baltimore, gave the package, and immediately returned to Pennsylvania. President John F. Kennedy was killed only a few days after that. Yes, Sheeran believed that the guns he carried in Baltimore were, for sure, used to shoot the president.

Sheeran added that a week after the president was killed, he visited Bufalino at the Vesuvio restaurant, and the Mafia boss was delighted.

CHAPTER 8

THE DISINTEGRATION

In the book's closing chapter, we'll see how, in the late 1970s, law enforcement found a way to successfully bring Mafia bosses like Tony Provenzano and Russell Bufalino to the court of law and in prison. Many members of the Bufalino crime family were imprisoned or died in the following years. In 1989, Bufalino suffered a stroke. Control of the Bufalino family passed to Billy D'Elia, who tried to expand its activities and territorial presence. We'll follow D'Elia's attempts after Bufalino's death and the final disintegration of the Bufalino crime family.

The Strange End of an Era

When, in August 1976, Johnny Roselli was found dead with evident signs of torture in a drum in a Miami bay, it was clear that the Church Committee could not complete its report on the relationship between organized crime and the CIA. It was the third murder of a person who testified to the committee after those of Giancana and—according to the committee—Hoffa. The committee delivered its report as it was by then.

In parallel, the investigations into Hoffa's disappearance could not bear fruit. The evidence was not enough to bring someone to the court of law, and as we saw, it would take nearly thirty years before the truth came out after the confession of near-death Frank Sheeran. There is always another solution, though, as we know since the famous Al Capone case. If the government can't catch the outlaws for their major criminal activities, the government can always hope to find a weak point in other criminal activities it chases them for.

In the case of Tony Provenzano, the boss of the Genovese family and a Teamsters union leader for years, that weak point the law enforcement was able to find was the murder of an official of the Teamsters back in 1961. So, Provenzano went to trial and was convicted in prison in 1978. Sheeran was first indicted in 1980 on two murders and a series of other cases, but he was found innocent, and he finally was convicted in 1981 in thirty-two years in prison for labor racketeering. On his part, Giacalone was found guilty of income tax fraud and convicted to ten years in prison. In the case of Briguglio, in the end, the authorities did not have to prove their suspicions that he was involved in the 1961 murder that condemned Provenzano, as someone shot him to death in March 1978 in New York.

Russell Bufalino Finally in Jail

For Russell Bufalino, the case the law enforcement managed to use to finally lock him in jail was the strangest of all. It all began when Jack Napoli, a bartender from Brooklyn, used Bufalino's name to come in contact with a jewelry dealer who had some stolen diamonds. Then Napoli paid $25,000 to buy the diamonds but with a bounced check. When Bufalino came to know that a bartender had used his name to buy stolen diamonds he didn't even have the money for, Bufalino went mad.

Napoli understood that he was in trouble with what he had done, and he immediately went to the FBI, asking for protection. The FBI agents did not lose the opportunity and told him he could help them a lot if he accepted to be wiretapped during his meeting with Bufalino, that they knew it was about to come. Indeed, the old don was furious and called Napoli to his Vesuvio restaurant to explain himself and order him to give back the diamonds, or else he was going to kill him with his own hands. Bufalino told Napoli: "I'm going to kill you, cocksucker, and I'm going to do it myself, and I'm going to jail just for you."

Bufalino was famous for his cool temper, never losing control and talking too much, and that was a factor in his success as a Mafia boss. But at that time, he was extremely angry with Napoli for using his name in that way, and he was for once caught off guard by law enforcement, as they had everything on tape.

In this way, on October 27, 1976, FBI agents arrested Bufalino at his home in Kingston and took him to a preliminary hearing in Wilkes-Barre. He was released after he paid a $50,000 bond, and that was just the beginning. The only solution for Bufalino was for Napoli to be killed and, thus, not to testify.

In September 1976, Bufalino was at the Rainbow Room in Manhattan just after he had attended Frank Sinatra's sold-out concert at the Westchester Premier Theater, the second after the one in April. The Westchester Premier Theater was a successful hall that earned hundreds of thousands of dollars for its owners. Still, it was under federal investigation, as it was owned by two New York gangsters, Gregory DePalma and Richard Fusco, and a securities salesman named Eliot Weisman. It was opened a year earlier with a concert by Diana Ross. Also, Carlo Gambino, boss of one of the New York Mafia families, had offered financial help for this luxury facility to open, with a 10% interest rate. Not surprisingly, mobsters from all over the United States were there for the Sinatra concert that night. One of them was Jimmy "the Weasel" Frattiano, who at the time was acting boss of the Los Angeles mob.

Frattiano had participated in ten murders in his criminal career, and in 1977, he would be charged with the murder of a union official named Danny Green. Green was killed in Cleveland with a bomb under his car, and Frattiano was the one who had introduced to the Cleveland mob the hitman that killed Green. Frattiano agreed to enter the Witness Protection Program and cooperate with the police as an informant under the term that he would serve no more than five years in prison; in fact, he would serve just twenty-one months. As a protected witness, Frattiano mentioned to the agents that Russell Bufalino planned to kill Jack Napoli.

After the Sinatra concert, Frattiano met Bufalino at the Rainbow Room in Manhattan, and Bufalino spoke to him in confidence about the grand jury that was investigating him. Bufalino told Frattiano that he needed to take out someone, i.e., Napoli, who was about to testify against him. The reason why Bufalino chose Frattiano to talk for the job is impressive. Thanks to the amazing connections he had in the government, Bufalino knew that Napoli was under FBI protection as the owner of a pork store in Walnut Creek, California. Walnut Creek was near the home of Frattiano in

San Francisco. Frattiano was the best person to help with that problem.

Bufalino and Frattiano talked for around twenty minutes at the Rainbow Room, and they gave an appointment for two days later at the Vesuvio restaurant. There was also Mike Rizzitello, another prominent member of the Los Angeles crime family. Frattiano agreed to do the job for Bufalino, and after he returned to San Francisco, he began looking for Napoli at Walnut Creek. But Napoli was nowhere to be found.

In May 1977, Frattiano went again to New York for a Frank Sinatra concert at the Westchester Premier Theater. After the concert, he went again to the Vesuvio restaurant in Manhattan with Rizzitello to see Bufalino. Frattiano told Bufalino that he couldn't find Napoli, and the latter responded that, obviously, Napoli had left town, so he had to find another way to get to him and take him out. In fact, nobody knew where Napoli was at the time since he had fled from Walnut Creek owing $3,000 to Wells Fargo Bank.

Later that year, Frattiano was arrested on the murder of Danny Green and many other charges, as already mentioned, and he agreed to cooperate with the FBI to reduce his sentence. Frattiano testified that Bufalino had asked him to kill Napoli, and on October 21, 1977, Bufalino was convicted to four years in jail. Ironically, it was his attempt to prevent Napoli from testifying that provoked the testimony that incriminated him through Frattiano.

Bufalino appealed, but the appeal was rejected. He stayed for six weeks at the Metropolitan Correctional Center in New York in August and September 1978, and the federal judge Morris Lasker gave him permission to celebrate the anniversary of his wedding, which was the 50th, in Pennsylvania. When he returned to New York after this furlough, initially, they sent him to the federal prison in Springfield, Missouri. Then, Bufalino was finally transferred to the Federal Institution at Danbury, Connecticut.

In that medium-security prison, Bufalino had a quite calm permanence, and he liked to play cards, to be more specific, pinochle. At the same time, he continued to supervise his crime family and his businesses. Everything had been discussed at the party for his wedding anniversary at his hotel at Howard Johnson. There were mobsters from Northeastern Pennsylvania, New York, Philadelphia, Buffalo, and other places, and apart from drinking and having fun, they talked about business, and it was determined that Bufalino would continue to be the head of his family even from inside prison, with Edward Sciandra, James Osticco, and Billy D'Elia acting like underbosses following his orders.

Bufalino was released on May 8, 1981, but not for long. Soon, he was put again on trial, where he was convicted to fifteen more years in prison, as the prosecutor Nathanial Akerman received from the judge permission to play the wiretap with Bufalino's death threat to Jack Napoli, and before the trial, the Pennsylvania Crime Commission published its report titled "A Decade of Organized Crime." During the previous years, Bufalino had also tried to get one of the other prisoners, Steven Fox, to find and kill Napoli after he was released from jail with parole. The evidence against Bufalino was now too much. Bufalino was out of the game and inside prison for good.

The Bufalino crime family members didn't know that in those years, the FBI had opened a special investigation named "Full-Time Surveillance of Members of the Russell A. Bufalino Family," commonly called RABFAM. Osticco was soon to be imprisoned as well, as he was sentenced to eight years in jail for fixing the trial of Louis DeNaples back in 1977. In July 1983, he was also charged, together with Casper Giumento, for having supplied dynamite to Frank Sheeran. Osticco would die in 1990 after he was released because of bad health two years earlier. On his part, consigliere Edward Sciandra was sentenced to two eighteen months in prison for not reporting income tax.

So, as the FBI noted during the 1980s, D'Elia became the undisputed leader of the Bufalino crime family, the one Russell Bufalino used to send his orders more often. In 1989, his close collaborator during those years, capo Anthony Guarnieri, was also sentenced for labor racketeering and many other charges to thirty years in jail. Frank Sheeran had been sentenced, too, after charges against him in 1980 of mail fraud, taking bribes, and, naturally, labor racketeering. His sentence was eighteen years in prison.

At the same time, all the older prominent members of the family were dead or imprisoned. Jack Parisi and Philip Medico died in December 1982 and February 1983, respectively. Soon after, the patriarch of the family, Steven LaTorre, who was one of the "Men of Montedoro" in the early 1900s, died in July 1984 at the age of 98. Casper "Cappy" Giumento would follow in March 1987. All of them died from natural causes, a sign that the time had passed for the crime family even though Russell Bufalino continued to be perfectly active even behind bars, now in his 80s.

That didn't mean that the Bufalino family faded away so easily. On the contrary, under D'Elia's leadership, the crime family collaborated closer with the Lucchese family in New York, established operations in Miami and Baltimore, and took control of the Edgewater Hotel and Casino in Laughlin, widening its reach in Nevada, as well. That move came after an agreement with Tony Spilotro, a violent gangster from Chicago who was portrayed in another famous gangster film, Martin Scorsese's "Casino" of 1995.

However, in December 1983, the FBI concluded the RABFAM investigation, considering that the Bufalino crime family had been essentially decimated, stating that at the time, its most important members had been convicted or in ongoing judicial proceedings.

In 1989, Russell Bufalino had a stroke and was transferred to the federal hospital in Springfield, Missouri. There, in a wheelchair, he finally retired, passing the next years doing lighter and calmer things, like playing bocce and attending mass regularly—that one had always been a central part of his life, not a retirement hobby. In Springfield, he also had the chance to reunite with Sheeran. He, too, transferred there because he suffered severely from arthritis.

Bufalino was released from prison in 1991, and they moved him to a nursing home in the Scranton area, where he lived his last years until his death of natural causes on February 25, 1994, at the age of 90. In those last years, he received many visitors who came to pay their respects to the great Mafia boss. There was also a ritual. Every visitor stopped and kissed the old gangster's feet after entering the room and approached the bed where he was lying.

The Bufalino Crime Family After Bufalino

As what went down as the "Bufalino crime family" had not started with Russell Bufalino, but even before he was born, it did not end with his death—not immediately. Indeed, what happened in 1994 was that Billy D'Elia, the acting boss for a while, became the actual boss of the family.

As mentioned earlier, D'Elia had made some pretty important moves under the supervision of Bufalino, expanding the family's reach and collaboration with other families of the country outside the previous geographical limits of action of the Bufalino family. After Bufalino's death, D'Elia tried to expand those limits and links even further. Under his leadership, the family worked with families in Philadelphia, southern Florida, New York, Pittsburgh, Los Angeles, Miami, Nevada, and even associates of Russian organized crime. In particular, D'Elia's collaboration with the Philadelfia Mafia family was so close that when their boss, John Stanfa, was convicted and put in jail, he thought about appointing D'Elia as acting boss of the Philadelfia family.

At the same time, though, the Bufalino crime family, in fact, was shrinking. It was becoming weaker as its historical leaders and members were leaving the scene. D'Elia tried to give new impetus and vigor to the family, replacing members who left, were imprisoned, or died with new ones. However, his attempts did not have great success. The era of traditional organized crime and of the Bufalino family was in decline.

The family's activities during the D'Elia leadership included money laundering—a scheme in which many people were operating in the gambling and prostitution sectors, as well as corrupt politicians, of course, and the Russian "Mafia" participated.

So, on May 31, 2001, D'Elia, Jeanie Stanton, who was his mistress, and Thomas Joseph all had search warrants executed at their homes by the agents from the Criminal Investigation Division of the IRS, US Postal Inspectors, and the Pennsylvania State Police. The agents also searched the home of a certain Marranca, who was an informant working simultaneously for the FBI and the Pennsylvania State Police. Marranca would also testify to the Fourth Statewide Investigating Grand Jury against Louis DeNaples, focusing on DeNaples' connections to the Mafia as well as his control of the Mount Airy Casino.

After the warrants, on February 26, 2003, the New Jersey Division of Gaming Enforcement barred D'Elia from accessing the casinos in Atlantic City, New Jersey. This decision was made based on information that had been supplied by the Federal Bureau of Investigation and the Pennsylvania Crime Commission.

Exactly five years after the warrants of 2001, on May 31, 2006, D'Elia was charged on federal allegations of having laundered $600,000 in illicit narcotics revenues collected from a member of the Bufalino crime family who was based in Florida, as well as from other individuals. One of them was an associate of the Lucchese crime family whose name was Phillip "Fipper" Forgione. The charges were brought against D'Elia by the United States Department of Justice. During the time that D'Elia was out of jail on bond, he tried to convince an informant working for the United States Customs and Border Protection to kill a witness. As a result, he was detained in custody until he eventually pleaded guilty and was sentenced.

D'Elia entered a guilty plea to charges of witness tampering and money laundering in March of 2008. He was given a jail term of nine years for his crime. In the end, D'Elia's sentence was reduced because he became an informant and gave evidence against Louis DeNaples, the proprietor of the Mount Airy Casino Resort in the Pocono Mountains, cooperating with the government and testifying against him. As a reward for his assistance in the government investigation into DeNaples, D'Elia received a two-year reduction in the length of his sentence in the year 2010.

The Bufalino crime family has been considered extinct since around 2010, after its last boss, D'Elia, pleaded guilty and cooperated with law enforcement. In 2011, a former investigator of the Pennsylvania Crime Commission, named James Kanavy, said during an interview with the author Dave Janoski that there probably wasn't a crime family based in Northeastern Pennsylvania anymore. Any remnants of the Bufalino crime family at that point would be part of the remaining New York crime families.

CONCLUSION

There is no doubt that in the history of organized crime in the United States, the Bufalino crime family occupies a prominent position. For a long time, it operated in a secretive and enigmatic fashion, staying away from the main focus of law enforcement and maintaining a veil of silence, which many erroneously thought of as a weakness or lack of importance. The truth was that the Bufalino crime family had a long story going back to the beginning of the 20th century and became one of the most powerful families of organized crime during the years of Russell Bufalino's leadership.

Bufalino was so successful and reigned for so long among the leading figures of organized crime that his family is named after him, even though its origins go back to the very first years of the 1900s. However, thanks to Bufalino, the Northeastern Pennsylvania crime family expanded its influence beyond Pittston and Scranton, reaching a national broad level comparable to that of New York, Chicago, and Los Angeles crime families. Bufalino's businesses and investments would get Cuba, his influence and links to the most significant labor unions in the United States and the government, and his ability and financial power with the Italian authorities. The Bufalino crime family was involved in numerous criminal activities, such as loan-sharking, illegal gambling, extortion, prostitution, and labor racketeering.

On the other hand, the stronger it grew, the more the law enforcement took notice of the Bufalino family and intensified its attention to disintegrate it. In those years, law enforcement grew in power and capability much more than the crime families, thanks to the technological and tactical progress, which made surveillance and data collecting and analyzing much faster, more massive, and more efficient. Law enforcement agencies used wiretapping, task teams, informants, and intensive surveillance with many agents to deal with organized crime and bring its leaders and members to the court and behind the bars of prison.

Indeed, by the late 1970s and the 1980s, many leaders and associates of the Mafia paid for their criminal operations and actions. Organized crime, particularly in the Bufalino family, began to decline. Its fall would become evident and accelerated after Russell Bufalino died at 90 in 1994. After that date, the Bufalino crime family would never be the formidable criminal organization it once was, despite the efforts of its past leaders.

We could say, in conclusion, that the story of the Bufalino crime family represents an emblematic example of American organized crime's rise and fall, glory and demise. It shows how a quiet, calm, and friendly attitude can be deadly and efficient if accompanied by determination, cynicism, and precision. At the same time, on the other hand, it proves that not even the most effective, secretive, silent, and attentive criminal organizations can escape the clutches of law enforcement forever if it's determined, organized, well prepared, and uses the technological, psychological, and tactical scientific knowledge of our times.

From a point of view, it could be a raw and criminal implementation of the American dream. From another point of view, it could be the aspect of what didn't work well with the American dream in the previous century, its bad version, a sickening way of pursuing the opportunity that America should represent. In any case, the history of the Bufalino crime family is part of an era and a society where success still used to pass often through violence and coercion, where organized crime was very present, even at the upper levels of society, business, and politics. An era we would prefer to have left behind, enjoying its fascinating aspects only through books, movies, and podcasts.

GLOSSARY

Aladena James Fratianno (1913-1993): Known as "Jimmy the Weasel," he was the acting boss of the Los Angeles crime family and spent over seven years in prison. He was accused of misrepresenting himself and conspiring towards Danny Greene's murder.

Angelo Bruno (1910-1980): He was a Sicilian-American mobster who was the boss of the Philadelphia crime family for two decades until his assassination in 1980. Born in Sicily, he immigrated to the U.S. and settled in South Philadelphia. Bruno was close to New York Gambino crime family boss Carlo Gambino and had a close relationship with mobster John Simone. He was married to Assunta "Sue" Maranca and owned various companies. Bruno's preference for conciliation over violence led to his assassination, sparking a mob war that claimed over 20 lives. His home was considered a historical landmark, but a committee ruled against it.

Anthony "Tony Jack" Joseph Giacalone (1919-2001): He was a Sicilian-American organized crime figure in Detroit who became known nationwide because of his role in the disappearance of Jimmy Hoffa in 1975. He was sentenced to 10 years in prison for tax evasion and was involved in the Hotel Gotham numbers racket.

Carlo Gambino (1902-1976): A Sicilian-American crime boss who took over the American Mafia Commission after Vito Genovese's imprisonment in 1959. He was part of a criminal organization led by Joe Masseria. After Genovese's death, Gambino took control of The Commission, which he despised for drug dealing. Gambino's death in 1976 was due to his heart condition and hospitalizations. His legacy continues to be portrayed in the media.

Charles "Lucky" Luciano (1897-1962): He was an Italian-born gangster who was a key figure in establishing the Commission in 1931 and organized crime in the United States. He was a key aide in Joe Masseria's criminal organization and was involved in the Castellammarese War, a rivalry between Masseria and Salvatore Maranzano. Luciano controlled lucrative criminal rackets in New York City and proposed a national Commission to settle disputes. In 1936, he was convicted of compulsory prostitution. His sentence was 30 to 50 years in prison. He was deported to Italy in 1946.

The Commission: Established in 1931 by Charles "Lucky" Luciano, was responsible for overseeing all Mafia activities in the United States and mediating conflicts among families. It consisted of seven family bosses, including New York's Five Families, Chicago Outfit boss Al Capone, and Buffalo family boss Stefano Magaddino. The Commission faced challenges, including the Apalachin meeting in 1957, a plot to kill members in 1963, and the Mafia Commission Trial in 1985. Luciano was convicted of being part of the "Combination" prostitution ring and sentenced to 30-50 years in state prison. The Commission's current membership consists of the Five Families and the Chicago Outfit.

Francis Joseph Sheeran (1920-2003): Often known as "The Irishman," Sheeran was a labor union official in the United States and an enforcer for Jimmy Hoffa and Russell Bufalino. He was suspected of having ties to the Bufalino criminal family and being engaged in organized crime infiltration into unions. In 1980, Sheeran was convicted of labor racketeering and sentenced to 13 years in jail. Before he died in 2003, he confessed to having assassinated Teamster leader Jimmy Hoffa. His story served as the inspiration for Martin Scorsese's 2019 film The Irishman.

Frank Costello (1891-1973): He was an Italian-American crime boss who was part of the Luciano crime family. Born in 1891, he joined the Morello gang in the U.S.**U.S.** in 1895. He controlled slot machine and bookmaking operations, bringing millions in profit. Costello faced multiple convictions and was stripped of U.S. citizenship in 1952.

Frank Edward Fitzsimmons (1908-1981): He was an American labor union leader, president of the Teamsters Union from 1971 to 1981, and before that, the acting president from 1967 to 1971. Fitzsimmons had worked as a bus driver and truck driver before joining Teamsters Local 299. He negotiated a national trucking contract and formed the Alliance for Labor Action in 1968. In 1971, Hoffa resigned as president, and Fitzsimmons was elected as international president.

James Riddle Hoffa (1913-1975): An American labor union leader and president of the International Brotherhood of Teamsters from 1957 to 1971. He became involved with organized crime in 1964 and resigned in 1971. Jimmy Hoffa, a Detroit truck driver, played a significant role in the Teamsters Union, defending them from raids and expanding their influence. Hoffa was convicted in 1964 of several charges. He resigned in 1971 but was barred from union activities until 1980. Hoffa disappeared on July 30, 1975, and is generally accepted to be murdered by the Mafia.

John Edgar Hoover (1895-1972): He was an American law-enforcement administrator who served as the final Director of the Bureau of Investigation and the first Director of the Federal Bureau of Investigation (FBI). Before the Apalachin Meeting, for a long time, he had denied that Mafia existed. He expanded the FBI and modernized policing technology. He was credited with overseeing several captures of outlaws and bank robbers and was credited with investigating Communist subversion and the "Top Hoodlum Program."

John Sciandra (1899-1949): He was the Italian-American crime boss of the Northeastern Pennsylvania crime family from 1933 to 1949. Born in Montedoro, Sicily, he immigrated to the United States in 1908 and worked as a coal miner before becoming an enforcer and bootlegger for Bufalino crime family boss Santo Volpe. In 1933, after being questioned about his involvement in the murder of Samuel Wichner, Santo Volpe appointed Sciandra as the new boss.

Joseph Mario Barbara (1905-1959): Also known as "Joe the Barber," Barbara was an Italian-American mobster who led the Bufalino crime family from 1949 to 1959. Born in Sicily, he worked as a hitman for the Northeastern Pennsylvania crime family and was arrested for multiple murders. In 1944, he bought a property in Apalachin, New York, and was convicted of illegally purchasing sugar. In 1957, he hosted the Apalachin meeting, where over 100 mafiosi discussed gambling, narcotics smuggling, and international narcotics trade.

Mike Rizzitello (1927-2005): He was an Italian-American mobster. He was involved in organized crime and illegal gambling. He served nine years in prison and was banned from casinos in Las Vegas.

Min Matheson (1909-1992): She was a labor union organizer of the International Ladies' Garment Workers Union (ILGWU). She is better known for his intense and fearless union activity in Northeastern Pennsylvania from 1945 to 1963. Born in Chicago, she faced violence in mafia-controlled labor industries. She joined the ILGWU in 1944 and faced opposition from organized crime bosses. Min contributed to workers' personal lives with education, health benefits, and maternity benefits. She was a founding member of the National Organization for Women, aiming for equal rights for women.

The Rainbow Room: This was a private event space in Midtown Manhattan, New York City, and was a popular destination for the elite and celebrities. Opened in 1934, it was a saloon and dance hall that hosted celebrities and royalty. After a decline in business, it closed in 2009 and reopened in 2014 after renovations. The restaurant was declared a landmark in 2012 and awarded an award for outstanding interior architecture by the American Institute of Architects in 2017. The restaurant features a revolving dance floor inspired by Murray's Roman Gardens and has received positive reviews but is rated as expensive.

Stefano Magaddino (1891-1974): He was an Italian-born Mafia boss of the Buffalo crime family in western New York. He was a charter member of the American Mafia's ruling council, The Commission. Born in Sicily, Magaddino led a clan allied with Giuseppe Bonanno and his brother. He orchestrated the murder of

Felice Buccellato in 1917 and was arrested in 1921 for murdering Camillo Caiozzo. Magaddino became a naturalized U.S. citizen in 1924 and made a fortune through several criminal activities like loan-sharking, illegal gambling, extortion, and labor racketeering. He was the longest-tenured boss in the American Mafia's history and was involved in nationwide Cosa Nostra affairs.

The Teamsters: The International Brotherhood of Teamsters is a labor union formed in 1903 by merging the Teamsters International Union and the Teamsters National Union. The union has a decentralized structure, with local unions governing themselves autonomously. Despite corruption during its early years, the IBT has grown significantly, becoming one of the most powerful unions in the country by World War II. The union faced political power struggles during the Great Depression and war, with Dave Beck and Jimmy Hoffa gaining control.

Tony Provenzano (1917-1988): He was a prominent American mobster and member of the Genovese crime family New Jersey faction. Born in 1917, he worked as a business agent and president at Teamsters Local 560 in Union City, New Jersey. Provenzano was indicted for extortion in 1963 and served four and a half years in prison. He was also indicted for conspiracy to violate the anti-kickback statute and sentenced to life imprisonment.

William "Mafia's Big Billy" D'Elia (1946): He was an American former mobster who was the boss of the Bufalino crime family after the death of Russell Bufalino in 1994. He grew up in Pittston, Pennsylvania, and worked with the family as a driver and gofer. After Bufalino's death, D'Elia tried to expand the family's activities, including money laundering. In 1990, he was implicated in a money laundering operation involving The Metro newspaper. D'Elia was indicted in 2008 on money laundering and cooperated with law enforcement.

Umberto "Albert" Anastasia (1902-1957): An Italian-American mobster and crime boss who founded the American Mafia and co-founded Murder, Inc. He controlled New York City's waterfront and was known as The Earthquake, The One-Man Army, Mad Hatter, and Lord High Executioner. Anastasia was part of the Luciano crime family and was involved in the murder of Morris Diamond and Peter Panto. Genovese sought control of Anastasia's family but was indicted on narcotics trafficking charges.

Vito Genovese (1897-1969): He was an Italian-born American mobster who rose to power during Prohibition and played a significant role in the American Mafia. He was a childhood friend of Lucky Luciano and played a role in the Castellammarese War, shaping organized crime in the United States. Genovese served as a mentor to Vincent "Chin" Gigante and later led Luciano's crime family, which was renamed the Genovese crime family in his honor. Genovese was convicted on narcotics conspiracy charges, and in 1959, he was sentenced to 15 years in prison. Genovese died in prison in 1969 and is buried in Saint John Cemetery in Middle Village, Queens.

REFERENCES

Beck L. (2019, November 28). *What happened to the Bufalino crime family from the Irishman?* Refinery 29. https://www.refinery29.com/en-us/2019/11/8643809/where-is-the-bufalino-crime-family-now-the-irishman#:~:text=According%20to%20the%20Times%20Leader

Birkbeck M. (2013). *The quiet Don: The untold story of mafia kingpin Russell Bufalino.* New York: Berkley Books.

Birkbeck M. (2023, July 8). *The real mafia was more involved in 'The Godfather' than anyone knew.* New York Post. https://nypost.com/2023/07/08/the-real-mafia-was-incredibly-involved-in-the-godfather/

Bruney G. (2019, November 27). *Russell Bufalino took the true story of the Irishman to his grave.* Esquire. https://www.esquire.com/entertainment/movies/a29961398/russell-bufalino-the-irishman-true-story/

Corsino, L. (2014). *The neighborhood outfit: Organized crime in Chicago Heights.* University of Illinois Press. http://www.jstor.org/stable/10.5406/j.ctt6wr6fx

Drapper_Don. (2011, July 17). *The Bufalino file: A look inside the massive FBI paper trail on NEPA's most notorious mobster.* Five

Families of New York City. http://www.fivefamiliesnyc.com/2011/07/bufalino-file-look-inside-massive-fbi.html

Hayes A. (2022, December 3). *Bootleggers, bathtub gin, & speakeasies: Organized crime in the 1920s.* The Collector. https://www.thecollector.com/organized-crime-roaring-twenties/

Role of the internal revenue service in law enforcement activities: Hearings before the Subcommittee on administrations of the internal revenue code of the committee on finance United States Senate, 94th Cong. (1975, 1976). https://bit.ly/3PCOSYy

Cheney J. (2023, April 10). *Exploring Scranton's Industrial History at the Anthracite Heritage Museum.* History in Northeastern Pennsylvania Archives. https://uncoveringpa.com/anthracite-heritage-museum

Krainc. A.E. (2022, March 10). *Prohibition & organized crime in the 1920s.* Study.com. https://study.com/learn/lesson/prohibition-organized-crime-1920s-history-aftermath.html

Lubasch A.H. (1977, October 22). *Bufalino sentenced on extortion charge.* The New York Times. https://www.nytimes.com/1977/10/22/archives/bufalino-sentenced-on-extortion-charge-reputed-mobster-gets-four.html

Lubasch A.H. (1981, October 21). *Trial of 2 crime figures told of plot to kill key witness.* The New York Times. https://www.nytimes.com/1981/10/21/nyregion/trial-of-2-crime-figures-told-of-plot-to-kill-key-witness.html

McBride J. (2022, October 11). *Bufalino crime family now & then: Does it exist today?* Heavy.com. https://heavy.com/entertainment/2019/11/bufalino-crime-family-today-now/

Organized crime in America: Hearings before the Committee on the Judiciary United States Senate. 98th Cong. (1983). https://www.ojp.gov/pdffiles1/Digitization/92732NCJRS.pdf

Kaiser, D. (2008). *The toad to Dallas: The assassination of John F. Kennedy.* Harvard University Press. https://doi.org/10.2307/j.ctt13x0j3v

Pennsylvania Crime Commission (1970). *Report on organized crime.* The American Mafia. https://mafiahistory.us/maf-pcc70.html

Pennsylvania Crime Commission (1989). *Report on organized crime.* Commonwealth of Pennsylvania. https://www.ojp.gov/pdffiles1/Digitization/138666NCJRS.pdf

Pennsylvania Historical & Museum Commission. (2015, August 26). *1861-1945: Era of industrial ascend*ancy. Pennsylvania Historical & Museum Commission. http://www.phmc.state.pa.us/portal/communities/pa-history/1861-1945.html

Serratore A. (2019, November 21). *The true history behind Martin Scorsese's 'The Irishman'.* Smithsonian Magazine. https://www.smithsonianmag.com/history/truth-behind-martin-scorseses-irishman-180973620/

Sokol T. (2019, November 29). *The Irishman: Real life gangsters from Philly and New York.* Den of Geek. https://www.denofgeek.com/culture/the-irishman-real-life-gangsters-history/

Tonry M., & Reuter P. (2020). *Organizing crime: Mafias, markets, and networks.* Chicago and London: The University of Chicago Press.

Valin E. (n.d.). *In Pittston, informing runs in the family.* The American Mafia. https://mafiahistory.us/rattrap/inflatorre.html

Waring E., & David Weisburd (2018). *Crime and social organization: Advances in criminological theory.* Routledge.

Wintermute, B. A. (2017). Crime and Punishment in Eastern Pennsylvania, 1903–18, Part 1. *Pennsylvania History: A Journal of Mid-Atlantic Studies, 84(3)*, 363–385. https://doi.org/10.5325/pennhistory.84.3.0363

Wolensky R. P. (2014). Organizing ladies' garment workers in Northeastern Pennsylvania: Min Matheson and the ILGWU. *Pennsylvania Legacies, 14(1)*, 20–25. https://doi.org/10.5215/pennlega.14.1.0020

Wright, C. (2019). The life and times of Jimmy Hoffa. *Class, Race and Corporate Power, 7(2).* https://www.jstor.org/stable/48645445

www.ingramcontent.com/pod-product-compliance
Lightning Source LLC
LaVergne TN
LVHW052027200926
848481LV00005B/1604